Pop Grenade

From Public Enemy to Pussy Riot:
Dispatches from Musical Frontlines

Pop Grenade

From Public Enemy to Pussy Riot:
Dispatches from Musical Frontlines

Matthew Collin

Winchester, UK
Washington, USA

First published by Zero Books, 2015
Zero Books is an imprint of John Hunt Publishing Ltd., Laurel House, Station Approach,
Alresford, Hants, SO24 9JH, UK
office1@jhpbooks.net
www.johnhuntpublishing.com
www.zero-books.net

For distributor details and how to order please visit the 'Ordering' section on our website.

Text copyright: Matthew Collin 2014

ISBN: 978 1 78279 831 6
Library of Congress Control Number: 2014951068

A CIP catalogue record for this book is available from the British Library.

Design: Stuart Davies

Printed and bound by CPI Group (UK) Ltd, Croydon, CR0 4YY, UK

We operate a distinctive and ethical publishing philosophy in all
areas of our business, from our global network of authors to
production and worldwide distribution.

CONTENTS

Matthew Collin has worked as a foreign correspondent for the BBC, Al Jazeera and Agence France-Presse, and as editor for *The Big Issue*, *i-D* magazine, the *Time Out* website and the Balkan Investigative Reporting Network. He has written for many newspapers and magazines, including *The Guardian*, *The Observer*, *The Wall Street Journal*, *Mixmag*, *The Wire* and *Mojo*. His other books are *Altered State*, *This is Serbia Calling* and *The Time of the Rebels*.

Introduction

Hamada Ben Amor was still living at his parents' house in the provincial Tunisian port city of Sfax when he finished a new hip-hop track he had been working on and uploaded it with a video clip to the internet.

The video opens with black-and-white archive images of Tunisian president Zine al-Abidine Ben Ali trying to comfort a terrified schoolboy in a classroom. His hair slicked back in vampiric style, the president looms over the cowering child and demands to know what is wrong: "Go on, tell me. Don't be afraid! Do you want to tell me something?"

It then cuts to the young rapper, wreathed in lugubrious shadow as he launches into a reply like a vengeful prosecutor reading an indictment for the most heinous of crimes: "Mr. President, today I am speaking to you in my name and in the name of all the people who are suffering... Today I speak fearlessly on behalf of the people crushed by the weight of injustice..."

As the 21-year-old rides the rolling groove, he looses off a barrage of lyrical punches, landing slug after slug on the Tunisian dictator. Corruption, poverty, unemployment, police brutality, repression - line by line, verse by verse, he batters away at Ben Ali in what must be one of the most vigorous takedowns in hip-hop history.

Rais Le Bled (*Head of State*), the song that the young MC recorded in November 2010 under his alias El Général, would go on to have more impact than he could ever have imagined over the weeks that followed, and wider political resonance than most other rap songs ever recorded.

"It was a direct message for the president, a message in the name of the people, for the people," he explained later. "I wanted it to reach the president, I wanted him to know what's happening

1

in the country."

The message got through. As tens of thousands of Tunisians took to the streets a month later, after a street trader set himself on fire in a symbolic act of self-sacrificial protest, *Rais Le Bled* went viral, becoming an anthem for their uprising, sharpening the rage and disgust of a people that had suffered too much and for too long.

El Général quickly struck again with another blast of insurrectionary lyricism, *Tounes Bledna* (*Tunisia My Country*), declaring that the protesters would never back down, never surrender: "Tunisia is our country, the entire people hand in hand!" This time his words so infuriated the authorities that police launched a dawn raid on his parents' home in Sfax, dragging him off to the National Security Bureau in the capital where he was handcuffed to a chair and interrogated for three days.

"They asked, how can you write such stuff? How dare you pass messages to the president, he has such an important position in our country, you can't criticise the chief directly! Why did you do it? What do you want? Who's behind you? Who are the people who told you to write such stuff?" he recalled.

"They asked a lot of questions, and I said: 'I belong to myself. I write about the things that I see from one day to the next. This is the voice of our everyday lives.'"

And it was already too late to stop him; the songs were out there and the days were counting down to president Ben Ali's flight from power and into exile. After El Général's release, he joined the protests too: "On the streets, I saw unity, I saw intelligent young people. I felt like I belonged."

The Tunisian uprising heralded the start of a remarkable few months in the Middle East and North Africa: what became known as the 'Arab Spring', a moment of revolutionary zeal which struck fear into the souls of dictators across the region and beyond. A time when rappers scrawled their lyrics behind the barricades, and when it seemed that the impossible had finally become achievable... for a brief moment, anyway, until some of those dreams turned into savage nightmares...

In Tahrir Square in Cairo, protesters thrilled to the sound of rapper Deeb declaiming a summons to action called *Egyptian, Stand Up!* over steely funk interlaced with sinewy Arabic motifs: "The revolution is not over yet, it has just begun," he urged. In the Palestinian territories, in Lebanon and Jordan, even in Syria, hip-hop had become a new medium of dissent for a younger generation of Arab youths.

Songs were lashed together from street slogans, quickly recorded, uploaded, file-shared, replayed back onto the streets on which they originated, creating a feedback loop that fed itself as it nurtured the resistance. "Today in the Arab world, when you want to pass on a message, rap is the best way," El Général declared. Chuck D of Public Enemy once described rap as the 'black CNN'; now it was as if Arab MCs were running their own rolling news channel, the hip-hop nation's Al Jazeera.

"Music is the weapon of the future; music is the weapon of the progressives; music is the weapon of the givers of life."
Fela Kuti

People have been using music to damn the iniquities of the powerful and narrate the emotions of changing times since the earliest days of recording, and for centuries before that. The story of how an obscure young rapper from a provincial Tunisian city became a revolutionary hero was just another example of how pop, in its widest definition, can still help to inspire and sustain movements for change, and in turn transform the lives of those who channel the energies of social turmoil into sound.

The six pieces of reportage that make up this book are about extraordinary moments like this - fleeting periods in recent history when music became a soundtrack to social transforma-tions, quickening the heartbeat and feeding the soul of cultural movements or alternative communities seeking, with the audacity of youth, to confront injustice, alter the consciousness of a generation, or at least create safe havens where they could freak freely until the police moved in.

The first and final chapters tell the stories of encounters with two unique groups of pop-cultural activists, Public Enemy and Pussy Riot, who came from very different times and places but both started out with the direct intent to set fires and smash icons. Despite being wounded by the energies that they unleashed but ultimately could not control, both succeeded in shining a light into the darkness at the heart of their own worlds.

Here too are tales from outside the traditions of the protest song and the history of politically-conscious pop - stories about intrepid attempts to create alternate realities or 'temporary autonomous zones' offering at least the illusion of a momentary escape from the tribulations of a rapacious Babylon.

Amid the chaotic hedonism that erupted after the fall of the Berlin Wall in 1989, the techno scene helped to create a new identity for the once-divided city, bringing youth from east and west together in the liberating darkness of subterranean night-clubs and helping them to build some kind of new community in what was once no man's land - or that's what some of those who were there at the time believe. Its most spectacular manifestation, the Love Parade, offered an alternative vision of the metropolis as a nexus for creative energies; a vision that managed to retain at least some of its resonance despite the brazen commodification and ultimate traumatic demise of the event itself.

In Britain in the nineties, there were also those who believed that the acid-house fantasy of love, peace and ecstatic bliss could be more than a weekend holiday in an altered state - the anarchistic sound-system techno-hippies who wanted the free party to go on forever, even after a series of laws were passed to make it stop. Some of these sonic extremists chose to leave their homeland behind and took to the roads of mainland Europe to live the rave dream full-time after they saw the illicit hedonist culture that they had loved selling itself for commercial rewards. Moving from country to country in their raggedy convoys, they sought out new spaces to create their own libertine enclaves in a symbolic rejection of capitalist realities.

Musicians have played vital supporting roles in a series of uprisings to oust undemocratic regimes in recent years - during the Arab Spring, and amid the revolutions in eastern European states like Serbia and Ukraine in the first decade of the twenty-first century, to the point when it has sometimes seemed that no popular rebellion is complete without its own theme song. This book documents a few dramatic days in the life of the uprising in Istanbul's Taksim Square in 2013, when young Turkish musicians braved the tear gas and plastic bullets to help resist what they saw as an assault on their liberty and their culture - an attempt to socially engineer a generation of dutiful Islamic conservatives - marking them as heirs to a little-documented history of rock'n'roll dissidence in Turkey that dates back to the sixties.

But young progressives like these hold no domain over the sonic realm. On the other side of the ideological barricades, music has long been a tool of propagandists trying to promote government ideology (and a means of torture, in the case of the Guantanamo Bay prisoners subjected to incessant rock music at extreme volume by US jailers trying to break their spirits). Another chapter in this book looks at a period when pop propaganda was taken to its most extraordinary extremes in recent history, in the former Soviet republic of Georgia under the rule of idiosyncratic president Mikheil Saakashvili, a man who seemed to have a catchy tune ready for any political situation, from election campaigns to battles against separatist rebels. But as optimism gave way to horror, these patriotic melodies became the soundtrack to his nation's terrifying descent into armed conflict.

Pop Grenade, then, is a series of personal dispatches from critical moments when music has been used as an agent of change, or as Fela Kuti put it, as a *weapon*. It is not intended to be a comprehensive history of pop and politics over the past couple of decades; rather, it is just what I managed to see with my own eyes - a series of dispatches from the some of the highest of times, acted out by an extraordinary cast of righteous preachers, libertine conspirators, delirious cultists, rock'n'roll visionaries, techno activists and holy fools, not all of whom are still with us anymore.

That's because, perhaps inevitably given the stakes that have sometimes been in play, not all of these stories have happy endings. Some of them end in despair, disillusionment and even death; there is failure and regret here as well as celebration. But one thread runs through all these dispatches from various time-zones and datelines: the belief that sometimes, at the right time in the right place with the right people, music can still be a genuinely inspirational force.

As a journalist, I've been privileged to witness some remarkable happenings on the frontlines of pop culture over the last couple of decades, often finding beauty and wonder in the most bizarre and desperate places. I've also met some exceedingly unusual people with very peculiar ideas about what music can do - incite a revolution, stop a war, revitalise a city, help to build a state...

And sometimes, some of them even managed to succeed.

Chapter One

The Prophets of Rage

Air-raid sirens howl out across the darkened hall as a platoon of young men in urban camouflage uniforms and red berets march purposefully onto the stage, paramilitary troopers clasping what look like semi-automatic pistols at shoulder height as they drill back and forth, their faces set hard in concentration. The sirens wail on, louder now, piercing the eardrums as the troopers raise their fists in a Black Power salute and their stern little sergeant-major yells out his defiant invocation: "Armageddon is now in effect!"

A volley of turntable scratches and jagged-edge samples rips through the wall of screeching noise and a martial drumbeat hammers out of the speakers, clattering closer like a robotic marching band. The paramilitaries with their replica Uzis stand to attention and their commander lifts the microphone and shouts again: "Alright, let's make some noise! Let's break this shit up!"

And it's on, the show is on... Chuck D is leaping, boxing the air and gesticulating frantically to emphasise the beats as they drop hard from the speakers, while his hype man Flavor Flav vamps and pranks his way around him, weaving demented figures-of-eight as he gambols across the floor: "Bass for your face!" he blurts out, as the Security of the First World troopers cock their ersatz weapons from podiums above the stage, their choreographed stop-motion poses halfway between militaristic menace and theatrical camp.

As they launch into *Rebel Without a Pause*, Chuck D looks set to spontaneously combust right here in front of the crowd, his eyes popping as his energy rush starts to hit escape velocity, as if the speeding rhythm might propel him upwards, out of the hall and away across the city skies. "Yo Chuck, you've got them running scared!" warns Flav as he sees his comrade about to catch fire...

It's hard to remember now, so long afterwards, just how Public Enemy dropped like a sonic cluster-bomb into the collective consciousness of British youth back in 1987 when they first toured the country - an experience that was to be as life-changing for them as it was for us.

The anticipation had been rising steadily since their first British release, *Public Enemy No. 1*, earlier that year. Most of us had still only read about the band in the music papers: the 'Black Panthers of rap', the new militants of the hip-hop age, incandescent with revolutionary zeal, come to blast our brains apart with the kind of electronic assault we didn't even have the strength of imagination to dream about. I remember getting my copy back from the record shop one evening: the matt-black sleeve, the iconic Def Jam Records logo - the definition of *where it's at*, at that time - and putting the needle to the groove for the first time... and then this unimaginable dervish howl, this frantic eruption of squalling frequencies that I would only later discover was sampled from Fred Wesley and the JBs' *Blow Your Head*... and indeed, my head was blown; a few short minutes later, nothing could be the same again.

In 1987, the time was right: much of the dominant pop music of the mid-eighties was either glossy and aspirational, as fitted the Reagan-Thatcher years, or had retreated into anomie and introspection. But now here was a crew that was sketching out a new iconography of pop dissent and filing the latest dispatches from the frontlines of racial politics in the US, while making a noise that was as radical as their message. How could we resist?

The hyperactively trend-searching British music press, which at the time still had a crucial influence on public taste and was staffed with highly literate critical partisans yearning for a new sound with the subversive energy of punk rock, instinctively embraced Public Enemy and helped stoke an appetite for their debut album *Yo! Bum Rush the Show*, which received a largely tepid reaction from the US media but became a cult artefact in the UK.

To a British listener, Public Enemy had that dark thrill of forbidden knowledge as well as the infernal energy of a musical genre that was not yet fully-formed, hurtling into the future unconstrained by custom and practice, while their contradictory vibrations gave them an urgent, nervous buzz. "The British tabloid music press found this package irresistible, and with a strange mixture of fanboy irony, Frankfurt School skepticism and thinly disguised racial fear, they began calling Public Enemy the world's most dangerous band. Their music was so good it was scary," suggested US author Jeff Chang in his essential hip-hop history, *Can't Stop Won't Stop*. [1]

A glance at some of the adoring articles written about Public Enemy in the British music press in 1987 gives an idea of what Chang meant. One journalist from the *NME* described the band as "street heavies with a PhD in Political Studies and a blade in their back pockets".[2] In the *Melody Maker*, another awestruck writer declared: "Nothing has ever looked so malicious or so venomous. So overstrung or so outraged. So excessively executed and so savagely *meant*."[3]

As well as ideologically-motivated music writers looking for something to dirty up the sterile façades of late-eighties corporate pop, Britain was also a relatively unsegregated country with a huge appetite for contemporary black music and a few crucial radio shows that promoted the most challenging of alternative sounds: from the late-night broadcasts of BBC veteran John Peel to the London pirate stations and regional radio DJs with specialist dance-music shows like Stu Allen in Manchester. The country also had its own racial tensions and right-wing government, making it fertile territory for Public Enemy, both musically and politically. "Public Enemy had much more cultural impact in England than they had in America when they came out," recalls Bill Adler, the band's former publicist at Def Jam. "It was remarkable. Public Enemy was hailed like the second coming."

Their first British tour in 1987, with LL Cool J and Eric B. & Rakim, came just a few months after a rambunctious visit by Def Jam label-mates Run-DMC and the Beastie Boys, who briefly served as pantomime villains in the tabloid press after violent altercations at a gig in Liverpool and a mini crime wave involving fans stealing Mercedes emblems from cars to hang around their necks as pendants in tribute to their bratty rap heroes' sartorial style.

When Public Enemy arrived however, the moral panic took on a more sinister, racial tone, with hip-hop linked to incidents of mass mugging by gangs of black youths running wild on Tube trains - 'steaming', the press called it. When the tour reached London's Hammersmith Odeon, squads of police officers were deployed along the route between the venue and the nearest Tube station, with busloads of reinforcements parked up in the back streets in case of unrest at what London newspaper the *Evening Standard* described as a "gangster music concert". A police spokesman explained to the BBC that hip-hop gigs attracted "thousands of the wrong types", and the Metropolitan force even appealed to the venue to cancel the gig, issuing an overtly racist statement that declared: "Rap music seems to encourage the worst elements."[4]

The disproportionate extremity of the reaction was grounded in fear, says Malu Halasa, a journalist who covered Public Enemy in their early years for the British magazine *Hip Hop Connection*: "It does seem amazing, but if you have strong black men, dressed in uniforms, in a position of prominence in society, talking articulate politics, I think you would still see that reaction even now," she suggests.

Although Chuck D dissed the Queen and prime minister

Margaret Thatcher from the Hammersmith Odeon stage and there were a few scuffles and a handful of arrests outside the venue, London did not burn that night - but the controversy did bolster Public Enemy's outlaw image and the tour unexpectedly turned Britain into their overseas stronghold, just as this country offered up its devotion to so many black American musical innovators before and afterwards, from the original Chicago bluesmen to the pioneers of Detroit techno.

Up to this point, the band had been speaking very specifically to their own people, their own community: to young black Americans, whose traumas they had set out to illuminate. Now they realised that they were being heard across the Atlantic Ocean, and by young whites too; something they had possibly never anticipated. "When we went to England and so many people embraced us and readily identified with what we were saying, that's when we realised that our message had gone through. It was like, *wow!*" marvels Professor Griff, Public Enemy's former 'minister of information', almost three decades later. For Chuck D, that 1987 tour was the "magical starting point" for much of the success that would follow.

In the audience at those first British gigs were the hardcore B-boys and B-girls, the original rockers who had been break-dancing and bodypopping to electro since the early eighties; there were the youths from the council estates and the teenage Def Jam obsessives who wore their bomber jackets festooned with hip-hop badges and purloined Mercedes emblems as pendants. But there were also disaffected post-punk renegades who had started getting into early rap, house and techno, seeking something with more spirit and purpose as independent rock lost its potency and vision. These were the people whose ideas about the transformative potential of pop had been shaped by punk rock and the more adventurous, politically-conscious bands that came in its wake, like The Slits, The Pop Group, the Au Pairs and the Gang of Four, who deconstructed capitalism and gender relations over serrated punk-funk grooves.

For many of us who rushed to buy the first Public Enemy records, they seemed to represent a fulfillment of the desire for genuinely progressive pop music. "When they came along, they just seemed like the perfect band because they gave you all this hinterland of politics and opened up the history of civil rights, challenged orthodoxies and tantalisingly raised issues like violence. People were just enthralled by this rebellious, noisy spirit," recalls journalist Stuart Cosgrove, who was one of Public Enemy's early supporters at the *NME*. Along with Mantronix, KRS-One, Run-DMC, the Beastie Boys and Eric B. & Rakim, here, it seemed, was music worth believing in again. Even if, in the beginning at least, we well knew that these records were never actually made for us, here was a sound, at last, that made us feel truly *alive*.

"The black artist's role in America is to aid in the destruction of America as he knows it. His role is to report and reflect so precisely the nature of the society, and of himself in that society, that other men will be moved by the exactness of his rendering and, if they are black men, grow strong through this moving, having seen their own strength, and weakness; and if they are white men, tremble, curse, and go mad, because they will be drenched with the filth of their evil."
Amiri Baraka, *Home*, 1965

Down on the Bowery, a place where all hopes have narrowed down to the next score, the next bagged bottle, the next panhandled quarter. A black man - or at least he looks like he could be, his face ingrained with dirt like a miner emerging from the pit-head, his eyes blank, his age unknowable - huddles in the cardboard bolt-hole he has built for himself in a corner shaded from the sun. He jerks to his feet as I pass, shrieking out high-pitched curses like he was blowing a feral soprano. Next to him, a man with one leg is rifling through plastic bags full of newsprint he has stacked away methodically in a shopping trolley, muttering a rhythmic monologue of staccato tics and clucks as he labours at his task: hobo glossolalia, the beatdown soundtrack of Skid Row, clacking out a nervy counterpart to his comrade's free-jazz screech.

Across the road, it's junkietown; the crackheads swaying and raving and sweating and tussling with each other over unknown petty disagreements. Black, white, Hispanic - critical cases of all races and colours, come together in desperation and the desire for oblivion, in the summer of 1988, in a New York City which has long since ceased to exist.

In the years before before mayor Rudy Giuliani came to office with his zero-tolerance mission to wash the scum off New York's streets, the area around the Bowery was still a raddled landscape of boarded-up storefronts and dilapidated apartment blocks with shattered windows, grimy façades spattered with cryptic graffiti, vacant lots strewn with tatty pieces of abandoned furniture, bits of broken-down cars and cast-off household detritus. When Chuck D told me later that day that "the American Dream is based on bullshit", I already had some idea what he was talking about.

Just over a year after I brought home that copy of *Public Enemy No. 1*, I was walking along the Bowery on the way to the nearby Def Jam offices, having quit my job to start writing about music. It was here, from the windows of his label's HQ on Elizabeth Street, that Chuck D had watched the cadaverous crack fiends and smack whores who inspired him to write *Night of the Living Baseheads*, his caustic sermon about the terrors that the devils of addiction were casting down upon his people. In the summer of 1988, Public Enemy were at their fearsome, compulsive, controversy-scorched peak, just days before the release of their masterwork, *It Takes a Nation of Millions to Hold Us Back* - and so, at this point, probably the most exciting band in the world.

"Challenge information, instead of taking it for what it is, do you know what I'm saying?" Chuck D instructs me, offering a bullet-point lecture in the basics of journalism within a few minutes of our meeting. This was his tactic with reporters at the time: confront, provoke, attack: "When you get information, challenge it, weigh it, use your logic. Try to get as much information as possible. Just don't believe all that *bullshit* they're throwing at you."

He's hurling out ideas, measuring up possibilities, scribbling down obscure diagrams on a piece of paper like a clandestine plotter as he talks - a stocky, muscled young man wrapped up in a black-and-tan leather bomber jacket, his eyes looking up momentarily from his arcane calligraphy and locking onto mine to demand acknowledgement. Then seemingly out of nowhere, he announces that he wants to make a film: a black *Star Trek* with Public Enemy's personnel in the lead roles. "Check out *Star Trek*, the only thing that makes an episode is that they're dealing with superior forces and they're the underdog. It's the same story," he insists.

Chuck, of course, would be the Captain Kirk figure: "Because I give all the orders and I make sure that if we're going to do this, we do it," he explains, before going on to outline a role for Professor Griff, the 'minister of information' who cries apocalypse as the band take to the stage: "Griff plays a role like Scotty; we can perform a task without Griff, but Griff has to be there to man the ship. He's the only one outside myself who can hold everything together."

The film never came to be, but the analogy of Public Enemy as a soul sonic force, boldly going where no band had gone before, was absolutely clear. Chuck as charismatic commander, doubting himself but always doing the right thing in the end; this made sense too. But Griff as his dour but faithful subordinate, moaning occasionally but always holding the conflict-battered ship together - well, this relationship would be tested in the tough times that were to come.

Then Chuck changes track yet again, his chain of thought switching to the possibility of the US electing a black president. That summer, veteran black activist Jesse Jackson was in the middle of a torrid and ultimately doomed bid for the Democratic presidential candidacy. But Chuck argues - to my surprise - that the US is not ready for a black leader. Jesse must lose, for the good of his people, he insists. "It's good that he runs; it's good that he puts up a fight. He shouldn't win, because Reagan has swept so much dirt under the rug that it's not fair to leave a man that's good and fair to deal with all that bullshit. Critics would rip him apart, black Americans would start believing in all that bullshit and they would lose every bit of hope and faith they have in the man. Right now it's a total mess and I'd rather see Bush or somebody else get stuck in the garbage."

George Herbert Walker Bush, he was referring to here - Bush Senior; Daddy Bush, who eventually won the presidency in that grubby contest to succeed Ronald Reagan in 1988. His son George W. Bush, 'Dubya', who would later become the 43rd president of the United States, was working for his father's campaign at the time, awaiting his own turn in the Oval Office.

"You can't talk about rebuilding a house when the foundation's got termites in it, which this whole system has. It has to be *torn* down and rebuilt," Chuck continues, before shutting the topic down: "Things are going to get worse before they get better." Of course, in 1988, we had no way of knowing how much worse they would get, in the bleak and violent years of the second Bush. Or how the hopes invested in a black president would be tested later still.

Just as the individualist materialism of the Margaret Thatcher era in Britain helped to summon up the collective utopian yearnings of the rave scene, Public Enemy were shaped by the tribulations of young black males during Ronald Reagan's presidency. The right-wing former actor's eight years in office saw a huge redistribution of wealth; like Robin Hood in reverse, the president and his men took from the poor - especially the black and Hispanic poor - and gave to the rich. New York saw urban neighbourhoods decay to the point of collapse, as hundreds of thousands of whites abandoned the city for the suburbs, leaving those behind to be terrorised by the homicidal demons of crack cocaine.

The civil rights victories of the previous generation now seemed a long way off; in the mid-eighties, the talk was of uniformed brutality and white vengeance: the police's fatal beating of a graffiti artist in Manhattan and killing of an elderly black woman in The Bronx, the assault on three black men by a white gang at Howard Beach, the shooting of four black youths on the New York subway by a white vigilante called Bernhard Goetz - an atmosphere of trepidation and retribution, raging iniquity and racist gunfire.

"This was 20 years after the civil rights movement; young black Americans were at a crossroads, they should have made gains, and they weren't making those gains, and I think that frustration came out in hip-hop," suggests Malu Halasa. This frustration made Public Enemy what they were, gave them the raw need to strike back and the fuel to charge their message.

Chuck D was also older than most of his peers in the hip-hop scene of the late eighties; old enough to remember what had been possible. Born Carlton Ridenhour in 1960, he had grown up amid the sixties struggles for pride and justice. His parents moved the family from Queens to the relatively middle-class but still effectively segregated 'black belt' neighbourhood of Roosevelt in Long Island. It might have looked more affluent than the urban projects, but that didn't mean that the black middle class could take anything for granted, he insisted. "There's no pattern to follow. If you become an exception to the rule, it's not a gift to your son and daughter, you know what I'm saying?" he told me.

"If I'm middle class, it doesn't mean that my little sister's middle class. Whites got it like that. Black people, like this: I could go to school, have a college education. My brother could be in jail, my sister could be on drugs and prostitution, because there is no pattern to follow."

Chuck's parents were into politics, and believed that he should know his history. He remembers the civil-rights marches on Washington, the murders of Martin Luther King and Malcolm X, which gave him a perspective that younger rappers could never have. The music that he loved in his youth was moulded by the turbulent currents of the times: hard, committed funk, like his childhood favourite James Brown singing *Say It Loud (I'm Black and I'm Proud)*. In his autobiography, *Fight the Power*, he gives the impression of being a somewhat introspective youth, thirsting for knowledge that lay beyond the outer limits, fascinated by space travel and the Apollo moon missions, avidly drawing and reading comics, those modern American fables that nurtured so many children's creative fantasies.

After he turned ten, he started going to African-American summertime study sessions for youngsters at a local college, organised by black activists from the ranks of the Nation of Islam and the Black Panthers, learning about the slave trade and African culture, honing his political worldview. Two other men who would play a crucial role in Public Enemy also attended these formative lectures, Richard Griffin - later to become known as Professor Griff - and Hank Boxley, who went on to become a sound system DJ and then the leader of PE's quartet of producers, the Bomb Squad, under the alias Hank Shocklee.

After enrolling at Long Island's Adelphi University to study graphic design and communications, Chuck also met Harry Allen, who would later become a hip-hop journalist and Public Enemy's self-proclaimed in-house 'media assassin'. Chuck then started rapping at parties staged by Shocklee's Spectrum City sound system, calling himself Chuckie D and delivering his rhymes over disco hits like Chic's *Good Times* and MFSB's Philadelphia classic *Love is the Message*.

In yet another serendipitous coincidence, the Adelphi University college radio station, WBAU, was one of the first in the US to champion hip-hop. Its programme director, Bill Stephney, would also go on to play a crucial role in creating Public Enemy. Clearly something of a musical visionary, Stephney gave Chuck and Hank their own show to play the early rap records, alongside DJ Keith Shocklee, Hank's brother and another future member of the Bomb Squad. Not long afterwards, Stephney also offered airtime to a hyperactive multi-instrumentalist and irrepressible joker called William Drayton, later to become known as Flavor Flav. A remarkable crew of talented, intelligent and highly ambitious young men had started to coalesce out of the Long Island 'black belt', and the dreams that they shared would take them further than they could ever have imagined.

By the time Chuck signed Public Enemy to Def Jam Records in 1986, he, Hank Shocklee and Bill Stephney had already defined the band conceptually as a cabal of politically-committed black outlaws, preaching the righteous truth and wreaking moral revenge on the oppressors. From Long Island, Chuck brought with him Flavor Flav, Spectrum City DJ Norman Rogers (renaming him Terminator X) and the sound system's bouncers, led by black Muslim martial arts trainer Professor Griff, restyling the heavies as a paramilitary defence force called the Security of the First World. The crew was complete.

It was a moment that Harry Allen describes as a "temporal sweet spot", a point when the cultural, social, political and technological energies of the age came together at the same place and time - an irrepressible force that seemed destined to prevail, whatever the odds. And through his own dedication and the fortuity of history, Chuck D was right at the centre of it all - as Allen says, "at the right time, at the right confluence of cultural streams... I don't think that happens often."

"African-American culture is Afrofuturist at its heart. With trickster élan, it retrofits, refunctions and wilfully misuses the technocommodities and science fictions generated by a dominant culture."
Mark Dery, *Black to the Future*, 1995

"We wanted to create something that was unique, a sort of mash-up of The Clash and Run-DMC, and that's what Public Enemy became," explains Bill Stephney, the WBAU programmer who shaped the concept of Public Enemy with Chuck D and Hank Shocklee, then went on to work for Def Jam. The Clash had been one of those bands whose lyrics, interviews, image and graphics had served as pointers to other musics and other cultures, to outsider literature and art, disseminating the spores of ideas about race, class and power in Britain. Like David Bowie with his talk of William Burroughs and Neu!, or Joy Division's references to Werner Herzog and J.G. Ballard, The Clash were what is now known as a 'portal band', musicians whose work takes its young acolytes by the hand and leads them through the gateway of the imagination into new realms of experience.

Stephney says that the creation of Public Enemy was influenced by New York's new wave scene as well as the early hip-hop of Grandmaster Flash, Kool Herc and Afrika Bambaataa in the late seventies and early eighties, a time when the city's clubs were throwing out new pop forms that would dominate the coming decades. "I once interviewed Malcolm McLaren for college radio, he came up to WBAU right around the time that he released *Buffalo Gals*, and he talked about the analogues between the punk movement in the UK and the hip-hop movement in New York City, and we saw that too. Public Enemy really reflected that era and all those influences coming together," Stephney insists, before adding with an ironic laugh: "There were folks who thought that our views were a little *exotic*, because usually black music tended to be conservative in its approach."

New York at the time was like a "racial crucible", he recalls; a city on the edge. "The times dictated that musicians should carry on the legacy of urgent statement art, of agit-pop. We felt that in hip-hop, with the exception of *The Message* by Grandmaster Flash and the Furious Five, there wasn't any group that reflected the times. We listened to *Sandinista!* by The Clash and said, why can't we do that?"

Like The Clash, Public Enemy tried to bring radical ideas to a mainstream audience, and arguably succeeded much better than black American predecessors like Gil Scott-Heron, the Last Poets or the Watts Prophets. Chuck D's lyrics were like a packed grenade: detonate it and all kinds of ideological shrapnel would burst outwards in a frantic shower of potential inspirations. His rhymes were densely studded with references to black history and politics, like hypertext links embedded in a web page, Harry Allen suggests: "It's like the words are a series of nodes that are connected to other ideas… it's almost like your job is to read and go through it really slowly later on and make a check on anything you don't understand and look that up."

While British art-rock bands referenced writers like Burroughs and Ballard, PE directed their listeners to Frantz Fanon and W.E.B. Du Bois. Chuck D once wanted to be a sports reporter, and as he threw down his lyrics like he was commentating on a fast-moving football match, listeners would pore over the obscure conundrums he was scattering like tickertape in a whirlwind.

Because there was no internet back then, virtually each one had to be carefully researched to decode its meaning. Who were these people he was referencing, these obscure names like Chesimard? (Black activist JoAnne Chesimard, better known as Assata Shakur, step-aunt of 2Pac, who escaped from jail after being convicted of shooting a policeman in 1973 and fled into exile in Cuba.) What was the party that "started right in '66"? (The Black Panthers.) What was a bolo? (A Sugar Ray Leonard punch.) And the "green, black and red"? (The pan-African flag.) Meanwhile the PE song *Party for Your Right to Fight* not only upended the Beastie Boys' hedonistic anthem but also sprinkled clues about the FBI's covert COINTELPRO operations to infiltrate and disrupt civil-rights and black resistance campaigns. "We want poems that kill," demanded African-American writer Amiri Baraka back in the sixties. "Assassin poems, poems that shoot guns." [5] Now here they were.

Professor Griff said that he later realised that PE had a remarkable and perhaps unprecedented opportunity - the chance to educate part of the white mainstream about black history, to bring the noise to the oppressor in his lair, or at least to his children who were hungry for new beats: "We got racism and white supremacy and we put it right in the face of white people and said, 'This is what we've had to deal with all our lives,'" he said.[6]

When Public Enemy toured Britain in 1987, they were already into an incredible run of hits that would redefine the possibilities of what both hip-hop and rock music could hope to be. This was sonic futurism - *Afro-futurism*, to be more precise - in full and total effect. Not just 'bass for your face', although there was plenty enough of that too, but something much more ambitious.

Hip-hop had always been intrinsically avant-garde music, from the funky bricolage of Grandmaster Flash's *Adventures on the Wheels of Steel* to the chilly Kraftwerk textures and cosmic reveries of Afrika Bambaataa's *Planet Rock*, with its utopian narrative of a world without earthly cares, "where nature's children dance inside a trance".

Exploring how early sampling technology could twist snippets of sound into unimaginable new forms, Public Enemy's production team, the Bomb Squad - Hank and Keith Shocklee,

Eric 'Vietnam' Sadler and Chuck D himself under the alias of 'Carl Ryder' - took this idea of irreverent recontextualisation right beyond the frontiers, setting out to be as revolutionary in sonic terms as they were in their lyrics. These were musical alchemists with a taste for the "shrillest, strangest and most dissonant amalgams of sound", as Luigi Russolo's Futurist manifesto *The Art of Noises* put it back in 1913.

"Hank and Chuck didn't want music. They wanted non-music, aggravation, noise," recalls Sadler. "They would do things that made absolutely no sense at all musically, but they were *funky*. Studio engineers kept telling us, 'you can't do this, you can't do that'. But I learned that there are no rules, you can do whatever you want."

Beats were overdubbed and overdubbed again until they were unrecognisable, loops of tape were stretched around studios to elongate grooves, samples were processed and re-sampled until they degenerated into grungey static, or re-layered over and over, until another, previously unimaginable sound emerged.

"We had to push the equipment to its limits because at the time, when we started, there was so little equipment available, and we had to invent new ways of doing things," Hank Shocklee explains. "This is where the hip-hop concept of the turntable being an instrument comes from - we used the turntable not as a record player but as a *sound-design* tool." Sounds were seized from all over Shocklee's huge library of discs: from Funkadelic, the Temptations, Isaac Hayes and other soul giants to metalheads Anthrax and even British glam-rockers The Sweet.

The music was intended to sound like an alarm call. "We were trying to make people think, 'What the *fuck* is this?'" says Chuck. "There was nothing 'appealing' about any of our music - it was *jarring*. We were trying to beat people over the head, to make them take notice."

It also had to embody the urgency of the moment: New York City in the dread times of vigilante killers, crack zombies and blood-lusting cops, all loose on the streets of the five rotten boroughs as the two eights clashed. "It was speaking for the underdog, the underclass, the have-nots. So it couldn't be melodic. It had to be atonal, to provoke a reaction with sound," Shocklee says.

The Bomb Squad tried to harness the raw power of rock'n'roll, the spirit of Jimi Hendrix as well as James Brown, to give the beats more aggression. "At the time when PE came out, nobody gave a shit about anything. People were lost, they didn't have any direction," Shocklee recalls. "PE came in and said: 'No! We need to be talking about what is going on, we need to wake everybody up, get everybody out of their trance.' So it had to be *abrasive*, it had to be *loud*, and it had to say things that no one would say but needed to be heard out there."

The Bomb Squad tried to drench Chuck's stentorian declamations in a roiling torrent of panicked energy. "Chuck's natural vocal is a baritone, he has a voice almost like a Baptist minister. If you put music around him that's melodic, the message and the energy will get lost because it will all blend in together," Shocklee explains.

"So the only way is to create a *thunderstorm* of sound so that he doesn't come across like a Baptist minister, but like the voice of God - a voice that resonates with fire and brimstone. The music had to be like lightning bolts coming from heaven, like hail-storms and tornados."

After the squalling racket of *Public Enemy No. 1* and the wrecking-ball beats of their debut album, *Yo! Bum Rush the Show*, Public Enemy fired off a series of singles that remains unparalleled in hip hop: *Rebel Without a Pause*, then *Bring the Noise* and *Don't Believe the Hype*, and the following year their best-known song, *Fight the Power*.

Inspired by the clarion call from the Isley Brothers' driving seventies funk groove - "you got to fight the powers that be!" - *Fight the Power* was commissioned by rising black film-maker

Spike Lee for the soundtrack of his 1989 film *Do the Right Thing*, a drama about the tempestuous racial relations between New York's African-Americans and Italians, set amid a broiling Brooklyn summer. "When this film came out, some people said it was going to cause riots all across America," Lee said later.[7] He had originally wanted to open the movie with a contemporary version of the 'negro national anthem', *Lift Ev'ry Voice and Sing*. The cherished old classic spoke of the "harmonies of liberty", but what Public Enemy gave Lee was a very different interpretation what that could mean.

"1989, the number, another summer," *Fight the Power* begins, as Chuck D, who once said that black people "should look at the American flag like a Jewish person looks at the swastika", used the song to take aim at two of conservative America's pop culture icons: Elvis Presley, who he accused of stealing the souls of black musical pioneers for his own profit, and John Wayne, the right-wing actor who once said that he believed in white supremacy "until the blacks are educated to a point of responsibility".[8]

The song plays again and throughout the film on a beatbox carried by one of the characters, Radio Raheem - and at the climax when an angry Italian pizza-parlour owner takes a baseball bat to the young rap fan's ghettoblaster in an act of symbolic repression intended to silence the voices of resistance.

But perhaps the most remarkable scene is the opening sequence, when the Puerto Rican actress Rosie Perez jacks her body to the PE track along a lamp-lit Brooklyn street. As her costume switches from a scarlet mini-dress to a skin-tight electric-blue leotard to boxing shorts and a bra, Perez hacks and slashes at the air, grimacing and pouting defiantly as she hustles her voluptuous frame back and forth across the shot, throwing punches at the camera in a display of insouciant sensuality that makes it very clear that she is the one fighting for the power over her own destiny, offering an entirely different interpretation of the song.

Spike Lee also directed the video for Public Enemy's single release of *Fight the Power*, a full-on statement of intent that was the counterpoint to Perez's display of female resistance. In its full, seven-minute version, PE's version opens with archive newsreel footage of civil-rights activists rallying in Washington in 1963, carrying placards demanding an "end to bias" and singing *We Will Overcome* as they gather to hear to Martin Luther King speak.

It then cuts to another rally, this time in full colour, with Chuck D addressing a teeming street full of demonstrators who are holding placards of Malcolm X, activist Angela Davis, boxer Muhammad Ali and the PE crew. "Yeah, check this out man, we rolling this way. That march in 1963, that was a bit of nonsense, we ain't rolling that way anymore!" Chuck declaims.

Flanked by the S1Ws in black fatigues and dark shades alongside various bow-tie-wearing members of the black Muslims' Fruit of Islam security detail, Chuck, Flav, Griff and Terminator X make their way to the stage through the cheering crowd that was assembled by Lee in Brooklyn to create a tableau that portrayed PE as the political oracles of a new and very different Black Power generation, with the gospel tones of the civil-rights marchers replaced by the insurgent rhythms of hip-hop.

Fight the Power was to become a rebel anthem that far transcended its original political context in eighties New York, in places where few people had even heard of Howard Beach or Bernhard Goetz. In March 1991, more than 4,000 miles away in Belgrade, the capital of the collapsing Yugoslavia, authoritarian leader Slobodan Milošević sent tanks onto the streets to crush protests, and the independent radio station B92 was ordered to stop broadcasting any information that was critical of the regime. The station's DJs responded with sonic resistance, playing records like *Fight the Power* over and over again to get their message across, with the policemen who had been stationed in the studio to guard against potential transgressions completely oblivious to Chuck D's defiant proclamation: "Our freedom of speech is freedom or death - we got to fight the powers that be." Public Enemy and other early hip-hop crews would have an influence on the rave scene too, even though Chuck D once said he disliked house music, describing it a yuppie groove expressing nothing but superficial escapism. But in the acid house pleasuredomes of late-eighties Britain, at clubs like Manchester's Haçienda, hip-hop tracks by Mantronix and Chubb Rock were anthems in the first dayglo months of the Ecstasy era, and even in 1989, during the blissed-out summer of rave, some British DJs continued to segue *Rebel Without a Pause* into their sets. Later still, *Fight the Power* would get played at outlaw parties thrown by anarchist sound systems who played cat-and-mouse games with the police as they took their travelling carnivals across the British countryside in the early nineties.

The rave scene was partly energised by breakbeat-driven house grooves turbocharged with hip hop and soul samples, snippets of barely-identifiable yelps, moans and grunts, as if in homage to the Bomb Squad - tracks like Frankie Bones' *Bonesbreaks* series; the template for what would become known as 'hardcore' and then jungle and drum'n'bass.

Many young British ravers, like Liam Howlett of The Prodigy, came to electronic dance music through hip-hop; "their love of PE's speed and attack and riotous blare translating into breakbeat hardcore", as British journalist Simon Reynolds put it. Crucially though, as the social context shifted, so did the meaning. "These B-boys turned E-boys stripped out the politics and turned PE's state of emergency into the panic rush of rave and jungle," Reynolds wrote.[9]

Perhaps the closest thing to Public Enemy that Britain ever produced was Shut Up and Dance, two tough-talking hip-hop heads from Hackney in east London called PJ and Smiley who made "what we thought was British rap", although it sounded more like English ragamuffin rave. "We'd take old Def Jam tracks, push them from 100 to 130 BPM, and let rip on the mike," Smiley once said.[10]

Shut Up and Dance were one of few crews to bring genuine social commentary to the UK scene with their street-corner broadsides against rip-off raves, crack dealers and police injustices. In the US meanwhile, the Detroit techno crew Underground Resistance adopted PE's black-power iconography and used it as ideological fuel for an even harsher sonic assault, channeling their fury at the Motor City's brutal decline into machine music that sought to break free of earthly oppression and blast off into the cosmos. In the 'techno museum' at the Underground Resistance headquarters in Detroit, one of the display cases honours their inspirations. There, behind the glass, alongside pictures of Geronimo, Bruce Lee, Sun Tzu and black pioneers like baseball legend Jackie Robinson and the Tuskegee Airmen of World War Two, is a photograph of Chuck D and Flavor Flav.

"Brothers and sisters, I don't know what this world is coming to..."
Jesse Jackson, speaking at the Wattstax festival in 1972, sampled by Public Enemy on *Rebel Without a Pause*

Public Enemy set out to become notorious - the Black Panthers of rap - but notoriety sometimes exacts its own price, as students of sixties radical history could perhaps have foreseen.

Anyone who had been alert to what PE had been saying would have noted the overt references to the Nation of Islam and its leader Louis Farrakhan in their lyrics; in *Bring the Noise*, Chuck hymns Farrakhan as a "prophet". And anyone who had been reading some of PE's interviews in the British music press in the summer of 1988, when Griff ranted obnoxiously about Jews and gays, would have realised that PE's 'minister of information' had the potential to unleash a controversy that they could not hope to rein in.

Both Chuck and Griff admired Farrakhan for his message of black self-empowerment and self-reliance, which made sense to people who no longer trusted in the utopian integrationist rhetoric of the sixties and were looking for a call to action that suited the times. As Bill Stephney told author Jeff Chang: "He [Farrakhan] was the only Black leader who said, 'You, Black man, can pick yourself up. You can have strong families. You can build your own businesses. You can do. He was the only affirming leader."[11] Chuck also admired the way that Nation of Islam hardliners roughed up drug dealers and shut down crack houses in black neighbourhoods: this was direct action, a justified use of force.

Farrakhan had also been a musician in his youth - a calypso singer and violinist nicknamed 'The Charmer' in the early fifties, who can still be heard, courtesy of the internet, crooning kooky little novelty numbers about a zombie jamboree in a New York cemetery and about post-war transsexual celebrity Christine Jorgensen ("Behind that lipstick, rouge and paint, I got to know: is she is, or is she ain't?" he sings). He gave up the stage for religion, eventually becoming leader of the Nation of Islam, a black Muslim movement whose founder taught that white people were a race of devils created by an evil scientist around 7,000 years ago. Farrakhan would also go on to exert a crucial influence over some of the best-known rappers of the eighties and nineties.

PE's admiration for the religious leader who was regularly accused of being anti-Semitic was hardly noticed in the US until Griff gave a provocative interview to the *Washington Times* newspaper in May 1989, in which he was reported as saying that Jews were responsible for "the majority of wickedness that goes on across the globe".[12] His words set in motion a scandal that gripped the band for months to come, from which they struggled to recover - and in some ways, never really did.

As the story went viral across the US television networks, it sparked demands for bans and boycotts, apologies and retractions. For a while, the heat got so intense that it was unclear whether Public Enemy would ever record again. "My memory of that time was mostly of us trying to figure out what to do, and if the band was going to continue or not," recalls Harry Allen. "We couldn't respond in a way that made sense, except to say, 'This is not what we're about.' That became a huge distraction because it was all for a while what anyone wanted to talk about. And we're still talking about it now, you know?"

Chuck held an emergency press conference in an attempt to limit the damage. "We are not anti-Jewish, we are not anti-anybody - we are pro-black, pro-black culture, pro-human race. Professor Griff's responsibility as minister of information for Public Enemy was to faithfully transmit those values - to everybody. In practice he sabotaged these values," he said.[13] But eventually, after taking advice from Farrakhan who told him to law low and try to ride out the controversy, he was forced to suspend his comrade from the band.

Among many of their white fans in Britain, the reaction was profound disappointment and confusion. Disappointment, because we had believed that they were better than this. Confusion, because anti-Semitism seemed so alien and anachronistic, and because what Griff had said seemed to be somehow a betrayal of so many of the people who had bought their records and their stance on black resistance. Of course, the genocidal history of slavery and racist oppression was undeniable, in Britain as it was in the US. If there was an international court that could put slave-traders and their political and military commanders on trial posthumously, it would not want for indictees. When Farrakhan told whites, "you have not been saints in the way you have acted toward the darker peoples of the world and toward even your own people", it could hardly be denied.[14] But for some of those who had invested a lot of belief in Public Enemy, it was hard now to see them as the heroes we had hoped they would be.

"I think it did damage them," says Stuart Cosgrove, who turned a showdown interview with Chuck and Griff over the politics of the Nation of Islam into a fascinating piece of confrontational journalism for *The Face* magazine in 1988. "It was shrill, racist and unnecessarily hostile. I felt they didn't really understand that what they were saying could be very hurtful to some people, and that wasn't good for them because people *wanted* to like them. There was a lot of goodwill towards Public Enemy that they lost. People had such passion for what they were doing, but then they started to mouth off and people started to say, 'What the hell are they really about?'"

The strange thing about the whole scandal was that judging by the company they kept, Public Enemy weren't racist or anti-Semitic at all. Many of Def Jam's staff were white and Jewish, like Rick Rubin, the man who signed them to the label, and their publicist, Bill Adler, as well as their managers and the photographer who shot their record covers.

Later, in his book *Analytixz*, Griff strongly denied that he was prejudiced: "I know and understand Jewish pain and Jewish hurt by meeting with Jewish people and going to the Holocaust museums on two continents," he wrote.[15] And more than two decades after that crucial *Washington Times* interview, he still continued to insist that he had been misquoted: "The media accused us of being anti-white, anti-Jew and anti-American, but they misinterpreted everything we said," he told me, insisting that he had only been targeted because he spoke the truth about his country's troubles: "If you hold up a mirror and let America see herself in the mirror, it's ugly, man; it's really ugly. And no one can deny that. So why blame it all on Professor Griff?"

For Bill Adler though, the reasons to blame Griff were clear: "Griff was a devotee of Farrakhan, and Farrakhan is an anti-Semite." Adler resigned as Public Enemy's publicist, considering himself unable to defend the indefensible, although he says that he thinks he understands why the Nation of Islam leader's teachings made sense to Griff.

"The benign way to look at it is that Griff is a young black man who has political consciousness and who asks himself a question - why is it that my people, black folks in America, remain second-class citizens? He's looking for answers, and Farrakhan *provides* answers. He's got a cosmology in place. There's nothing that happens to black folks in America that Farrakhan can't explain, and that's very satisfying to someone like Griff," he suggests.

The scandal also highlighted other contradictions about PE. Although they preached about political progress, they were always in some way socially conservative, with Chuck promoting family values and rejecting homosexuality and feminism as threats to the healthy rehabilitation of the race: "Man is husband and woman is wife. Men should be men and women should be women. And there's no room in the black race for gays... Lines have to be set," he told Simon Reynolds.[16] Stories of the S1Ws playing tapes of Nation of Islam sermons while doing physical jerks on their tour bus added to the image of rigid masculine asceticism - although Flav clearly didn't live like a clean-cut Islamic scholar.

Perhaps because of our sheer desire to believe in Public Enemy, we had ignored the more illiberal side of their worldview. Some black American writers, however, had under-stood what was going on almost right away. "Since PE show sound reasoning when they focus on racism as a tool of the US power structure, they should be intelligent enough to realise that dehumanising gays, women and Jews isn't going to set black people free," Greg Tate wrote in New York's *Village Voice* in 1988.[17]

But maybe it was hardly reasonable to hold up a group of young musicians as political sages, as Bill Stephney once pointed out: "Woe be it unto a community that has to rely on rappers for political leadership. Because that doesn't signify progress, that signifies default. Now that our community leaders cannot take up their responsibility, you're gonna leave it up to an 18-year-old kid who has mad flow? What is the criteria by which he has risen to his leadership? He can flow? That's the extent of it? If our leadership is to be determined by an eighteen-year-old without a plan, then we're in trouble. We're *fucked.*"[18]

But this was the role that PE had claimed for themselves, and it was by these standards that they would be judged, and it was these contradictions that would help to tear them apart.

"Remember - revolution is not an event, it's a process."
Professor Griff's answering machine message, 2014

In the reportage sequences that make up part of Public Enemy's 1987 UK tour documentary, *London Invasion*, they first appear like a crack squad of determined and tightly-drilled young men on a special mission into the unknown, dressed for action in uniform black fatigues and combat caps: a tough little unit; indomitable, indivisible, incorruptible. But as the documentary continues, this picture changes, and it starts to become apparent that there are fissures in the façade of unity.

From the start, Chuck had tried to maintain creative harmony while flanked by two characters with seemingly irreconcilable differences: the stern hardliner Griff and the wayward joker Flav; one a Nation of Islam teetotaller, the other a substance abuser; one into discipline and order, the other a blithe spirit of chaos.

"One of the group's greatest strengths was also one of its greatest contradictions," says Bill Adler. "The very idea that you would have Flavor and Griff in the same group - that's a recipe for dysfunction! But at the same time it's also very attractive, because they represent two different poles of black manhood. Flavor is the street-corner cat and Griff is the would-be Nation of

Islam recruit. Flavor is all about wildness and license and fun, and Griff is all about discipline and sobriety."

Unlike Griff, Flav never caused Public Enemy any political damage, but his drug use and his arrests for domestic violence chimed harshly with the idea of black self-improvement and empowerment that Chuck was promoting. Although Flav has insisted that he was never a "dysfunctional addict", he was already smoking crack around the time that the band shot the video for their anti-drugs track *Night of the Living Baseheads* in 1988. In one documentary film about PE, Griff addressed Flav directly: "We're trying to save our people, but we have to drag you out of the crack house."[19]

Flav's later reinvention as a television reality-show lothario, starring in the series *Strange Love* with his actress girlfriend Brigitte Nielsen and then hosting his own dating game show, *Flavor of Love*, disgusted Griff almost as much as his drug consumption. "It's very hard trying to get the message across when girls are taking off their bras and throwing them onstage at Flavor instead of throwing their fists in the air," he said.

Chuck, who also didn't drink alcohol or take drugs, tried to explain Flav's drug use as an example of the genuine struggles of an ordinary black man in contemporary America: how could one band remain unaffected by this all-consuming narcotic plague? "When Flavor had his problems with drugs and the police, some said: 'Why are you talking against drugs and you can't even keep Flavor off of drugs. Public Enemy is a contradiction.' That's bullshit. That's a dumb-ass statement. Public Enemy is real. We've never tried to hide that fact," he wrote in his autobiography.[20]

There's no doubt that Chuck had the courage of his convictions, though: when malt-liquor manufacturers St. Ides used his voice without permission for a commercial, he sued them and wrote a furious anti-booze track called *One Million Bottlebags* - a huge contrast to the shamelessly avaricious rappers of the twenty-first century, who actively promote luxury alcohol brands, cutting endorsement deals or even buying shares in vodka, cognac and champagne firms and then plugging them in their lyrics and videos to boost sales to their gullible admirers.

But the pressures on Public Enemy to be political leaders as well as cutting-edge recording artists were immense, and coupled with their personal discontents, it created a "perfect storm" of destructive energies, says Bill Stephney.

"There were very different personalities and there was the pressure of trying to be political and social saviours and at the same time trying to make great music - we've seen that before, it presented incredible challenges to Marvin Gaye and to the Beatles," he explains. "I don't want to compare Public Enemy with the Beatles, but there was a point for both groups where the music was hitting and the social impact was hitting at the same time, but at the same time that situation is incredibly combustible."

After the release of their third album in 1990, *Fear of a Black Planet*, the original PE team - that remarkably gifted alliance of young thinkers, musicians, activists and their record-company allies - had busted apart. Griff was gone, PE were at odds with Def Jam executive Russell Simmons, publicist Bill Adler had quit, and Stephney and Bomb Squad maestro Hank Shocklee had left to start their own label. "It was the beginning of the end of an era," says Adler.

And the mood in rap had changed. Just months earlier, PE seemed to be riding the crest of a fierce and righteous wave of black-power rappers, a generation of young iconoclasts who would remake hip-hop as more than just another musical product. "We literally saw the consciousness rising in the masses of black people in America, we saw people taking off those nasty-ass gold chains and putting on African medallions, we saw them joining revolutionary organisations - it was a beautiful thing!" Griff recalls.

But within a couple of years, 'Afrocentrism' was no longer chic and the hardcore politics of conscious hip-hop were becoming unfashionable. Gangsta rap was taking over, with its ideology captured in the early lyrics of NWA: "Life ain't nothing but bitches and money." A few months after the LA riots in the spring of 1992, NWA alumnus Dr. Dre would set the tone with his keynote album *The Chronic*, adding dope and hooch to the gangsta formula. Although rappers would continue to use their music to condemn social injustices in the decades to come, this was a consciousness shift that ensured that Public Enemy would be fixed in history as a unique phenomenon in hip-hop - the men who put black radicalism on the global stage - but whose time as a defining force for a culture had passed.

The balance of power - or rather, influence - had shifted away from Chuck D and his crew, forever, and hip-hop would develop into a massive corporate consumerist venture, selling sportswear, sneakers, fizzy drinks, junk food and booze. In his autobiography, Chuck recalls being at a sponsored gig ten years after *Public Enemy No. 1* was released, and wondering "how the control of hip-hop and rap music had changed hands and got swallowed up by the corporate pimps of soul".[21] Somehow it had slipped through his hands, much of that influence he had once wielded, seeping away invisibly until he was back on the margins of a culture he had once dominated.

Gangsta rap fetishised everything that he had stood against: heedless consumerism, internecine violence and political nihilism, all packaged up and sold for profit by white corporations, Chuck explained in his book. "This whole gangster kick, you have to ask, where does it benefit us? The sad truth is - it doesn't," he concluded.[22]

Even when I first interviewed him back in 1988, he was already warning about the evils of amoral materialism. "I have to try and shoot down most black people's values," he said, pumping his fist to emphasise his determination. "They want gold, they want a car; right, that's it, that's all they want. These things are nothing!

"It's the whole mentality of America - 'I want it now, I want it, I don't care if I have to step on top of and crush heads, I want it now.'"

Back then, he thought he could fight this and win. But although he certainly fought as best he could, it didn't really turn out as he might have wanted. If hip-hop in its early days was, in some way at least, about challenging America's elites, by the end of the nineties many rappers simply wanted to *become* them. "There was a battle of ideologies in the early nineties between so-called 'conscious rap' and so-called 'gangsta rap'. And the gangstas won," says Adler.

But the emergence of gangsta rap wasn't the only thing that changed the hip-hop game. When British MOR singer Gilbert O'Sullivan sued rapper Biz Markie for purloining a snippet from his twee seventies hit *Alone Again (Naturally)* in 1991, a court handed down the landmark ruling that sampling was copyright theft. "'Thou shalt not steal' has been an admonition followed since the dawn of civilisation," the judge declared, and from that point on, payments had to be made for every piece of music sampled on a record.[23] Public Enemy's albums, particularly *It Takes a Nation of Millions to Hold Us Back* and *Fear of a Black Planet*, had been layered and relayered with scores or possibly even hundreds of samples, but the Bomb Squad's kleptomaniac techniques were now rendered so costly as to be almost obsolete.

Chuck insists that the blow was not as devastating as it appeared: "It affected our style - the making of music from music," he admitted. "But you've got to understand, when we started out, Public Enemy's mission in music was to never repeat ourselves twice. So even when we found something that worked, we scraped it off the board and started something else."

But for Hank Shocklee, this was not only a major creative setback but a critical ideological defeat. "It changed the way we worked but it also changed the entire landscape of the music industry and how it worked. Everyone started going back and seeing what samples people used in their records and how much money they could get off of it," he recalled.

"So yes, it did change the work dramatically, because my whole idea was to use sampling as an art form and not as a means of stealing people's ideas, you know? So now when you can no longer do that anymore, you have to reinvent yourself. So you go have to *backwards*, to where you came from, which is where you didn't want to be in the first place - recreating the sounds you hear from live instruments," he said despondently.

In other words, the music had to change, and Public Enemy would never really find another way to recreate that blazing alchemical brilliance that lit up their early recordings. Their first single of 1990, *Welcome to the Terrordome*, seemed to sum up all frustrations that had assailed Chuck over the past year - his every move tracked, his every utterance held up for public inspection. He condensed all the rage and paranoia of the moment into a song that burns with furious defiance from the confessional gambit of its opening line: "I got so much trouble on my mind..."

"Today I speak fearlessly on behalf of the people crushed by the weight of injustice..."
Tunisian rapper El Général, *Rais Le Bled*, 2010

It's 2014 and I'm standing in another darkened hall, amid the genteel Regency lanes of Leamington Spa in the English Midlands, about 50 miles away from where I saw Public Enemy for the first time, watching some of the same men, now in their fifties, run through the same routine.

Near the stage, they're selling T-shirts commemorating Public Enemy's recent induction into the music-business establishment in the shape of the Rock'n'Roll Hall of Fame, and the largely middle-aged crowd, many of them wearing newly-bought PE merchandise, are taking souvenir snaps of themselves in front of the band's sniper-sight logo banner. Public Enemy have become a 'heritage act', it seems; there is no nameless menace at loose in the house tonight.

As the sirens wail out once more and the bass drops hard again, hundreds of fists pump the air, while Flav, skinny as a pipe-cleaner, prowls the stage, eyes boggling out of his pixie face and limbs contorting epileptically, urging the crowd to join him in chanting his trademark interjection of "Yeah, boyeeee!" Chuck meanwhile is the consummate showman, leading a tribute to hip-hop's old school with renditions of classics like Grandmaster Flash's *Adventures of the Wheels of Steel* as well as funked-up versions of PE's own hits. The S1Ws run through their martial routines in desert camouflage uniforms, like mechanical Gulf War action dolls. DJ Lord, who replaced original PE DJ Terminator X when he left the group to start an ostrich farm in North Carolina, takes the spotlight for a mind-bending cut-and-scratch interlude. Flav has his own solo segment in the show too, inviting some of the local ladies up onto the stage to get jiggy with him. This is a showbiz revue, in which all the well-known characters play their well-honed stage roles and everyone goes home feeling happy that they were there.

It's a thing of warmth and charm, and the music remains incredibly powerful. But it's not dangerous anymore; how could it be? I remember briefly what Malu Halasa told me: "The nature of rap and of the music business in general is that it moves on really quickly. The times move on as well. Can someone who was the voice of a generation all those years ago still be the voice of today's generation?" And I start to understand why Chuck had begun to refer to PE as 'the Rolling Stones of the rap game' - they are brilliant live, but their new records could never recreate the impact of their peak-hour hits. Because that peak hour has passed.

The next day, I met Chuck at a Hilton hotel in a business park on the outskirts of Coventry. As we sat down to talk in the faux-sophisticated surroundings of the bizarrely-named Voyeurs Bar, Andy Williams was crooning ballads through the PA system. It was a long way from the Bowery, although even that has been gentrified since the eighties.

At the age of 53, Chuck said that he didn't see himself as an elder statesman but as a "cultural spokesperson", explicitly framing himself in the sixties tradition of conscious bards who used their eminence as a platform to dispense wisdom as they understood it. "If you want to be a cultural spokesperson, you've got to study other cultural spokespersons - be it Pete Seeger, Harry Belafonte, Bob Dylan, Nina Simone, Joan Baez, you've got to study those people, you've got to understand some of their pain and you've got to study the times they lived in to see what made them work," he explained.

He was now using his celebrity to promote younger rappers from around the world through his online radio show, just as he once promoted early hip-hop in his pre-Public Enemy broadcasts on WBAU. He remained, at heart, an activist and an educator, shaped by that same sixties tradition in which he grew up. "But being an educator as a musician is still not as important as being an educator as a teacher in the school system," he cautioned sternly. "*That* is the real deal."

When I asked him if he felt more 'American' now that there was a black man in the White House - something that was almost unimaginable when I interviewed him in 1988 - he responded with an exasperated smile.

"I'm not a citizen of any place, I'm a citizen of Earth," he snapped. "I totally disbelieve in all governments. They're all full of crap. Culture is my religion; I think the closest thing to my cultural inner religion is Islam, but we all share our human soul; our blood, sweat and tears."

Professor Griff had long ago been readmitted to the band, but he didn't make the UK tour because of some kind of passport problems with the British authorities. Through his own online radio programme, *NMEMindz*, and his public lectures across the US, he had begun to emerge as something of a player on the conspiracy theory scene, a hip-hop counterpart to gonzo tinfoil-hatters like David Icke and talk-show host Alex Jones, propagating 'truths' about the transglobal power of the Illuminati and the US government's 9/11 'false flag operation' - in Griff's case, from a Black Power/Nation of Islam perspective.

The peculiar thing about Griff though, despite his predilections for the wilder fringes of political reasoning, is that he also sometimes talks a lot of sense. When we spoke on the phone a few days before the Leamington Spa gig, he set out a decent case that rappers like Public Enemy, by bringing an understanding of black consciousness to the white mainstream of American youth - by helping to *desegregate pop*, essentially - had helped to lay the groundwork for a situation in which a black man could be elected president of the United States.

"We actually educated an entire generation," he insisted. "I think we educated masses of young blacks of course but surprisingly we also educated a whole bunch of young white people who grew up and went to the polls and said: 'Let's give this a try.' Hip-hop played a very important role in making that happen."

But Griff and Chuck weren't optimistic that Barack Obama could really achieve much, though; this was not the PE dream come true, not yet. "I think he's a good man, but the president of the United States, regardless of whether they might be a good person, wears a dirty set of clothes, with bloodstains on them," explained Chuck. "It's unavoidable. You can't wash those dirty clothes in any washing machine." As he spoke, it sounded like he was sketching out the lyrics for another song in his mind.

Now that the controversies that assailed his group in its youth were in the distant past, Chuck said he wanted to focus on the fact that despite all that, Public Enemy had managed to survive.

"We've been together for 28 years, and that is a miracle in music, not to mention as a rap group. And as a group of black males, statistics say there's a greater chance that we all should have been in jail," he said.

Griff was in a mellow mood too, insisting that he carried no more grudges: "I'm not angry. I've forgiven Chuck, I've forgiven Public Enemy for throwing me under the bus. I've moved on," he said. "I'm still able to travel around and people say to me they appreciate what I have done, that it changed their life - and that is a beautiful thing."

And those old recordings still have the power to show and prove, even as their origins in the social tensions of the New York City of the mid-eighties are gradually fading into the haze of the past. When I interviewed rapper Tareq Abu Kwaik, alias El Far3i, a young Palestinian from a refugee family living in Jordan whose songs address subjects like colonialism, oppression and contemporary Arab identity, he told me that early hip-hop had showed him how popular music could work as "social commentary for our people".

"The general idea of hip hop, it clearly being a reflection of the struggle of black people, was indeed an inspiration when I was young. All you have to see is someone being able to comment on what they are seeing and letting out the frustration in music to be inspired," he explained.

The eighties idea of 'conscious rap' may seem quaintly earnest in a hip-hop era dominated by bejewelled braggarts and sexual exhibitionists, but Malu Halasa, who moved from music journalism to writing about the culture and politics of the Middle East, is convinced that it is still having an impact in places where young people are searching for ways to make themselves heard.

"Rap and graffiti are forms of expression that haven't lost their power yet, young people are still discovering what they can do with them. So these forms are having a new lease of life in an area where there is trouble and strife," she explained. "It's about resistance and having a voice; these art forms have a power because ordinary people can pick them up and communicate their thoughts and their politics."

As an ardent admirer of General Gaddafi, Griff was none too happy about the Libyan leader's bloody demise during the 'Arab Spring', but he was proud that something he had helped to create still had the power to inspire. "Public Enemy will one day get old and weary, but the mind revolution still continues," he declared. "The oppressed and the dispossessed will always be looking for a theme music that is going to serve as a backdrop for their revolution."

And perhaps it's the greatest testament to Public Enemy's sheer will to power that in these songs from faraway lands, in the music of people like Tareq Abu Kwaik and El Général and so many others, you can still feel the vibrations of *Rebel Without a Pause* and *Fight the Power* humming through the turbulence of twenty-first century conflicts like the dark rumble of a far-distant thunderstorm.

Between the zeroes and ones of digital-age hip-hop, across countries and continents, the voice of Chuck D still seems to boom outwards, like an undying ghost in the machine.

Chapter Two

Berlin Zero Hour

And then the skies opened and the rain came down... lightning flashed like a celestial strobe and thunderclaps crashed off the walls, hammering out a counterpoint to the crackle of snare drums from the sound systems as our disorderly procession of trucks pulled into Wittenbergplatz... and as the deluge raged harder, arms reached upwards to embrace the downpour like a benediction from above, slashing geometric patterns out of the clouds of white mist rolling low overhead from the fog machines on the trucks, screaming in rapture as dirty blurts of electronic bass and the vicious screech of a synthesiser tore out of the speakers out yet again, the anthem of this moment and this day, *Der Klang Der Familie*, the sound of the family - as the collective ritual was sanctified with pure water from the low Berlin skies ...

And on the glistening pavements, at the eye of the storm, lithe young bodies crouched down and lit torches and capered in reckless circles around them like revellers at a pagan jamboree, as girls held on to boys - and girls to girls, and boys to boys - clinging tight as they watched the plumes of smoke drift away over the bomb-shattered spire of the nearby church. And as the parade came to an end, distorted rhythms echoed back off the façades of office blocks and then outwards again, into the distance...

The summer of 1992, Berlin, in that glorious period of liminal grace after the Wall came down. "There is a sense of lawlessness, a millennial party being played out at top speed," I wrote in a report that I filed at the time - a sense that anything was possible in this city hurtling into its future, where the old rules had ceased to exist and new ones were yet to be written.[1] Where children like us could frolic amid the ruins of the past, with history providing the backdrop to our festivities. In any abandoned space, in any deserted building, it seemed, fresh flowers could bloom overnight in the darkness. If you looked down across the city from its highest point, the rotating eyeball of the television tower above Alexanderplatz, it was almost as if you could see the landscape shifting before your eyes, like watching the present race forwards in time-lapse motion. Decades of inertia had suddenly come to an end, and now the city was rushing, rushing onwards - to where exactly, it hardly seemed to matter, the only important thing in that moment was to hold on tight and ride the wild energies that were surging through the air...

Back in 1992, the Berlin Love Parade was still a relatively obscure domestic German phenomenon which that year attracted around 15,000 hardline technoheads - a figure that seemed phenomenal to us then, and yet tiny in comparison with the 1.5 million ravers who would join the dance just seven years later. In 1992, the Love Parade was still a gathering of the clans from across the reunited country to revel in the sheer exuberance of their own existence, to show off their extravagant beauty in all its polymorphous perversity, out there on the Kurfürstendamm, right in the city centre. To give the Saturday straights doing their shopping on the upmarket Ku'damm a little jolt of surprise, certainly, but also to stake a claim on the urban landscape not just as a place for buying and selling, but as the forum for a carnival: our carnival, our Love Parade, with its youthful innocence that could not and did not last.

The story of how all this came to be is a remarkable take of historical serendipity, daredevil brinkmanship, creative oppor-tunism and sheer luck: the right place, the right time... What was even more remarkable was not just that this annual procession of techno sound systems through the city centre took such a hold on the popular imagination, but also that it gave Berlin a shot of pure adrenaline just when it was needed. The Love Parade, and the techno scene that nurtured it, helped to create a new narrative for contemporary Berlin - and yes, even for the reunited country itself - which nobody could have predicted beforehand and, in retrospect, still seems astonishing. The long decline of the parade and the horror that marked its ultimate demise may have tainted its historical legacy, but in its early years at least, it was a symbol of hope, ambition and sheer hedonistic release for a metropolis where old shadows still lurked: a mass exorcism of the ghosts of the past.

In 1992, I arrived in Berlin for the first time in six years, and it was as if all its old monochrome shades had somehow been transformed into glowing technicolour. In 1986, I had taken a 26-hour train journey across western Europe to its furthest outpost: the divided city, where all roads came to an end at that concrete barrier which rejected all rational discourse. So I behaved like any good tourist should: had my photo taken in front of the Wall, mourned quietly by the markers commemorating those who had been killed trying to escape the Communist dictatorship, made the obligatory day-trip to East Berlin where I was lucky enough to be able to get rid of most of my almost-worthless Ostmarks paying fines for jaywalking and then buying beers for the clientele of the only bar playing half-decent music that I could find before it was time to head back west as the midnight curfew drew close.

By 1992, traces of this Cold War ambience could still be felt despite the cranes that loomed over the huge building sites on what once was no man's land, where corporate office complexes were under construction as Berlin prepared itself to become the political capital of a united Germany once more. These were chaotic and unpredictable times, and their perfect soundtrack was this new music which had not even been named when I was there in the mid-eighties: this music which seemed to embody the feeling of vertiginous acceleration, like a careering unmanned vehicle with no programmed destination, only the sheer terrifying pleasure of hurtling forwards towards whatever came next - *techno*...

The Love Parade still felt raw and delightfully ramshackle in 1992 as well, as if everything had been lashed together at the last minute by a bunch of random urban freaks on a comedown from the previous night's party - which in some senses was true. The pre-scripted scenarios that would follow when it became a global media event were yet to be laid out and defined. The story was still being written, right in the moment.

The sound-system trucks that made their way down the Ku'damm that year illustrated this glorious anarchic spirit. In later years, Love Parade floats would become lavish productions: huge trucks laden with corporate sponsorship from the legal drug lords of cigarettes and booze, sonically-advanced water-cooled sound systems and preening, narcissistic 'superstar DJs'. But in 1992, some of the floats weren't even really floats at all. I remember seeing a sleek white limousine with blissed-out ravers sprawled wasted over its long bonnet, and a flame-haired female fire-breather in shocking orange showering sparks as she paraded in front of a multicoloured Manila 'jeepney'; an eccentric gent in full military dress driving what looked like a motorised wheelchair, and another man - for reasons that perhaps only made sense to himself - pushing a shopping trolley along, wearing just his boots and underpants, while others skimmed through the crowd on rollerskates and on bicycles... There was none of the crush and hustle that would typify the parade's later years; there was still space for the twisted imaginations of cultural outcasts to run riot along the city's main consumer thoroughfare at the height of a Saturday afternoon.

Among the bigger trucks, the Planet club's vehicle was tricked out as a huge pink cartoon rabbit with its floppy bunny ears lolling down over the cab. But the East German trucks, which were taking part in the parade for the first time that year, were much more dowdy, hung together on the cheap with crudely spray-painted banners; financially at least, the East-West divide had yet to be overcome.

And then there was Tanith's truck... Tanith was an ex-punk turned DJ from provincial Wiesbaden called Thomas Andrezak who had renamed himself after a character he found while flicking through a book on mysticism - to avoid being given a 'punk' nickname like 'Rat' or 'Sid', he told me - although he would later discover that he had named himself after the Phoenician goddess of love and war: perfect for a man who became Berlin's hardcore maestro, the gaunt-faced ringleader of a gang of wilful outcasts on a brain-scrambling journey to the outer limits.

Tanith also had an immaculate sense of punk-rock theatre. His truck in 1992 resembled Martin Sheen's patrol boat on its doped-out pyrotechnic voyage through the spooked jungle waterways of *Apocalypse Now*, but with weapons-grade techno blasting out instead of the Rolling Stones. "It's decked out like a tank, all camouflage and netting, with the DJ as a demented military commandant leading the troops from his gun turret," I wrote at the time. "As the bassdrum powerdrills, his comrades set off smoking orange flares. But just when it starts to look frighteningly militaristic, one of the stormtroopers in combat gear turns to display the peace sign painted on the back of his uniform."[2]

The stormtroopers of peace: a vision of Berlin techno distilled to its essence... The next year, Tanith went even further, arriving at the Love Parade with a decommissioned Soviet tank that he had somehow obtained. There is an iconic photograph of him from that time: standing high and mighty on top of the Russian behemoth, swathed in camouflage and raising aloft a voodoo skull as if invoking the spirits to put his mutant crew under the spell of his music. A man at the peak of his powers, at the height of an era never to be repeated.

There was no shortage of utopian rhetoric swirling in the

ether at that time - considering the amount of MDMA that was percolating through most people's nervous systems, it's hardly surprising - and a lot of it, inevitably, sounds naïvely optimistic in hindsight. Further out than most however was the perennial idealist who invented the Love Parade in 1989, a few months before the Wall came down: Matthias Roeingh, better known as Dr Motte, a Berlin-born DJ who played in a punk band in the early eighties and then went on to run some of the city's first acid house clubs. "He was a carefree, reckless kind of rogue, good-natured and always ready for a joke or prank," as his girlfriend of the time, fashion designer and artist Danielle de Picciotto, said in her Berlin memoir *The Beauty of Transgression*.[3] Or as my friend, the Berlin-based writer Dave Rimmer, put it to me once: "Motte is a holy fool, a brilliant man, a force for good, but completely crazy."

Acid house, for Motte, was an escape hatch from the walled city of the eighties into realms of consciousness where, with the right chemical assistance, dreamers could slip the bonds of reality and float freely. "It was like discovering a new territory," he explained later. "There was a wall in Berlin and then suddenly there is a door in that wall, and you can look *behind*... it was incredible. It opened up our minds and we discovered ourselves."

Motte was seen by some of the Berlin scene's more pragmatic operators as a clownish showman mouthing recycled hippie platitudes, but others saw in him a kind of carefree naïvety that was very much of its time. Dave Rimmer remembers one night at Berlin's E-Werk club when Motte appeared to crash right through the doors of perception: "Motte came in, and he was completely out there, saying he had seen God. Then he stripped off all his clothes, clambered up onto the speaker stacks and danced there, completely bollock-naked, for the next five hours. But somehow Motte stripping off and dancing naked on the speakers was kind of *inspiring* in a way that it wouldn't have been if it had been

48

anyone else, because he somehow represented the spirit of the place."

Motte's own inspiration came from a trip to Britain during 1988's acid house 'Summer of Love'. In her book, de Picciotto recalled how the couple went to a club in London where "we stood, dumbfounded, listening and experiencing the dawn of a new era".[4] Acid house started in London after four working-class British DJs, Danny Rampling, Paul Oakenfold, Nicky Holloway and Johnny Walker, discovered Ecstasy on a summer holiday in Ibiza in 1987 and then tried to recreate their mind-altering experience at home, starting clubs like Shoom, Spectrum, Future and The Trip and inadvertently instigating a dance-drug scene that would dominate European youth culture for years to come. Like them, Motte also wanted to bring his holiday back with him.

"Friends of mine told me about underground parties they went to in London, Manchester and Sheffield, where police came and stopped the parties and took the sound system but people were still dancing outside in the streets with ghettoblasters, having a street party," he told me, his eyes glittering with nostalgic fervour. "Ah, *street party*! It was immediately in my mind, how can we do that here? A spontaneous street party - *how*?"

Late one night in 1989, Motte came up with the most monumental prank of his life, one which would help to define the decade that would follow and even help to transform the image of the entire city, although he could hardly have known this at the time. Like the Paradise Garage in New York, the Warehouse in Chicago, Shoom and Spectrum in London or the Hacienda in Manchester, it would become one of those unique moments in dance culture whose resonance continued to be felt across the decades that followed, endlessly reimagined and reinterpreted by those who come afterwards. Motte decided to hold a demonstration for happiness and unity in the heart of his still-divided metropolis, marooned for decades like some bizarre island in a sea of Communist decay, a protest *against nothing* but rather *for* all that he believed was right and good: a ravers' promenade, bringing his people out of the subterranean darkness and into the light - a *Love Parade*...

"As is conventional, islands have their castaways. This one was full of them."
Dave Rimmer, *Once Upon a Time in the East*

"Berlin was always hardcore," Tanith once told me. Certainly, Berlin had always been *different*; different from the rest of Germany, and a haven for creative free-thinkers for significant periods of the twentieth century.

Between the end of World War One and Hitler's rise to power, amid the social upheaval, economic chaos, poverty and political violence of the Weimar Republic, Berlin seethed with a remarkable and rarely paralleled upsurge of artistic innovation. This was the time of the Berlin Dadaists, people like George Grosz and John Heartfield who exposed the horror of the 'war to end all wars' and its turbulent aftermath. The Berlin Dadaists gave the irreverent playfulness of the original Zurich-based anti-art movement a harder political edge that reflected the tougher environment of the German capital between the wars: "Life appears as a simultaneous confusion of noises, colours and spiritual rhythms, and is thus incorporated - with all the sensational screams and feverish excitements of its audacious everyday psyche and the entirety of its brutal reality - unwaveringly into Dadaist art," said the 1918 Berlin Dada manifesto.

It was also the time of Bertolt Brecht, of Kurt Weill, Hanns Eisler and Arnold Schoenberg, of Fritz Lang and FW Murnau and Marlene Dietrich and Lotte Lenya, of Walter Gropius, László Moholy-Nagy and the Bauhaus school of architects and designers, of Arthur Koestler, WH Auden and Christopher Isherwood, whose stories of decadent Berlin life in the shadow of the Nazis would inspire the film *Cabaret*... "Above all, Berlin in the 1920s represented a state of mind, a sense of freedom and exhilaration. And because it was so utterly destroyed after a flowering of less than 15 years, it has become a kind of mythical city, a lost paradise," Otto Friedrich wrote in his superb history of the Weimar Republic, *Before the Deluge*.[5]

Unsurprisingly, the Nazis didn't care for cosmopolitan, 'un-German' Berlin. They despised its culture and its relative tolerance for the avant-garde, its racial and sexual minorities and its libidinous nightlife. The city was, a Nazi Party newspaper once fumed, "a melting pot of everything that is evil - prostitution, drinking houses, cinemas, Marxism, Jews, strippers, negroes dancing and all the vile offshoots of so-called 'modern art'".[6] The feeling was mutual; most Berliners voted against the Nazis until they no longer had the choice. Indeed Hitler, who once described Berlin as "that sinful Babel", even dreamed of transforming the city into a grandiose fascist metropolis which would be renamed Germania.[7] Instead his regime was crushed, and Berlin was bombed to rubble.

That sinful Babel... after the Wall went up in the early sixties, Berlin became a refuge for young people who could evade military service by living there, where social benefits were better, rents were cheaper and parents were a long way off. It became a new home to hundreds of thousands of immigrants and a bolt-hole for nonconformists: anarchists and squatters, avant-garde musicians and artists attracted by its dark glamour - an image that also drew David Bowie and Iggy Pop to the city in the seventies to record some of their most remarkable albums, *Heroes* and *The Idiot*.

What gave the early Berlin techno scene its edgy vitality - and what it would come to lose as the years passed - was its roots in these subcultures of the seventies and eighties, in post-punk thrash, industrial noise, avant-garde art and the contrarian turbulence of the city's nightlife. Techno itself was created in the eighties by a trio of young black musicians from Detroit: Juan Atkins, Derrick May and Kevin Saunderson, the 'Belleville Three' whose 'high-tech soul' music became so ubiquitous around the world that its black American roots were sometimes forgotten. But even before techno even had a name, some of the Berlin scene's originators were already active in the city's post-punk and electro subcults.

Dimitri Hegemann, who would later launch the seminal club Tresor club, was involved in organising the Atonal festivals which brought industrial heroes like Psychic TV to the city. Mark Reeder, an expatriate from Manchester whose MfS label would later define the early years of trance, was promoting and recording for New Order's Factory label. Motte and another future DJ star, Westbam, made appearances in 1981 at the Geniale Dilletanten festival, a forum for DIY sonic aggressors which also featured the shredded industrial noise of Einstürzende Neubauten. A manifesto for the event celebrated chaos, cacophony and iconoclastic vitality, echoing the Berlin Dadaists' "sensational screams and feverish excitements".

Einstürzende Neubauten, like Bowie in the previous decade, thrived on the city's esoteric vibrations, and when Nick Cave and his band The Birthday Party joined them in Berlin in 1982, it became a nexus for a certain kind of seeker after dark eighties cool. This was the time captured in prose by *Berlin Blues*, one of the novels by Sven Regener (who was also a singer in the band Element of Crime), with its slacker anti-hero slouching around the tattered fringes of Kreuzberg's anarchist enclave. Dave Rimmer's *Once Upon a Time in the East* is another vital snapshot of that time; a thrilling ride through the last days of the divided city that shuttles back and forth across the Wall as its hashbiscuit-munching protagonists play cat-and-mouse games with the authorities on both sides.

"Berlin was like this strange oasis where people didn't have to work very hard to live, they could rent property cheaply and wander around just doing what they wanted," Dave explained, recalling the time when he first arrived in the city in the early eighties. "It attracted eccentrics, and a lot of young people coming in to avoid the draft. Because of the lack of pressure and expense, people could live in a different way and be as extreme as they wanted. "

The feeling of disconnection from Western consensus reality began at the point when the East German border guards climbed aboard the train in their cheap acrylic uniforms, before it rattled down the enclosed line that sealed it from the DDR, past the decaying smokestack towns and the barren roads almost empty but for the occasional peculiar little Trabant car puttering slowly past, while the barbed wire fences flashed relentlessly past the windows of the carriages as they clattered towards their final destination. The city was still divided into American, British, French and Soviet sectors and the Wall seemed to overshadow every journey across it, infusing everything with its constant reminder of venal sins, unpunished crimes and the poignancy of loss. Although the Wall was possible to ignore and many Berliners did so, because they could get out by road, rail or plane any time they wanted, unlike their eastern counterparts through the looking-glass, this was still a "haunted city", as architectural historian Brian Ladd has written, "a city whose buildings, ruins and voids groan under the burden of painful memories".[8]

The Wall - or the 'anti-fascist protection barrier', as the East German regime called it - started to go up when the border was sealed on August 13, 1961, first with barbed wire and later with a reinforced concrete wall stretching more than 100 kilometres, whose fortifications would become more entrenched and oppressive as the years passed. Next to it was the 'death strip' with its watchtowers, searchlights, trenches, bunkers and armed guards, where scores of people would die trying to escape during the Wall's 28 years of existence.

Even in 1989, just months before the Wall fell, Motte said that he had no idea that this could change so quickly. "Growing up in Berlin, knowing the situation, you could never ever think that system would collapse. How? Impossible. To break this Iron Curtain and to reunify Germany? Impossible," he insisted.

Even as mass protests grew across East Germany and thousands of people started to escape through Hungary and Czechoslovakia, the breaching of the Wall, when it came, was almost completely unexpected. On November 9, 1989, East Berlin's ruling party boss Gunter Schabowski gave a televised press conference during which he suddenly announced that East Germans could leave the country at any border crossing - effective immediately. People began rushing to the Wall, demanding to be let out, chanting for the gates to be opened - and finally, incredibly, they were. Thousands surged across into West Berlin in their Trabants and on foot, to be met with flowers, champagne, beer and passionate embraces from West Berliners on the other side. As a spontaneous street party erupted, people scrambled up onto the Wall, dancing and screaming, trans-forming the symbol of captivity into an improvised disco, attacking it with hammers, chisels and any other implement they could find as they beat out the rhythms of release.

Some parts of the Wall were sold off by local entrepreneurs or at auctions abroad; other slabs were carted away and ground down into gravel to be reused as building materials; one piece is kept at former President Ronald Reagan's library in the US as a trophy of his Cold War triumph, and now only a few small sections remain standing in Berlin itself as permanent reminders. I still have a small piece myself, which I bought on Potsdamer Platz in 1992, packed inside a cheap little plastic gift box which also contains a replica of a Trabant and an East German officer's badge. Whether it is actually genuine or not doesn't matter much to me: its questionable authenticity does not diminish its emotional charge.

And as the Wall began to disappear, the Berlin of the eighties started to go with it, like an old black-and-white photograph too long exposed to the light, and a new picture started to come into focus.

"At last mad, at last redeemed!"
Berlin pedestrian in Wim Wenders' *Wings of Desire*

Stunde null - zero hour - the German phrase for the end of Nazi rule in 1945. And again, in 1989, the clock seemed to have been rewound and the past swept aside, ready for a new beginning.

Into the zero-hour vacuum came techno: a new music with its new drug, Ecstasy, with new spaces in which to thrive, spaces left derelict or abandoned by the collapse of what had been but now had ceased to exist, and a new community of eager youths united across the former divide for the first time as they explored the simultaneous novelties together in unique, unexpected circumstances. Berlin, as one writer put it, had become the "abstract city of fantasy", the ultimate raver's dreamscape where there were no limits to how high you could soar or how far you could go.[9] Techno inevitably became identified as the soundtrack to Berlin's newly altered state. "We call it the liberation dance," DJ Westbam told me at the time - and the Love Parade was to become its international symbol.

This kind of enthusiasm was still simmering when I talked to Tanith during the Love Parade in 1992. For a man with a reputation as a full-on provocateur surrounded by a clan of wild-eyed acolytes, his rhetoric sounded surprisingly utopian, all about unity, togetherness, one nation reborn under a groove. "The clubs were the first place that East and West came together and people recognised they are not different," he told me, his voice full of optimism about the possibilities that had opened up.[10]

Meeting him again two decades later, at a bar in East Berlin's now-gentrified bohemian district of Prenzlauer Berg, a couple of weeks before his fiftieth birthday, his hair greying under his trademark combat cap but his striking gaunt features and the subterranean rumble of his voice undiminished by the decades that had passed since we last spoke, he said that he still believed that the dreams of the early nineties were valid.

"It's funny to explain, but it was really true. It fulfilled even my most optimistic views, at least in the beginning," he explained. "East and West, we started at zero together. Techno was the first youth culture that started at zero on both sides. So the myth is true." The East-West disputes elsewhere in Germany after reunification and the emergence of violent neo-Nazism showed that in the clubs of Berlin, at least, something genuinely positive was developing, he insisted: "When you saw these other situations in Germany at that time, you can say that we did something good."

This analysis was not unique: one of the Love Parade organisers who I got to know in the early nineties, Jürgen Laarmann, also said that he still believed that the idea of techno as a unifying force is valid: "On the dancefloor, under the stroboscopes and lasers, that was the first place where the reunification really worked, and where people were really equal," he said.

But this was not just happening in Berlin, insists the photographer Wolfgang Tillmans, who went with me to take pictures at the 1992 Love Parade and was to become one of the most important artists of his generation. Techno was also thriving at the same time in other German cities like Cologne, Frankfurt, Hamburg and Munich, with an equivalent sense of innocent abandon.

"It was the same in the gay scene at the time as well, everything felt like you were breaking new ground, that there was no template for this," Wolfgang recalled. "Obviously it's a question of perceived experience and age, what made that special or if one can really say it was special. But I clearly had a sense that this meant something, that it was political in the sense that it was creating new realities, like at that time, the idea of European people being together and dancing together and seeing each other as part of one family seemed a very liberated and exciting idea, while at the same time there was war in Europe [in the former Yugoslavia]. There was a sense of utopia and a utopian reality alive in clubland."

The mythologisation of techno as the 'liberation dance' for German youth was as much a self-made construct as a reality: a few thousand people blissed out on E in nightclubs cannot transform the mentality of an entire society... Even after the official dismantling of the Wall and German unification in 1990, there was still talk of the social, cultural and economic divisions between people from East and West, 'Ossies' and 'Wessies' - of a 'Wall inside the head', which after decades of living apart was harder to tear down than the concrete structure itself.

"This was not a time of ease and comfort and no worries polit-ically - people were worried how this was all going to work out," Wolfgang explained. "These were hard times, especially in the East, they experienced real hardship when whole towns almost shut down. The Yugoslav war brought a lot of refugees to Germany, and there was neo-Nazi violence. It was a time when there was a sense of history in the air, a sense of urgency, a feeling of the pain of growing up, perhaps."

Down underground, in the darkness, it was easier to cast doubts aside. Tresor was the ultimate hardcore electronic music club, in the basement vault of the abandoned former Wertheim department store on Leipziger Strasse with its metre-thick walls isolating the bodies within from reality; a temple to techno, or *tekkno* as it was sometimes written in the early nineties in an attempt to convey a sense of its harsh assault. The first time I went down there, the sound was so physical that it felt like it might punch my heart out through my ribcage.

Tresor was one of the clubs that took over spaces left abandoned by the fall of the Wall and the collapse of East

German industry. Berlin had long had a tradition of squatting; the idea of liberating abandoned buildings was not new here, but suddenly the possibilities had become seemingly limitless. Discovering the space that would become Tresor, its founder Dimitri Hegemann once said, was "like opening a pyramid".[11] There was no water or electricity, and the vault's old deposit boxes were still there, rusting on the walls. Like at most early Berlin techno clubs, all this was left in place. Any decor - *anything*, even - was provisional: no one knew how long it would last before the developers moved in to clean up as Berlin became Germany's political capital again, another factor that enhanced the impression of dancing on the cusp of change.

You could almost feel the psychogeographical vibrations shuddering through Tresor, which had years earlier been expropriated from its Jewish owners by the Nazis. The club stood close to Potsdamer Platz, which in the twenties and thirties had been the heart of the capital, a vibrant crossroads full of restaurants and cafes, beer halls and hotels; a churning metropolitan hub and place of perpetual movement where "the Babylonian, immeasurable depth, chaos and might of Berlin" was on show, according to Weimar-era diarist Harry Kessler.[12] Later it became home to Nazi administration centres, with Gestapo and SS headquarters close by, as well as the bunker where Hitler died, until the area was bombed into oblivion during World War Two, and when the Wall's 'death strip' cut right across it, it became a wasteland.

In one scene from Wim Wenders' film *Wings of Desire*, an elderly man hobbles past the Wall and through the windswept bleakness of the deserted square with its muddy potholes, discarded rubbish and scrubby patches of grass, searching for his memories - the cafes where he used to sip coffee, the Wertheim store where he once shopped: "I cannot find the Potsdamer Platz," he frets to himself. "Here? It cannot be here... This cannot be the Potsdamer Platz."[13]

"There was nothing there. Absolutely nothing," Tresor staffer Alexandra Droener recalled later. "Rocks, debris, a fence here and there. Today you can't imagine how it was. The buildings were derelict. Plus the odd tower block from the eighties. Like a ghost town. Like after the Second World War. A real zero hour atmosphere."[14] What better place than this, then, to exorcise the ghosts of history?

"Everything was improvised then - *everything*. It was paradise, full-on, we could do anything and no one cared," Dr Motte said. This absence of official oversight in the months after the collapse of the East German Communist government not only allowed young West Berliners with their avant-garde heritage and young East Berliners desperate to celebrate their new freedoms to come together, but also provided the spaces in which techno could flourish.

Berlin, as several writers have suggested, had become a 'temporary autonomous zone' - anarchist philosopher Hakim Bey's phrase describing what he called a 'pirate utopia', a space liberated for brief period from the forces of authority; a concept often used to theorise the outlaw rave scene in Britain in the late eighties and early nineties when outlaw parties were staged in disused warehouses, factories, aircraft hangars, quarries and open fields.

"There are a lot of senses in which the Second World War didn't end in Berlin until the Wall came down," said Dave Rimmer. "Once it did come down, everything started changing *really fast*, and you had no idea where the changes were going to stop. It was absolutely the right time for a new kind of music - a genuine *stunde null* feeling - and techno also had that sense of ripping up the past, kicking out the old, accelerating into the future."

Faster, faster... the remorseless velocity of techno recalled the opening minutes of Walter Ruttmann's experimental documentary film about Berlin from 1927, *Die Sinfonie der*

Grossstadt, when the hypnotic flashing of abstract horizontal lines cuts into the kinetic patterns of railtracks rushing past as a train charges towards the metropolis. Sheer speed, sheer vitality; the rage to live, like the heroine of Tom Twyker's 1998 film *Run Lola Run*, in perpetual motion as she hurtles through nineties Berlin, energised by the electronic beats that fizz across the soundtrack.

Harder, harder... With their camouflage fatigues, army boots, gas masks and radiation suits, it was as if some of Berlin's ravers had created a kind of millennial survivalist cult, arming themselves for a final showdown with the forces of darkness, clad in the cast-offs of obsolete armies finally retreating from the Cold War frontlines. The Tresor record label's first release, *Sonic Destroyer* by X-101, could not have been a more perfect statement, even though it was actually recorded by the Underground Resistance crew in Detroit.

Inside the Tresor vault, *Sonic Destroyer* sounded like an apocalyptic call to arms: a jagged electronic riff that explodes out of a vacuum before being jerked into time by a brutal volley of snares like steel mallets smashing into reinforced concrete, then launches into a fierce motorik groove with sinister drones surging low around it. If the Berlin techno scene was a kind of ritual exorcism, *Sonic Destroyer* could have been its ultimate soundtrack... although, as Tanith pointed out, this was hardly a moment for any kind of abstract thinking: "Historically, from the outside, maybe the idea of exorcising the demons of the past might be correct," he said. "But from the inside, at the time, we didn't even think about that. We thought: we have a new playground, we can do what we want now."

"The art of reporting fails to convey the feelings that one experienced in those beautiful moments."
DJ Westbam

Back to 1992 again: my friend Vanya Balogh came rushing into the office in London where I was editing the latest edition of the pop-culture magazine *i-D*. He was clutching a sheaf of black-and-white prints and gabbling about a colossal rave he had just been to in Germany where he had witnessed an apocalyptic vision of "10,000 madmen shouting for more, harder, faster"; rampaging hordes of stoned freaks who had come together at an ice rink in Cologne, clad in the cast-off uniforms of post-industrial disintegration and glowing with chemical energy from behind the gas masks and radiation suits they were wearing: "Cybermen, robots, goggles, Oxy cans, hand lasers, space suits, mutoid dustmen, cosmic babies," as he wrote in the article that the magazine subsequently published.

Vanya was an energetic scene-chronicler from the Croatian capital Zagreb, my big-hearted travelling companion on several eventful and occasionally hazardous reporting trips across Europe in the nineties, who had worked as a war photographer during the conflict in Yugoslavia, seeing things in his homeland that he wished he had never seen.

"You would not fucking believe it!" he raved, enthusing about something called the Love Parade, a kind of exhibitionist carnival on Berlin's main shopping street, insisting that we had to go there together, that our impoverished little magazine should even pay to run a float in the event... "There was so much energy in Berlin at that time, I had never seen anything like it before and in some ways I haven't experienced anything like it since then," he said when we spoke about it again, many years later. "Coming from the former Yugoslavia, it was very significant for me, all these political changes after the Berlin Wall came down. There was some emotional investment in it for me, for sure."

Although techno could hardly have been less fashionable in London at the time - it was stereotyped as the musical juvenilia of ill-clad proletarian trolls and teenage amphetamine casualties - its savage energies were irresistible; the fierce electronic riffs of

Belgium, Holland and Germany that seemed to want to bludgeon the musical iconography of the past into dust, as well as the more emotional sounds of the music's Detroit birthplace. Trusting in Vanya's instinct to seek out exactly the right kind of madness, I somehow managed to secure backing from NovaMute, a techno label that had recently been launched by Daniel Miller's record company Mute, and rent a sound system and a truck in Berlin, which we hurriedly and haphazardly decorated just in time to get to Wittenbergplatz with a few minutes to go before the start of the Parade…

And then we were off: "For a lot of people, drugs work!" declaimed the voice from the sound system as our little blue truck jerked and jolted its way down the Ku'Damm carrying its random crew of British and German, black and white, hardcore boys in techno T-shirts and gyrating girls in skin-tight shorts, all bouncing on the boards until they were close to cracking and the speakers started to sway with the beat.

The freaks were already out, cutting loose outside the department stores and the supermarkets… buffed muscle boys, stripped to the waist to show off their gym-toned chests, prancing and twirling behind us while a longhair in a fractal shirt vogued like a hippie fairy… a little boy wandering through the swirl of dancers, eyes wide in wonder, grasping hold of one of the heart-shaped balloons that drifted down from our truck… the ambient DJ Mixmaster Morris, in a silver stovepipe hat with matching jacket and trousers, drifting gracefully past then suddenly leaping into the air like a frisky colt… One man skipping along in a chemical warfare suit and gas mask, another lying prone in the very middle of the road, naked apart from his underpants, staring intently at the cosmos inside his head…

"For a lot of people, drugs work!" the voice from our sound system declaimed, over and over again. Bemused tourists snapped off photos and shoppers stared out from the pavements in confusion; an elderly gent in immaculately-pressed shorts pumped his arms to the rhythm as we passed by while bored cops nodded their heads in time... A stunning middle-aged woman walked her chihuahua daintily through the crowd, ignoring the whole mess completely...

The music sounded roughly-hewn and ungentrified too, its harsh edges left raw enough to spike the consciousness, unlike the sumptuously upholstered trance that would follow in later years, smugly confident in its power to manipulate the emotions of the E-heads coming up on their pills. Cheers went up as the raggedy screech of synthesised strings ripped out again - *Der Klang Der Familie* by 3Phase and Dr Motte, the anthem of the day and the meaning of it all - and then that Biblical thunderstorm, ending weeks of drought... as the rain came down...

But even the 15,000 people who were there that day in 1992 would have been unthinkable in July 1989, when Motte's first Love Parade got under way. At the very beginning, he chose *Friede, Freude, Eierkuchen* as the event's slogan, an ironically humorous German expression that translates as 'Peace, Joy and Pancakes'. Motte claimed that this meant that the event was a protest for peace, global understanding through music and equitable food distribution, and he applied for the event to be registered as a political demonstration, which meant that he wouldn't have to pay for policing or the post-party clean-up. The authorities took him seriously and he got the permit. (Some of Motte's allies at the time believed this was just a cheeky scam to get permission to hold a rave right in the heart of the city. "It was a trick, and I liked the idea because it was a typical Berlin anarchistic thing," said Westbam. "But I think later on, Motte really started to believe that it was a political movement.")

That first-ever Love Parade in 1989 saw around 150 ravers trip gaily down the Ku'Damm, waving their arms in the air in the acid house style of the time, some dressed in smiley T-shirts and bandanas, others in eighties casualwear or the monochrome shades of the post-punk era. "We started from Wittenbergplatz, we were standing there with our three little vans and loudspeakers and generators. And tape decks! We were using tape decks!" Motte recalled.

"At first, there was no one there. There was a fine rain, like British weather, raining but not exactly raining. We stood there and didn't know when to start. Then the police came and asked us: 'Do you want to start now?'" He laughed at the absurdity: officers of the law asking the drug-crazed insurgents when they wanted to start their shambolic little uprising. "We had no clue! Nobody had done it before..."

Among the dancers that day was the nucleus of what would become the Berlin techno scene, the original motivators like Motte and Westbam, looking like fresh-faced college boys revelling in the audacity of their prank. "It was like a shiver down the back, an energy I had never felt before," Motte said.[15] Westbam insists that there was, even then, a sense that this would become something important: "Even though it was just this handful of people, in a crazy way we felt that we were writing history. But would anybody on that day have said that in a few years there would be a million people? I don't think so. If you had told me the Wall would come down a few months later? No, no!"

There was a lot of debate about *what it all meant* back then: debate that has never really been successfully resolved and probably never will be. Tanith said he believes that the idea was "to have a demonstration *for* something, not *against* something - for us, our music, for acceptance, for the idea that everyone can join in - a demonstration for goodwill".

Hundreds of articles and a sheaf of academic studies have been written trying to analyse what this opportunistic stunt that Motte dreamed up one night outside a Berlin disco signified in socio-political terms for Germany in the nineties. But in the end, I prefer Dave Rimmer's definition of the Love Parade: "a demonstration for one's right simply to be weird and have a good time - to live, in this city noted for its tolerance of marginality, a different kind of life".[16]

For Wolfgang Tillmans, the sheer "non-sense" of the techno scene was also crucial; its determined rejection of "normal reasonable behaviour".

"It had such conviction and such power and such volume, and for no good reason other than fun," he said. "It hugely inspired me - the strange contradiction between this alien, hostile, dystopian music and all this love and friendliness, it was something that touched me greatly. The desire for this hardness when it's all soft at the core, this reversing of meanings, turning things upside down - it was artistically inspiring.

"That's what I tried to do with my pictures as well, to paint a world I wanted to live in and present it as reality, portraying these happy people together in an international, pan-gender, non-racist way. It was an energy that I could not have cooked up myself alone."

Optimism among some of the scene's most garrulous boosters rapidly ballooned into wild hubris. Some, like Westbam and his ally Jürgen Laarmann, even began to speak about a utopian 'Raving Society', whose members would presumably spend their nights dancing towards dawn on the very purest MDMA and their days lounging in a flotation tank, hooked up to consciousness-enhancing 'brain machines', nourishing their intellects with 'smart drugs' and sipping guarana cocktails while tapping out new electronic masterworks on their computers. The wired-up raver was to be the prototype human of the future, like an avatar from an old Kraftwerk song brought to life in order to rescue a doomed planet from oblivion.

In an article he wrote in 1995, Laarmann declared that techno was a "revolutionary medium of liberation and freedom" that "will lead to greater global changes than the '68 movement ever succeeded in realising". Its peaceful, non-xenophobic, non-sexist collectivism "could function as a role model beyond the limits of the dancefloor", he suggested.[17]

"The techno generation is the vanguard of the age of commu-
nication, and due to its values of Love, Peace and Unity, repre-
sents the shining hope that things may still take a turn for the
better in this world," his manifesto concluded.[18]

At a time of unrestrained hyperbole, Laarmann himself was
certainly in the vanguard. His words were published in *Localizer
1.0*, a book featuring similar tracts that attempted to position
techno as the lifestyle of a better era to come, but which now, seen
from a distance, with its gaudy, era-specific 'futuristic' graphics
and naïve electro-shamanic philosophising, is as charmingly
quaint as an underground newspaper from 1968 or a punk
fanzine from 1977. (It is rendered even more dated by the two
pages it dedicates to explaining what the internet is and how to
use it: "This is possible with a so-called 'modem'," it points out
helpfully.)

Even back then, however, it's not clear whether anyone really
took the idea of a 'Raving Society' all that seriously, or if it was
just another attempt to put the life-changing experiences of youth
into some kind of context: to assemble an ideological framework
that proved that it *really meant something* more than just a
fractured series of drug-induced nocturnal epiphanies.

At the time, Laarmann was running the German techno
fanzine *Frontpage*, which rose vertiginously to become a mass-
distribution publication in the mid-nineties. When the magazine
eventually went bust in 1997, he went through some tough times
and lost almost everything he owned, but years later, he
remained essentially unapologetic about his nineties rhetoric.

"The Raving Society was the idea that through techno, and
technology like the internet, things would be more democratic
and everything would lead to more creativity. One can still
discuss whether that happened or not," he said, knowing that the
enthusiasms of youth are sometimes too easily ridiculed.
"Anyway," he added, "we were so crazy and had so much fun
and took so many drugs that we're just happy to be alive these

days."

I met Laarmann and Westbam again in July 2012 on fashionable Kollwitzplatz at a pavement café where no one appeared to be wired up to a 'brain machine', and 'smart drugs' were not on the menu. I hadn't spoken to either of them for more than a decade, although Westbam still looked like the archetypal superstar DJ with a trucker's cap perched on his head and his eyes masked behind aviator shades.

Born Maximilian Lenz in 1965, this canny character from Münster in provincial Westphalia had originally styled himself Frank Xerox in his early punk-rock days but then chose the DJ pseudonym Westphalia Bambaataa, in tribute to South Bronx hip-hop pioneer Afrika Bambaataa, before finally shortening it to Westbam. He made his first primitive electro-pop single in 1985 (titled *17 - This is Not a Boris Becker Song*), and played dance music at Berlin's Die Macht der Nacht parties in the pre-techno eighties while others were still swilling the dregs of industrial rock.

With his Low Spirit record label, Westbam helped to turn techno into pop in Germany, but was inevitably accused by idealists like Tanith of selling out the scene's ideals and commercialising its sound in pursuit of ever greater audiences and more money. It created a philosophical split within Berlin techno, but I got the impression that he didn't care much what anyone thought of him, either then or afterwards.

His sarcastic wit had not been softened by time either: in a hint at the subject of our conversation, he ordered a plate of *Eierkuchen* with a sly grin on the side. "Ah yes, the *Raving Society*," he said, as if acknowledging in advance the ludicrousness of the peace-love-and-pancakes era that he was about to discuss.

"Jürgen [Laarmann] was the Taliban of the Raving Society, he was the fundamentalist," he continued, poking his friend in the arm just to check that the quip had hit home. "I was more the realist; for me it was just a term that described what was going on. Jürgen painted it more like a utopia, like in the future everyone would be either be DJing or writing a techno newspaper or selling guarana or something, and everyone would be dancing and *being happy*."

He chuckled again, but then deftly changed tack and argued that a concept that seemed naïve with hindsight could only be truly understood within the context of its own time. : "That was really an idea of the nineties, after the Wall came down and the West won and it was all going to be democratic and we were all going to live happily ever after and freedom would reign," he said.

"The spirit of the time was carefree belief in technology, *Friede, Freude, Eierkuchen* and all that - it was that period between the fall of the Wall and the fall of the New York towers. That era ended with Osama bin Laden."

It was a smoothly-delivered theory, probably well-rehearsed over years of interviews, but - maybe - there was a sense back then, in that brief period between the first Gulf War and the attack on the World Trade Centre, that somehow the fantasies of a more peaceful world could prevail: liberty and prosperity for all... although if you were living in Bosnia or Rwanda or Burma or Somalia or East Timor or Iraqi Kurdistan or Nagorno-Karabakh around this time, maybe your view might have been a little different...

"It seems as if every raver in Europe is assembled here. Orange hair, red hair, green hair, blue hair, no hair. The men sport studded codpieces and see-through flares, army camouflage T-shirts with dayglo CND logos; hearts, flowers and stars decorate nipples; beards are like ornate facial topiary."
Report on the 1995 Love Parade in *The Observer*

From 1992 onwards, the Love Parade tripled in size each year, and by 1996, it had to move from the Kurfürstendamm because it had become too massive to be constrained by the tight confines of the city-centre thoroughfare. But although this marked a clear break with its subcultural past as an annual reclaiming of an urban consumer space, its new venue was laden with different but equally powerful psychogeographical significance: the Strasse des 17. Juni, which runs from the Brandenburg Gate through the lush expanse of the Tiergarten park, past the Siegessäule, the Prussian victory column topped by a golden winged statue, to the Ernst-Reuter-Platz.

This was the street that Adolf Hitler had used for his Nazi parades; the street renamed after the failed uprising against the East German communist regime in 1953. The Brandenburg Gate was where US President Ronald Reagan demanded in 1987 that the Soviets must "tear down this wall", and where the German people themselves started to rip it down with their own hands two years later; where they danced in the ecstasy of liberation and where the world's television correspondents broadcast their breathless reports. During the Cold War years, the Brandenburg Gate had been a symbol of the division of Berlin - and, by extension, of Germany, of Europe and of the world - but now it was no more toxic than the scene for a colossal rave. For the new, united Germany, with Berlin again its capital, the symbolism could not have been clearer.

"The Love Parade made it possible to have a million people on a street like that and not think of Hitler. It really changed the perception of Germany and of Germans," said Sven von Thülen, one of the authors of the crucial oral history of the peak years of Berlin techno, also titled *Der Klang Der Familie*. It was also a sign that a new generation of young Germans were refusing to be defined by the past any longer: "It was a kind of reinvention of post-war Germany after the Wall came down," said Westbam. "It painted a completely different picture."

But simultaneously, new tensions were emerging as what had started out as a quirky little local *schnickschnack* turned into a pan-European phenomenon. Three-quarters of a million ravers joined the Love Parade in 1996: a new turning point. It was now a genuine mass event; a 'brand', even, which was increasingly attractive to corporate sponsors seeking to seduce that most desirable market: youth. And what had once been makeshift and anarchic was also becoming increasingly formularised, particularly in the way it was portrayed by the media: the images of voluptuous bikini-clad ravegirls writhing lasciviously on speaker stacks as their fluorescent plastic pistols spurted jets of water over the grateful crowd, the bare-chested raveboys screaming out encouragement as they hung from lamp-posts, the provincial teenage tourists in comedy felt hats giggling and screaming in unison for the cameras, the DJ titans pumping their fists in the air as they blasted out their 'uplifting trance anthems' while laser beams played across the Siegessäule...

Captured in thousands of press photographs and beamed across the world by the television networks, such pictures were so powerful that they set a template for the Love Parade which would endure until its demise, and which meant that it was unable to continue developing creatively because it was trapped by its own self-image - an image far removed from the pre-Wall, countercultural Berlin of the event's creators.

The madness had become ritualised, the event regimented to the point where it no longer possible for piratical renegades to do their own crazy thing. In 1996, it would have been almost unimaginable for a man in full battledress to trundle through the parade in a wheelchair, or a nutter in his knickers to gaily push a shopping trolley behind the sound-system trucks. If anything, the financial charges that were now levied for running a float in the parade had now effectively prohibited random amateur interventions.

In another sign that things were changing, some of the scene's originators no longer wanted to descend into the frenzied crush, preferring to stay on their floats or to hang out backstage, doing drugs with the DJs and their entourages but not getting directly involved with the ordinary ravers any more. Vanya Balogh wrote in an article in 1995 that the Parade was a "display of love, friendship and unity" with a "sense of freedom and pure undiluted excitement", but he later told me that actually, he wasn't really so sure.[19] "It was not comfortable. I did not want to hang out on the street because I couldn't dance or even move around," he recalled. "I felt so small, minuscule in that crowd. It was way too much."

And a blizzard of white powder was swirling through the VIP hideaways: cocaine, the ultimate hubristic drug for the high rollers of the European techno elite. Vanya remembers a narcotic frenzy that resembled something from a grotesque George Grosz caricature of Berlin's decadent rich in the twenties. "The Love Parade had become a big brand, big money was rolling in, big amounts of coke were being delivered and everybody was getting off their heads," he said. "All the money was being spunked on Charlie. Behind the scenes it really was like that - suitcases full of coke...

"From that point onwards, I felt that for me, this was the end," he continued. "When the Love Parade started, it was an authentic celebration. I think it was really genuine, I don't think there was anything superficial or manipulative about it. But as it got big, it lost its link to the underground, and it lost its magic. A great idea was turned into a commodity - a caricature of itself in a way.

"We were interested in genuinely discovering a new world, but after a while, it was not a new world any more, just this big entertainment event."

In the heavyweight German press, the pundits were divided too: was this a force for good or a frivolous waste of time and brain cells - or maybe something more sinister? Some newspaper commentators argued that it brought hundreds of thousands of people together - people who might have little in common in their everyday lives - to celebrate in peace without any cult of personality or reanimation of the demons of the past. Others said it was an ominous signifier of mass uniformity, huge crowds marching in step to the beat of the same drum, like a choreographed North Korean parade... or perhaps even a Nazi rally... Some said that such a gargantuan display of apolitical unity was a welcome sign that the ideological tensions of the past were being left behind, while others argued that it was implicitly conservative because it involved no critical thought and mindlessly collaborated in its own commercialisation...

The music, too, started to become ossified, frozen in time by its own success. A big crowd inevitably needed the 'big tunes': the anthems guaranteed to get hundreds of thousands of hands in the air. The obscure and inventive was eclipsed while the renegade ultraspeed thrash of gabba and breakcore was cast out. The 'Love Parade anthems', promotional tracks made annually by DJs like Motte and Westbam with suitably meaningful-yet-meaningless titles like *One World One Future*, came to represent the deracinated trance which began to dominate the event - a long way from the politically-charged fury of Underground Resistance and the original Berlin underground. Musical dissidents like Tanith, who hoped the party could retain whatever was left of its provocative edge, started to feel that they no longer belonged.

"Low Spirit [Westbam's company] wanted to make it bigger and bigger; they kept saying, 'It's a big success.' But I was saying, 'What is success - the number of people there, the amount of money you make, or the way people feel?'" Tanith recalled. "The original intention was to include everybody - but with *our* music. But then it got so big that the music was becoming watered down too." Even if they weren't up for a hardcore screechfest, others agreed: we did not come here for a pop disco.

And something strange had happened as the nineties progressed: as the number of visiting ravers grew, the Love Parade became a major source of revenue for the city. People would come for the weekend, spend their money in Berlin's clubs, restaurants, bars and hotels, and turn the city into a massive boombox where electronic rhythms seemed to resound from every street corner.

In 1996, the city's economics chief Wolfgang Branoner called the Love Parade "the most important tourist event of the year", suggesting that it would bring in a 110-million Deutschmark bounty; by 2001, a Berlin tourism official would claim that the estimated income to Berlin had risen to 250 million Deutschmarks. "A spontaneous happening, which sprang from a unique time and place, has developed into a huge money-making opportunity," or so I said in an article I wrote at the time.[20]

The revenue was important for Berlin because the economic boom that was expected to follow reunification never really happened. In 1992, Potsdamer Platz had been Europe's biggest construction site as companies like Daimler-Benz and Sony began to build showpiece offices there. But the massive influx of corporate capital largely failed to materialise: none of the top 100 companies listed on the Frankfurt stock exchange moved its headquarters to the city. Berlin had remained, in its mayor Klaus Wowereit's memorable phrase, "poor but sexy", or at least by the standards of other major western European capitals.

While sponsorship had hardly been visible at the Love Parade at the beginning, it soon became dominant; the sheer size of the party meant that it needed serious cash input to survive. Tobacco companies, in particular, had seen some kind of marketing synergy between their legal narcotics and the drug-gobbling rave generation. But the increasing profile of business interests inevitably marked another departure from the event's subcultural roots. As Hakim Bey once noted of sponsored raves: "If

Pepsi Cola is involved then that is by definition from the very start to the very finish not a Temporary Autonomous Zone. Maybe it's a zone and maybe it's temporary. But it sure isn't fucking autonomous."[21]

Westbam, the eternal realist, would always argue that sponsorship was necessary to stage an event on such a scale - even Michaelangelo's Sistine Chapel masterpiece could only have existed because of financial patronage, he once said. In other words, the price of admittance to a massive free party was implicit acquiescence to commercial bombardment - although of course the Roman popes of the sixteenth century did not insist on positioning their logos around *The Creation of Adam*...

But the feeling that cynical businessmen were encroaching on our pleasures was an issue that everyone seemed to be grappling with in 1996 as we tried to comprehend the changing of the times. As I asked myself in an article I wrote, obviously not too sure of the answers: "While the organisers stress the financial realpolitik - if no-one underwrote the Parade, it wouldn't happen - as corporate concerns and government close in on a vision of unity and togetherness that is necessarily nebulous and fragile because its ideology is so loosely defined, does the dream evaporate, does the symbolic resistance to conformism lose its power?"[22]

The Berlin techno scene was also becoming increasingly institutionalised and regulated, part of the city's entertainment environment, signalling an end to the chaotic years of post-Wall creativity as techno's initial frantic rush started to decelerate. The Bunker club was shut down by police; E-Werk's lease expired and redevelopers moved in; Jürgen Laarman's *Frontpage* magazine went bust soon afterwards.

The Love Parade also lost some of its impact by moving to the enclosed environment of Strasse des 17. Juni, where it could no longer interact with the everyday life of the city. In terms of safety, this was a smart move. But it made the event, as Dave Rimmer noted, "a giant playpen fenced off from the general public".[24]

At that point though, we still wanted to see hope amidst the crowds of dancing strangers. Dave Rimmer took heart when he saw clubbers spilling out of Tresor as Sven Väth played a Love Parade after-party, chasing off the police and blocking the road outside the club, turning part of Leipziger Strasse into an improvised street rave - the temporary autonomous zone, revived for a moment. A touch of punkish defiance, Dave suggested, "was precisely what Love Parade 1996 seemed to lack".[24]

Later that evening, I watched a German television broadcast of a lengthy documentary celebrating the Love Parade's history, and fell into nostalgic reveries about the years gone by so fast. Maybe it was just the MDMA afterglow, maybe it was the hypnotic chords of Underworld's *Rez* shimmering through the windows as Sven Väth played on at Tresor just down the road. Maybe I was just deluding myself, but I obviously decided that I still wanted to believe: "When you see it presented like this, through the prism of mainstream broadcasting, it really does look special, a celebration of the communal will to pleasure and peaceful co-existence about which Dr Motte dreams: the restatement of the power of some indefinable 'spirit' that is not yet subsumed by hype and commerce," I wrote. "Looking back, will people really remember MTV or Reynolds Tobacco's presence here? Probably not. But they will remember the exquisite thrill of mass celebration."[25]

"In an idealistic way, it would have been great if the original spirit could have been sustained somehow. But we are humans..."
DJ Tanith

In 2001, the Love Parade finally lost its status as a demonstration, meaning that the organisers had to pay for policing and the clean-up operation. At the same time, numbers started to fall back below the one million mark, reflecting disillusionment with the creeping institutionalisation of dance culture that also damaged the mainstream club scene in Britain after the millennium. Although similar techno street parades were held around that time in cities as far off as Mexico City, San Francisco, Caracas, Santiago de Chile, Rotterdam and Leeds, it was clear that some kind of summit had been reached.

The Love Parade had always been in crisis, on the brink of implosion or falling apart. Environmentalists criticised it because revellers were poisoning the grass in the Tiergarten by pissing out gallons of urine, disrupting the breeding patterns of animals in the nearby zoo and scaring the birds with their deafening beats, causing a strange standoff between greens and ravers which highlighted the E-heads' blithe ignorance of any consequence of their pleasures and gave conservative moralists a platform to rant.

"The so-called 'Love Parade'," harrumphed the historian David Clay Large in 2001 in his book *Berlin: A Modern History*, was little more than an invasion of "beer-swilling, whistle-blowing, dope-ingesting louts, who trampled the vegetation in the park and left tons of garbage in their wake". However, even he had to grudgingly admit that "for all its offensive qualities, this celebration of youthful hedonism was rather less ominous in its implications than many of the other demonstrations that had transpired in this historic district".[26]

Increasingly though, it was not just the conservationists and conservatives who were complaining. As the years went on, criticism from former Love Parade supporters escalated: the event had become no more than a disco version of Germany's annual Oktoberfest beer festival, some said. The DJ Sven Väth, so flamboyantly extrovert on the parade in 1992, like a bizarre peacock splaying out his plumage, decided that he wanted no more of it: "The Love Parade has sold its soul in the truest sense of the phrase," he declared in 2001.[27] Even former 'Raving

Society' booster Jürgen Laarmann said that year that "musically, the Love Parade has no meaning at all" and mourned the loss of its political subtext as a "demonstration against the restriction of civil liberties".[28]

German writer Wolfgang Sterneck argued however that in one respect, it was still genuinely radical: an unrestrained drugfest on the streets of the capital constituted a genuine if unintentional mass protest for change: "The Love Parade is tantamount to a gigantic demonstration for the legalisation of psychoactive substances. The organisers have never planned this or framed it in this way, but in this respect the Love Parade has nonetheless taken its own direction," he wrote. "When people in such groups defy a legal prohibition, it takes on a political dimension, even if it isn't articulated explicitly by the participants."[29]

Disillusionment with the Love Parade had already created an annual counter-demonstration organised by hardcore ravers appalled by the antics of the city's techno elite. As I walked back past the Brandenburg Gate after the 1996 Love Parade had run its course, I stumbled across this group of people whose anger had taken physical shape: a scrofulous bunch of breakbeat-freaks, anarchist *Chaoten*, black-clad crusties, squatters and random acidheads who had turned a nearby parking lot into a temporary protest camp.

"The dusty ground is populated by five or six outlaw systems, their encampments built from tarpaulins draped over VW camper vans, selling tequila shots and spinning rabid Chicago Relief trax," I wrote in a report for *i-D*. "At the far end, the Reverends of Rhythm loop-generate hypnotic acid in sharp, crystalline stereo separation, ringing out over the skyline, their rig framed by scores of cranes overhanging the reconstruction zone in the real-estate treasure trove of Potsdamer Platz; a beautifully juxtaposed image of venture capital and its refusenik children under the sunset."[30]

The camp, I would find out later, was part of something called the Hate Parade - which was quickly renamed the Fuck Parade - a protest against the shutdown of their beloved Bunker club, an extremist techno den in a former air raid shelter which proclaimed itself 'the hardest club in the world' but was sold off for redevelopment and would eventually become an advertising mogul's personal art gallery and penthouse residence. They were also demanding that the Love Parade's opaque finances be made public, accusing Motte, Westbam and the rest of the event's registered owners of being profiteers who were selling the soul of the party.

"The Love Parade claimed to be political, but 'peace, joy and pancakes' is not really a political statement," said one of Hate Parade's organisers, Thomas Rupp. "They were piling up stacks of money from sponsors and trashing Tiergarten with all those thousands of people. The other thing is that they would not allow our music because it was not commercial. At the beginning there were trucks playing hardcore music but then they wiped them out."

The Fuck Parade was a counterstrike for nonconformism, according to Rupp, a former punk rocker turned techno DJ who also played in a Krautrock band and worked as a research chemist by day, developing cures for debilitating diseases (he said that he was known to his fellows as the 'mad scientist').

"The Fuck Parade is for free parties in free spaces and against gentrification. We have no sponsors and no commercial ambitions," he explained. "The idea of the Love Parade was only about sponsors and only about money. The Love Parade organisers were always claiming that they were supporting the subculture but they were not, so we were fighting against that. This was underground against mainstream." As the Love Parade once was...

The Fuck Parade also gradually turned into a forum for anti-capitalist campaigners and green activists - a symbolic annual reclaiming of public spaces that were increasingly under threat as the German capital was slowly redeveloped and the space for alternatives started to shrink. It changed route each year in order to pass by buildings which were under threat of repossession, blasting out its relentless terrorcore breakbeats and psychotic acid tracks as it made its way through the heart of the city, upholding the legacy of Berlin's punk-rock squat scene and the Kreuzberg anarchists' annual May Day riots: a ragged standard held high against the sanitising sweep of gentrification.

In a sense it was a counterpart to the Reclaim the Streets demonstrations, noisily theatrical environmentalist rave-protests that took over public highways in Britain in the mid-nineties in an attempt to halt the UK government's road-building programme. But while the British police did all they could to break up the Reclaim the Streets parties, seeing them as a threat to public order, German officers were deployed to *protect* the Fuck Parade because it was officially licensed as a political event. In the end, the counterdemonstration would even outlast the Love Parade itself. "Ironic, isn't it?" laughed Rupp.

By the turn of the millennium, the tiny avant-garde which had started the Berlin techno scene was no longer in total control of it, and to some of them, a phenomenon that had grown out of a specific place and time - and a set of circumstances that could never be reproduced - had been transformed into something unrecognisable, even reprehensible. Others however, like DJs Westbam and Mark Spoon, appeared to embrace the idea of being techno superstars playing to a stadium-sized crowd as if they were Bono or Mick Jagger.

There is a moment in the film *be.Angeled* - the only movie drama centred around the Love Parade, shot at the event in 2000 at the peak of its excess - where the heavily-tattooed Mark Spoon ascends like a conquering hero to the DJ podium on the Siegessäule, smirking superciliously as he acknowledges the crowd's acclaim: the lord of the dance luxuriating in his pomp.

This is not the ramshackle do-it-yourself vibe of *Friede, Freude, Eierkuchen*, it is something else entirely: something entirely grotesque - but yes, in its own way, wondrous - although it is not the Love Parade as some of its creators who managed to breathe fresh air in the shadow of the Wall had understood it.

A few lines from Dave Rimmer - about how he couldn't manage to meet up with old friends amid the roiling chaos of the 1996 Love Parade - seem to capture, at least for me, the feeling of a cherished moment slipping through your hands.

"I made lots of plans, but nothing turned out the way I expected it to," he wrote.

"A bit like the whole Love Parade, really.

"A bit like life itself."[31]

Mark Spoon - real name Markus Löffel - died of a heart attack in his Berlin apartment in 2006, at the age of 39. I knew him briefly from his hometown Frankfurt in the early nineties when he and his recording partner Rolf Ellmer (alias Jam El Mar) were making intoxicating proto-trance tracks like *Stella* and *The Age of Love*, and then a song whose title maybe said all that needs to be said about those days - *Right in the Night* - but already a man with monstrous appetites, a playboy princeling with a lust for cocaine and hard liquor, but somehow a kind person, at least to me, or that's how I remember it now when I think again of the brief time I spent with him so long ago.

Later his corpulent body became increasingly muscled, toned for action, his demeanour increasingly louche but at the same time determined, focused. Physically he seemed to grow into the moment: *his* moment, as he saw it. For the observer looking on, strung between fascination and disgust, this was decadence on a last-days-of-Rome scale: the repulsive attractiveness of the DJ emperor enjoying the oligarchic excess provided by weekend after weekend of ready cash, women and drugs. You could see it in *be.Angeled*, in Spoon's lopsided vulture's grin and his extrovert's tattoos: I am here, now - and *this is what I want*.

Or was he just playing a role? Even several years after his death, the comments on Spoon's tribute website showed that there was still a lot of love for him. Somehow he, and his music, had touched people: "You were larger than life and lived like a star, wherever you are now mate I'm sure you are still shining," read one of the hundreds of messages of condolence.[32] A couple of people posted comments warning about the dangers of cocaine abuse, but for me, this seemed impolite and misplaced. We knew who this man was - a "robber baron", Westbam once called him. And he seemed to know what he was doing; after all, one of his own tattoos declared: "We reap what we sow."

"When we buried Spoon, we buried the nineties with him," Westbam told me, with a smirk from behind his sunglasses that seemed to acknowledge that he knew he was being ironically disrespectful but at the same time respectfully honest. Like the financial crash that ended the bloated decadence of the 'superclub' era in Britain at the end of the nineties and crippled the Love Parade at around the same time, the death of Markus Löffel showed there was no way back to what had been. He was a symbol of an age that was over. History would take a different course, as it must sometimes, and Mark Spoon would not be part of it any more.

"In the end the Love Parade had little to do with love and was no longer a parade."
The Economist, 2010

Westbam was getting older. He could feel it; in his forties, the signs could no longer be ignored. At the Love Parade in 2009, he hardly recognised anyone anymore; the friendly faces of the past had long since drifted away, never to return. Like all DJs with careers spanning decades, he was destined to age while the ravers who danced in ecstasy as he played his music remained the same - "in the eternal zenith of youth", as he once said in a long confessional interview with his friend Jürgen Laarmann. During their conversation, he sketched out an image of a veteran DJ walking out of his booth, scanning the fresh clear faces in the nightclub crowd and then going into the toilets, only to see his own ageing features staring back at him from the mirror.[33]

At the Love Parade's peak in Berlin in the late nineties, Westbam had released a track called *We'll Never Stop Living This Way*: an implicit denial of creeping disinterest in youthful enthusiasms, of humanity's inevitable physical decay, even of death itself - an impulsive raging against the dying of the light. In interviews with the German press, he had spoken of the Love Parade outliving him and its contemporary participants, carrying on for another 50 or 100 years or more into the future, becoming some kind of carnival institution whose roots by the old forgotten Wall would slowly become obscured by the gathering dust of passing time. His predictions, unfortunately, would not come true.

In 2004 and 2005, the Parade was cancelled because the organisers could no longer afford to stage it now that they had to pay for the clean-up and policing themselves, while the corporate sponsors who had once seen techno as a perfect vehicle for pushing 'brand awareness' had started to back off.

Enter a German tycoon called Rainer Schaller, president of the low-cost exercise-club chain McFit, which bought the Love Parade name and supplied the cash so the event could return to Berlin's Strasse des 17. Juni in 2006. "The Love Parade is brought to you by McFit... Simply look good," one of its advertisements urged.

Dr Motte was infuriated by the sell-off and cut his links with the event he had founded and which had shaped his life. "I said I cannot do this anymore because I am not supporting a fitness chain with my name. For any amount of money, I will not do it," he told me.

"This is the question I have: if you have a culture and a happening that goes with it, does this happening belong to the culture, or in private hands? I thought it should be not-for-profit forever because this youth culture belongs to everybody. You can sell a brand, but not a spirit."

Motte was deeply hurt by his decision to quit, his former girlfriend Danielle de Picciotto suggested in her book: "It was a difficult step to take, since the Love Parade had been our child, but it had turned into a ghost, empty of meaning and seduced by uninspired commercialism," she wrote.[34]

Suddenly becoming an outspoken critic of his own creation, Motte even turned up at the Fuck Parade in 2006 to make a rambling speech about the natural vibrations of the universe, the insanity of warfare, the duplicity of politicians, the demise of the music industry and the healing powers of rave culture. This was not an apathetic generation, he insisted, but one that had chosen to express its dissent "not in the form of spoken words, but in the form of pounding rhythms".[35]

The perennially pragmatic Westbam, on the other hand, initially warmed to the fitness-club entrepreneur for stepping in to rescue the event: "He took Love Parade out of the grave because it hadn't happened for three years. I respected his guts. You always have these people that criticise the 'money-grabbers' but they have never done anything themselves. I have respect for people who have the guts to do something highly risky. But he was willing to take risks to the point of ruthlessness," he said.

"I would say it was a disaster now, but you are always wise after the event."

The 2006 Love Parade would be the last to be held in Berlin. The following year, the authorities refused to issue a permit for the event, and Schaller made the decision to move it to the post-industrial Ruhr Valley. "Berlin is losing the biggest party in the world," he said.[36]

Motte was bitter about this too, and blamed the city's political leaders for squandering financial and promotional opportunities that they had no part in creating: "We built up this culture, these clubs, this Love Parade, this new image of Berlin all around the world. Politicians wanted the image of a young creative city and we gave them this picture. But then they killed an event that was such a worldwide advertisement for Berlin and brought so much money to the city every year."

Whether an event with such specific historical roots even made sense in a different city was another question, but at first the move to the Ruhr Valley was seen as a success, with the parade drawing huge crowds in Essen in 2007 and Dortmund in 2008, even though critics like the writer Wolfgang Sterneck described it a "commercialised remix" of what had gone before.[37]

"The Love Parade was part of the Ruhr's post-industrial coming-out party," suggested *The Economist*, assessing it from the magazine's coolly unemotional liberal-capitalist angle. "The soot-coated centre of Germany's coal and steel industries" was looking for a new image as a creative centre for the information age, its correspondent wrote - and the Love Parade "added a jolt of Dionysian exuberance".[38]

But in 2009, the Ruhr city of Bochum decided it could not accommodate so many ravers safely, and the event was cancelled. The plan for 2010 in the city of Duisburg represented a new departure: the Parade would no longer circulate through the streets, but was to be confined to an enclosed arena. This was a tawdry fake; the dancers were to be corralled in a disused freight train yard and the sound-system trucks were to do no more than simply trundle around the bleak industrial arena, never interacting with the everyday life of the city. It was, as one German newspaper noted all too accurately, "a perversion of the original philosophy of rave culture".[39]

But Duisburg wanted it badly: to bring in the tourists who rarely visited this greyest of Ruhr settlements where glamour, as one German commentator noted dryly, "is in short supply".[40] The event's media sponsor, the tabloid *Bild*, tried to compensate by playing up the Love Parade's 'wild' image by publishing a series of photographs of nubile ravers with bared breasts.

Of course many of those who had joined the Parade in the nineties - myself included - were no longer paying much attention to any of this; the emotional bonds had long ago loosened and fallen away. "By that time, I felt absolutely no connection to it. Nobody I knew had been going for years," as Dave Rimmer said.

The trucks started to roll at 2pm in Duisburg, but an hour later, it became clear that something had gone badly wrong. The main entrance to the arena, a low, claustrophobic tunnel, was becoming overcrowded as security guards were overwhelmed by impatient ravers eager to get in. There were no emergency exits, and no way out as the crush began to intensify. As panic set in, people scrambled towards a small staircase at the tunnel exit in an attempt to escape, and then sheer animal fear took hold, and the stampede became overwhelming.

By the end of the day, 21 people had been killed in the crush and more than 500 others injured. Ravers had literally trampled each other to death as they struggled to survive. "I saw I was lying on dead people," one young woman said. "There were dead people beneath us with blue lips. I won't be able to forget those faces for the rest of my life."[41]

As the ravers started to die, the video screen kept on flashing out psychedelic images and the techno beats kept on pumping. Just a few metres away, technoheads blew their whistles obliviously and waved peace signs at video cameras even as the screams grew louder and the sirens of the ambulances blared out. The mayor of Duisburg gave a televised interview, salivating over the "1.4 million people" who were either there or on their way.[42]

Video footage of the disaster has been posted on the internet but it's hard to look at it for too long: arms reaching out desperately from the panicked crowd, people stretching to pull each other free, others almost reaching safety then falling back onto the concrete; the desperate, confused shrieks for salvation, the twisted bodies being lifted from the crush. I watched it once, out of a sense of duty, but I never want to see it again.

Some of the most moving testimony came in an article written by a Reuters photographer who arrived after the disaster to try to capture an image that would sum up what had happened. He found it amid the debris that the stampede had left behind.

"Sunglasses. I found dozens of mangled sunglasses. Red ones, yellow ones, pink ones. Some were heart-shaped," he wrote. "They were cheap models, those that people wear to have fun, not to protect themselves from the sun. Each one had belonged to someone for whom this party had turned into a nightmare. I found them driven into the ground by hundreds of feet...

"I took a picture of every one I could find. That was the best I could do to tell this sad story."[43]

What had begun in the shadow of the Berlin Wall had come to an end by another concrete barrier, far away in provincial Duisburg. As one of the notes laid in mourning outside the tunnel read: "July 24, 2010 - nothing will ever be the same."[44]

Westbam had flown in on a plane for the Duisburg event, which he had already announced would be his last Love Parade appearance; he had played every year since it started in 1989, but now he wanted out. He remembers receiving a series of text messages of commiseration on his mobile phone: "How sad it is that it had to end like this..."

Hold on, he thought, confused - surely the fact that I'm quitting the Love Parade isn't such a great tragedy? Then more messages flashed up on the screen, and he realised what had happened.

He was asked if he would still be willing to play, to keep the crowd calm and avoid an even more dangerous stampede for the exit. "I thought for a minute and said no, I don't believe that's right. I believe it's OK to play some music at a low volume, but not 'pump up the volume, top DJs playing slamming tunes'. How tasteless is that?"

He said that one of the organisers urged him to reconsider: "But why can't you play? It's still Love Parade."

"'It's still Love Parade...'" the DJ mused, his usual exuberance suddenly muted. "That's just fucked up."

In the days that followed, the German news magazine *Der Spiegel* reported that the tragedy was far from a random accident: "It was the result of a series of failures made by the city, the police and the event organisers."[45] The authorities in Duisburg needed the Parade to boost the city's image and were determined to have it, even if that meant ignoring safety warnings. A permit had been issued for 250,000 partygoers but the organisers reportedly expected 485,000. Entrances, exits and escape routes were known to be inadequate for a crowd of such a size, but all this was overlooked.

"Out of respect for the victims, the Love Parade will never take place again," McFit boss Schaller announced.[46]

It was finally over.

In a grim coincidence, Westbam had just released a CD compilation of his Love Parade anthems, entitled *A Love Story 89-10*, intended to commemorate the end of his involvement with an event that had been part of his life for more than two decades - but an artefact that inevitably came to be seen, in retrospect, as an obituary for innocence lost.

"It's so weird because there is even a photo [on the CD's cover] where I'm standing in front of a tunnel with debris behind me, like there's been a disaster," he said. "But it came out four weeks before Duisburg."

He paused, thinking again: "1989 to 2010... now it looks like a tombstone..."

There was a failed attempt two years later to bring back the Love Parade to Berlin, or at least an imitation of it called the 'B-Parade'. Despite receiving official permission, the organisers cancelled shortly beforehand, citing financial difficulties caused by unpleasant memories of Duisburg that had unsettled potential sponsors.

While Berlin's techno scene continued to thrive and its countercultural hardcore continued to struggle against gentrification and changing times, zero hour had long passed. The old Wall was a fading memory and there were no physical monuments to this remarkable era in Berlin's recent cultural history - a time when music helped to transform a city. It's said that Dimitri Hegemann once dreamed of building a huge 'Tresor Tower' on Potsdamer Platz, but it came to nothing.

Vanya Balogh, who brought me to Berlin for my first Love Parade in 1992, said he felt no nostalgia for those days anymore; what's gone is gone, and that's the way it must be.

"It just seemed right, back then - at that time, in that place, it seemed right," he said. "But I remember, even at the time, I thought: 'This is fantastic, but it cannot go on forever. We cannot do this forever.'"

Maybe, in the end, it is better that way. A temporary autonomous zone, by its very nature, is never meant to last.

Chapter Three

A Free Zone in Babylon

Four days in, time had started to lose its meaning. I looked at my watch, unsure of the hour, then turned the clock face upside down: was it half past 11, or five o'clock? It no longer seemed to matter.

I mentioned this to the French techno-skinhead who was standing next to me. He was stripped to the waist, his dirty combat trousers slung low, his pupils obsidian discs, light glinting off them under the sun. I don't remember who he was now, and I'm not sure that I ever knew.

"Time has stretched. It is bent out of shape," he replied. "This clock - put it away now, it is no use to you here."

Then the DJ on the nearest sound system dropped a ferocious breakbeat, and the skinhead leapt screaming into the air, the blue veins on his cranium straining out from his pallid skin as if they were trying to hoist him upwards into the heavens and clods of earth from his heavy boots sprayed out around him like debris caught in a tornado.

"Bad boy sound! Bad boy! Bad boy!" he yelled, his face contorting in drug-fucked rapture, as if the bassline itself was screwing him senseless, right here in this open field...

That night, rain again. The Teknival site glistened surreally, lit by flashes of lightning and billows of orange smoke from the bonfires, the intermittent rumble of thunder pounding like timpani under the cackle and screech of multiple Roland 303s. Around 12 sound systems were here now, all raging with infernal noise. The smell of wood smoke on khakis, caustic powders on the winds, a debauched tableau of bizarre gyrations, barbarous writhings, crazed muezzin shrieks... Teknival fever!

The message had already gone out on clandestine information lines all over the continent - Paris, London, Berlin, Prague - and the tribes had started to gather. Creeping in from the darkness, spewing fumes from their ancient trucks and patched-up buses: the acid monsters, gabbaheads, skunk punks, squat crazies, kitchen-sink alchemists and bug-eyed believers of many nations who had long ago lost their grip on consensus reality. Here in this Frence field, they would set up their temporary anarchist camp - the sound system jamboree that they called the Teknival - which appears, burns brightly for a few days then dissolves into the daylight, to reconvene elsewhere and elsewhen on a timetable that nobody really knows for sure, or if they do, they keep it well hidden from outsiders.

And within a few hours, a small conurbation had sprung up out of nothing: a 24-hour city with its own main street, its own generator-powered electricity, its own entertainment, catering, refreshments, shelter. One of the few things it didn't have was toilets, just a clearing in the nearby woods where you could escape into the darkness...

"ON TOP NON STOP. Teknivals are hardcore, spontaneous, free-form events. Coalitions of sound systems gravitate towards a spot, set up and then play for as long as possible. The uniting factor is techno's relentless pulse. The only barrier is the one inside your head. TEKNIVAL 23. FUK ME UP HARD STYLE."
Spiral Tribe leaflet, 1996

The Teknival: a last stand against the forces of commerce which had transformed the rave dream into a corporate-sponsored fantasy, against the military-industrial-entertainment complex which had, yet again, turned rebellion into money... or so they told me... a determined rearguard action against the amoral cynicism of encroaching consumerism, even against time itself: "Remember how we became controlled by time, by the concept of the clock?" demanded a freak manifesto that I picked up at one Teknival. "Inspiration is all about escaping the clock…"

Across the site, sound-system diehards had lashed together some formidable temporary constructions out of tarpaulins, tree trunks and rope. The biggest of all the systems, the Spiral Tribe rig, was in prime position at the heart of the main drag, and even had a fully-stocked bar and its own little record shop.

The Spirals! …but of course the notorious Spiral Tribe had invented the Teknival concept when they fled Britain for Europe in the early nineties, on the run from the conspiracy charges they were facing. They were being prosecuted for allegedly organising the country's biggest-ever illegal festival-rave at Castlemorton Common in May 1992; a week-long debauch that saw 25,000 or more ravers create mayhem in a rural idyll, setting off a nationwide moral panic. As the party wound down, the Tribe's core members were arrested for conspiring to cause a public nuisance. (They were tried two years later, but ultimately acquitted.)

After the arrests, they left the country to propagandise their confrontational brand of hardcore techno activism across the continental mainland, moving onwards through France and Germany, where they briefly occupied Potsdamer Platz during one brutal Berlin winter, then on into Austria and Italy, leaving cells of converts in their wake, all getting their own rigs together, all based on the Spiral blueprint of brutal beats, temporary land seizures and *make-some-fucking-noise* attitude. In their more sober moments, the Spirals liked to claim that they were using technology to invoke timeless energies from Mother Earth, taking back the land seized by the faceless capitalist oppressors and deploying extremes of sound and chemistry to traverse the boundaries of consciousness and push humanity to a new stage of evolution through a digitally-enhanced tribe-rite that fused the ancient and the modern… believe that or not, what was never in doubt was that they knew how to throw a seriously wild party.

"The unspoken rule or initiation with Spiral Tribe was that you had to live it, 24 hours a day. There was this incredible amount of focus and concentration," the Spirals' grinning, messianic leader, Mark Harrison, once told me.[1] To outsiders, the Tribe seemed to be like some kind of weird Gnostic sect, materially ascetic but pharmacologically excessive. Harrison seemed to enjoy the confusion that his crew caused, the perennial questions about who they were and what exactly they wanted: "[Are we] an army of insomniac cyberpunk DJs - bent on reclaiming the land and eco-revolution? A techno-pagan cult? Demons of chaos?" he once asked. "Or just a bunch of rag-tag chancers with big boots and bass bins?"[2]

In their self-imposed exile, the Spirals developed the Castlemorton techno-festival blueprint into what they called the Teknival. Within a couple of years, there was an entire summertime circuit of these outlaw extravaganzas which saw sound systems and their hardcore followers chase the illicit buzz back and forth across borders, seeking unpoliced spaces in which they could lose it without sanctions.

This particular Teknival, hidden away in the Champagne region of France in the spring of 1996, was typical, at least in terms of the music that the rigs were playing: there were drums, some basslines, a few disembodied screams, but nobody singing, not ever. Amidst the screeching acid and tribal junglism, there was a lot of gabba, the ultraspeed psychobeat of the Netherlands, battering the senses like the oppressive surround-sound chunter of an MRI scanner. Gabba was so fast that it was impossible to dance to in the conventional sense. In front of one small rig, a lone raver jerked and shuddered while the drums nipped at his limbs, as if he was trying to force his physique into the inhuman shapes of the music. He appeared to be in considerable pain, but maybe he was enjoying his solitary masochistic ritual.

Several non-aligned DJs had also turned up on site with bags of records in an attempt to blag guest spots on the established rigs. One of them, a hard-faced woman who appeared to be at least eight months' pregnant, was spinning equally fierce, industrial-strength hardcore.

My friend Simon Lee from London's United Systems crew had arrived too with a bagful of jungle tunes. Simon, an irrepressibly jovial character who, it sometimes seemed to me, would rather laugh than speak, said that he had cadged a lift to the Teknival in a Mercedes with a psychedelic adventurer from Guildford who had run over a wild boar in the forest on the way in. This twisted suburbanite was right now hunkered down behind a tree, half-naked with his face painted like a feral woodsman, wielding a sharpened stave, waiting for the wounded beast to emerge so he could spear it, cook it and eat it, he said. Either this was a joke or Simon had lost the plot completely, I thought. There were no wild boars here, just bad hallucinations on the road to oblivion.

But not for the last time in this unknown territory, I was wrong: a couple of days later, I saw the strung-out Mercedes driver attempting to roast the boar over a log fire. The creature was real enough but many hours dead, and after long exposure to the elements, its carcass was rotten, riddled with maggots and stinking horribly. The putrid flesh peeled off it like skin from a burns case. Nevertheless, the man remained insistent on eating the rancid beast, until one of the Teknival DJs stepped in and kicked it out of his grasp and into a ditch, where it lay festering as its noxious odours wafted out towards the tents of unfortunates camped nearby.

This was not really a major problem, however. There were more important things to worry about. The day before - was it Friday afternoon? - we had spotted the vans crawling in a sharp white line towards a cluster of farm buildings on the horizon; the only civilisation for miles around. They had parked up about half a mile away from the Teknival's guerrilla encampment, wedged between a glorious patchwork of rolling farmland and a small forest, a couple of hours' drive east from Paris.

From one of the trucks' weird arsenals of utility kit, a sound system DJ had produced a telescope, set it up on a tripod and zoomed in on one of the barns. The vans were full of CRS - France's fearsome riot police - and they were unloading their batons and shields; tooling up for a crackdown. They had already blocked off all the dirt-tracks leading to the Teknival site, preventing anyone coming in apart from those who had managed to sneak through the woods. As a police helicopter swooped low over our truck, a cloak of paranoia descended on the camp: we were trapped, surrounded. "About 6.30, that's when they'll come," one of the DJs said. "First light."

When first light came, he and I were the only ones still awake. Everyone else seemed to have disappeared, out of it or asleep. All the speaker boxes on our truck were strapped down, ready for a quick exit. As the sun started to rise, he faded a mournful melody into the mix, its machine coda chiming out over the fields and forests. Paranoid, exhausted, in a strange reverie amid this monochromatic dawn, we scanned the horizon for signs of their advance, willing ourselves to hold them back with only the strength of the bassline.

"It's then that I get an idea of what this trip is all about: it's more than just a party, it's a mission to build a temporary Eden, a lawless paradise free from the constraints of everyday existence"... or at least that's what my scribbled notes from the time appeared to say when I tried to read them again later, when it was all over. In the end though, the riot police never moved in, choosing instead to set up spot-checks for documents and drugs along the approach roads, ensuring that the paranoia refused to lift and the party mood turned restless and edgy, as if this was not any kind of release, just a stay of execution.

It had taken us 36 hours to reach this field and it was long after midnight when we arrived. The Desert Storm sound-system crew had picked me up on a blustery morning just off the M25 motorway on the flat green outskirts of London. I opened the side door of the truck - fragrant smoke ballooned out - and clambered into the dank little box which would be home for the next day or so. It was already full of bodies, sleeping bags, rucksacks, torn Rizla packets and sound equipment.

The truck itself was a marvellous conversion. It was an elderly DAF which had been fitted with a tiny kitchen, a triple tier of bunk beds and side panels which could open wide enough so a DJ could blast out music over the speakers while the truck crawled through the streets: what Desert Storm called a 'drive-by'. Its doors were painted with a stark energy-flash logo, adapted from the *Rogue Troopers* comic strip about biochip-etched commandos - "genetic infantrymen" - in the cult magazine *2000AD*. It was a kind of armoured personnel carrier for militant ravers; they called it their Rapid Deployment Vehicle - the 'RDV'. Desert Storm used to run with a real armoured car, painted camouflage with a built-in sound system, but it was apparently stolen somewhere it their hometown of Glasgow, towed away in broad daylight and never seen again.

Inside the truck were posters from recent raves and a clutter of dayglo orange Desert Storm stickers. They left a trail of these across Europe, on walls and doors, on postboxes and in people's homes. Over the months to come, that year in 1996, I would see them in the most unlikely places - a student radio station in the Slovenian capital Ljubljana, a terraced house in West London... The slogan on the stickers was their ideology distilled: "Lock up yer women and drugs - Storm is coming to town."

Inside the RDV, a random collection of young bodies: the sound system DJs, plus two student crusties who were planning to play live techno at the rave and were already worrying about the safety of their electronic equipment, a young French acolyte who had read about Desert Storm's exploits in a magazine and decided to join up, and me - the reporter, the 'participant observer', just along for the ride, wherever it might lead.

(Although they had also told me that I might prove useful making tea to sell to the Teknival punters.)

There were no windows in the back of the truck, so the grey coastal skies of Dover felt oppressive when the door swung back and we piled out to stock up on supplies - pasta, bread, rice; cheap high-carbohydrate sustenance. Everyone threw in £30 for diesel and passage across the Channel to France. But it turned out, to my initial confusion, that there were only two ferry tickets. The rest of us had to hide in the back of the van, quiet and still to avoid detection, as we slid past Customs and into the hold of the cross-Channel ship. I looked at Fish, the youngest of the Desert Storm crew, a 16-year-old illegal immigrant from Bosnia with no papers, who would be detained and probably deported if we were caught, and I thought of my comfortable apartment back in London, and buried myself under the nearest stinking blanket.

Fish: unlike the rest of the crew, who came from Glasgow, Manchester and Nottingham, Fish was from Tuzla, a town that was hit hard during the Bosnian war in the early nineties. He had become a fighter at the age of 14 and was given his nickname by fellow militiamen when he jumped into a trench full of water on his first day on the frontline. He was a hyperactive character who rarely slept and had an English vocabulary which mainly seemed to consist of the word 'fuck'.

By the following night, we had reached a small town called Vitry-le-François, somewhere south of Reims. We pulled up at the railway station to make another of many calls to the Teknival's organisers, and were met by Josie, a small, bespectacled black woman in an old Renault van, one of the first French converts to the outlaw techno cause. She and her boyfriend, a gaunt, friendly white man with the shaven head and combat fatigues that were ubiquitous on the Teknival scene, led us a convoluted route through remote farmlands and down dark lanes to our destination.

"Here is the site," Josie gestured, a little nervous, worried that we might have been followed by the gendarmes who had briefly quizzed her outside the station earlier.

"But first, you must work." She pointed to a ditch that divided the field and the lane. "There is a hole. You must fill this hole. Dig. Build a path."

It was 2am and there was no artificial light for miles around except the truck's headlamps. We all got digging in the blackness, shifting soil and rubble using whatever was at hand: two small spades, some children's seaside buckets, a hammer, a broom, our fingers. An hour's labour, and a kind of pass had been constructed, wide enough to get the RDV over the ditch. We were the first system here; we had 'taken' the site. A little cheer of self-congratulatory triumph went up as Keith swung the truck in.

"We urge all brothers and sisters of the underground to transmit their tones and frequencies no matter how primitive their equipment might be. Transmit these tones and wreak havoc on the programmers!"
Underground Resistance manifesto, Detroit, 1992

His name was Keith Robinson. Wearing an orange Celtic FC shirt under a fluorescent roadmender's waistcoat, Keith was Desert Storm's charismatic commandant, its irresistible force. All the way down to the site in France, he'd been pulsing with enthusiasm and chattering about this and that plot: the routes, the destinations, the possibilities, the unknowns.

It was only because of Keith that I went to France with Desert Storm, to be honest. We had met for the first time just a few weeks beforehand in Nottingham, where he had set up his ramshackle headquarters in the squatlands which had bloomed amid the decaying red-brick corporation estates on the fringes of the city centre: cheap dosses and perfect psychogeographical landscapes for the kind of unlikely schemes which he constantly obsessed over and often managed to pull off.

We met at a pub near Trent Bridge on a Saturday afternoon, not long before kick-off at the nearby Nottingham Forest football ground. Keith could hardly be missed amid the match-day lads with their beer bellies and toxic aftershave getting a few pints down their necks before the game, especially with his manic Mohican-cropped comrade Danny Baxter in a lurid orange-and-purple sweatshirt by his side. We ordered some lager, and then some more.

May 1996: Keith at 27 years old, lean and hard-bodied from his self-imposed itinerant existence, honed to optimum physicality like a fighter ready to enter the ring; the optimum weight for his chosen profession. I know that ascetic look, I thought: this person is serious, not just another wastrel from outer limits of the lysergic frontier. He had a collected, authoritative manner and the force of personality to inspire people to follow him. A man who thrived on perpetual motion and someone, it seemed to me at the time, who could make things happen.

The more I got to know about Keith, the more fascinating he became. Raised in flux, he was a restless soul, always plotting the next coup. He was also utterly fearless. Policemen and customs officers were simply stuffed dummies around which he would dance, weaving his anarchic patterns while they blundered in his wake, unable to comprehend the maverick logic that drove him forwards.

"My dad's a revolutionary. I've never met him. It doesn't really bother me so much now so I can tell you," he said to me a few months after we first met.

"My mum was in Russia studying communism, she's a doctor in politics, she was over in Russia and met my dad and he was a Sudanese revolutionary in the Communist Party. He'd had to leave, the revolution had failed, so he went to Russia; being a Communist, he thought it would be the place to be. He met my mum and that was it.

"I'm half-Sudanese, my mother's half-Viking, from Orkney. I grew up in Glasgow but my family always moved; there was never a stable place where we lived."

Keith started out as a nightclub DJ in the eighties but the flash of revelation came when he got turned on to techno. He threw the first Desert Storm party in a disused bank in Glasgow in 1991 amid the "clean surgical operations" (his ironic description) of the first Gulf War. "It was like Saddam's bunker, we put all these pictures of fighter jets and Saddam on the walls, put his face on the tickets. We were anti-war but we were also storming it, getting in there, doing it and getting out..."

Then there were raves in barns and tunnels and other unlikely places throughout the high times of the early nineties, until the bad boys with weapons started to pay visits, attracted by the untaxed money that was being made, mugging and coshing and knifing the rave to death. One night, at the biggest and most profitable party Keith had ever organised in Glasgow, he realised that it was time to get out when he saw who was in his 'VIP' area: "I looked around the room and there was just nobody I knew, there were all these E'd-out maniacs with machetes, all totally wired. 'Fuck this,' I thought. I had made the most money I'd ever made in one night but it just wasn't what it was about for me."

The fag-end of the acid house era, when our dreams were confronted by reality and found wanting - I had seen it at the Haçienda in Manchester at the end of the eighties: in the beginning, one nation under a groove and everyone on one matey - "What's your name? Where you from? What you had?" - the hooligans and small-time badboys loved-up and hugging strangers rather than hitting them, all mixed in with the students and the townies and the alternative types and all loving it. But within a couple of years came the scams, the betrayals, the threats, the beatings, and the lust for profit overwhelmed the love vibes; a culture that was all about letting down human defences obviously had little chance when it suddenly needed those fight-or-flight impulses to fend off attack. "You don't realise what's going on until it's too late," as Keith said.

A chance meeting in London with Mark Harrison of Spiral Tribe offered him a solution: take money out of the equation, and you disperse the vultures that feed off nightlife's black economy. "I told him what our problem was, and he said: 'Why don't you just go back up the road to Glasgow, kick in a couple of warehouse doors and do it for nothing?'" Keith recalled. "I thought: 'Do it for nothing? How are we going to pay the DJs?' He said: 'No, you'll be amazed what people will do for nothing.' I was really doubtful but he's quite a persuasive guy. I liked what I was hearing, I liked the idea that there were other people around who were prepared to do these things."

And so Desert Storm were on the road; destination unknown.

"We were all, in a way, seeking kindred spirits," I wrote in my notes after that first meeting with Keith and Danny. "To them, I was a potentially sympathetic journalist, perhaps able to assist in publicising their mission, another link in a network of friendly contacts upon which they survived. To me, they represented a potential escape route from my disillusionment with what we had become, a possible answer to the questions which crowded my mind these days: What were we doing? What did we really believe?"

For years, it had felt that there was something genuinely liberating about acid house and the rave scene. But a few months earlier, I had felt some kind of turning point. "It was New Year's Eve, and we were in a club, as ever - purportedly the most 'underground' in town and yet owned by a big leisure corporation who employed scene 'faces' to front what was essentially a commerce-driven project with nothing invested in the culture it said it was representing," I wrote at the time.

"The tickets retailed at a preposterous £35, and the rooms, stairwells and corridors were meticulously policed to excise any unwanted manifestations of delinquent abandon. We thought ourselves 'out of control' but were constantly under control. There were bouncers in the toilets, patrolling for signs of illicit drug-taking, and the DJ, an itinerant punchclock who was capitalising on some loose affiliation to a club in Ibiza, was banging out the vilest lowest-common-denominator house-by-numbers, each tacky riff and 'atmospheric' breakdown cynically programmed to excite the formulaic raptures of the Ecstasy user.

"And then come midnight, as the New Year dawned - there was nothing. None of the communal celebration, the hugging and kissing of complete strangers, the spontaneous smiles that had once made all this so unique. The party was over. It was the end of the night."

Just like in Berlin with the spiritual decline of the Love Parade, we seemed to be losing faith in some of the dreams that had sustained us for the past few years. In Dom Phillips' brutally incisive book *Superstar DJs - Here We Go!*, which documents the nineties 'superclub' years of excess and exploitation that bloated towards an inevitable crash on New Year's Eve 1999, what strikes me most is the main protagonists' almost complete moral disconnection from the outside world; their flight from both reality and idealism as a tsunami of cash and cocaine washed the soul out of a scene that had once been starry-eyed and loved-up.

Phillips saw these ugly moments closer than most because he was the editor of the British dance music journal *Mixmag* during its most vital creative period in the mid-nineties. In his book, Phillips lets the narcissistic princelings of the DJ booth and their partners-in-powder, the club promoters, babble on carelessly until they impale themselves on their own absurdities. I had interviewed people like this several years earlier for my own book about the origins of acid house and rave culture, *Altered State*, and I was depressed by how depraved some of them had become during the high-living years of 'caning it', 'larging it' and 'having it' that followed.

Some of the people that Phillips spoke to were self-aware

enough, however, in hindsight - the book was published several years after the millennial crash - to see exactly what had gone wrong. "Money and cocaine," said one of them.[3]

The preposterous excess of the era - a time of rampant decadence and blind hubris when hundreds of thousands were blown on luxury cars and drug abuse; the antithesis of all that was special about acid house - helped to draw people like me to diehards like Keith Robinson. Keith still believed. He wasn't earning thousands of pounds from his parties, or even getting paid at all, most of the time. He just did what he did because he loved it and thought it had to be done his way, and fuck the consequences.

"To the beat of the drum: *bang!*"
Desert Storm's Bosnian war favourite, *To the Beat of the Drum*

There weren't many 'superstar DJs' playing in Bosnia-Herzegovina during the war that broke out as Yugoslavia collapsed in the early nineties. Amid the most horrific conflict in Europe since World War Two, the continent's best-paid nightclub entertainers were understandably not too enthusiastic about the idea of spinning records while snipers took shots at them, even if they had have been invited, which of course they weren't because Bosnia had more pressing problems than a lack of raves. But Keith Robinson, obviously, was a man who thought a little differently, and towards the end of 1994, Desert Storm set out in their RDV with a food convoy organised by Workers' Aid for Bosnia, heading for the ravaged mining town of Tuzla.

The United Nations had declared Tuzla a 'safe haven', which meant that it wasn't very safe at all: a badly-shelled industrial settlement which had become a temporary destination for refugees fleeing from Bosnian Serb forces' ethnic cleansing campaign, and which would suffer one of the war's most terrible massacres in the months that followed. Keith and his crew arrived in the snowbound town just in time to throw a New Year's Eve party.

"We didn't know what was going to happen but we certainly didn't expect what did," he recalled later. "We were supposed to play in a basketball stadium and it fell through, so we set up the system in the truck and just drove about. We had the music turned on for about five minutes and all these soldiers with guns came running up. We thought, 'Oh shit, we've really done it now!' But they were saying, 'Turn the lights down and the music up.' We said, 'Are you sure you've got that right, you don't mean the other way round?' 'No, we have orders from the commander, turn the lights down and the music up!'

"So we turned the music up, soldiers were jumping onto the truck, and off we went. We came past the police station and the police were outside, firing into the air with revolvers, blue lights on, dancing on the bonnet of the police car. We got to the town hall and more soldiers came running out with a message: 'When you're finished, come to the mayor's house, he has wine and food for you.'

"Then we got to the first housing estate, pulled up, and within five minutes, doors opened and people were coming out from everywhere, running out of apartment blocks with AKs, just firing into the air. People everywhere, guns going mental, shouting and screaming and dancing."

The anthem that set the Kalashnikovs blazing was a minimalist jacktrack called *To the Beat of the Drum*, which had a compulsive "bang bang!" refrain that obviously transcended language barriers.

"Every time the track went 'bang bang!', they were firing in the air... *Jesus!* It was the first night that the curfew had been lifted in the city for about three years, it was New Year and they were just going crazy. I was a bit worried at times that they were going to go too insane and start shooting each other."

The drug of choice in Tuzla at that time was Artane, a

prescription chemical used to treat Parkinson's Disease which, if the dose is right, can create feelings of euphoria. (In the following decade, it would also be used by Iraqi troops to ease the terrors of patrolling post-war Baghdad: "I can't bear working without taking Artane. It makes me happy and high, but I still can control myself," one soldier told the *New York Times* in 2008.)[4]

"It's a bit like E but when you're faced with any aggression you become tense and aggressive yourself," one of the Desert Storm crew explained. "It's mad, you have a good time but if anything goes wrong, you just explode like dynamite. And everybody's taking this there - they're just putting drugs into bottles of home-made wine, shaking it up and downing the lot!"

The Tuzla trip was just one of several Desert Storm missions to Bosnia; the last, just after the Dayton peace agreement in December 1995 that ended the war, saw them linking up with Spiral Tribe and traversing the entire country, from Bihać to Mostar and Sarajevo, playing over 20 gigs. "Driving to Sarajevo in the winter with a dodgy truck and almost no cash is probably not the most sensible thing to try and do, but after hearing about the ceasefire, we just had to get there and take part in the peace celebrations," Keith said at the time.[5]

Photographer Adrian Fisk, who accompanied them on that journey, remembers his initial shock after crossing the border into Bosnia, seeing children throwing stones at unexploded landmines, trying to set them off, in the midst of a bomb-blasted landscape made yet more ominous by threatening wartime graffiti.

When they reached Mostar, where Croats had fought their Muslim neighbours across the glassy green waters of the Neretva river that divides the picturesque little town, Desert Storm staged the first major multi-ethnic party since the war. "It's a beautiful town, a tiny place where everyone knew everyone, but it was the scene of some very ugly war crimes," Fisk recalled. "If you went over the bridge from the Bosniak [Muslim] side to the Croat side, there was a very clear no-man's-land of about 300 to 400 metres that was absolutely shot to shit. You had to be really careful where you walked because of all the unexploded ordnance - it was a proper frontline."

This frontline was where Desert Storm decided to throw their party. "They handed out photocopied flyers they'd made, and come the night, people arrived," said Fisk. "But when they came, it was either older people or much younger people, a lot of young kids. There was not really anyone in their twenties because most of them were dead.

"So you had this extraordinary scene; you have to imagine, it's Mostar, just after the war has finished, you've got that really dark, minimal, unforgiving techno playing and the strobe firing off and the smoke machine going, so what they've actually done is recreated a mini war zone... And all these young kids just went absolutely crazy because they had so much tension and so much energy, they were so fucked up after all the damage that had been done to them, and these people had come all the way from England to put on a party just for them, and they absolutely fucking loved it. It was a magical moment."

In Sarajevo, Desert Storm staged the first all-night party since the three-and-a-half-year siege of the city was lifted; the only drawback was that because there was still a curfew, the club doors had to be locked, and until 5am, no one could be allowed to leave. It was about as far away from a British 'superclub' as it was possible to get.

Keith said that he saw Desert Storm's Bosnian sorties as a kind of 'cultural aid'; a direct connection on the level of the basic human desire to celebrate and dance. "People have been cut off from enjoyment and fun through being involved in this nightmare of war for so long," he told me. "Going there for a few weeks is not that risky, but the cumulative risk of being there all the time gets to you psychologically. Day in, day out, with this constant threat of death, nothing to do, a nightmare just trying to survive - it's going to get to your head, isn't it? So someone comes in with a bit of music and enthusiasm, it gets you going, gives you something different to do for a while..."

Or as another of the Desert Storm DJs, James Thomason, put it: "Music is a part of normal life that's been lacking. Food, yes, obviously you need it to live, but it's not everything - you need to feel that there's a point in living."

That still didn't answer questions about why people like Keith invested so much of their time and energy and money - so much of their young lives - in trying to make such things happen. Techno activists had to be mechanics, electricians, DJs, sound-and-lights experts and long-distance lorry drivers, all at the same time, unrecompensed apart from the marginal income from irregular paid parties, donations, unemployment benefits and perhaps for the more nefariously minded, selling drugs on the side. On their final trip to Sarajevo, Desert Storm had to hustle up cash with impromptu parties at almost every stop before reaching Bosnia and then camp out in sub-zero temperatures in the Slovenian mountains for a week, working on the truck after it broke down.

"It's amazing what you can do when you've got so much determination. Anything is possible," James said. Or as Sex Pistols biographers Fred and Judy Vermorel once said about Malcolm McLaren, sound system activists had to possess "the vision of an artist, the heart of an anarchist, and the imagination of a spiv".[6]

"I get something out of it as well though," Keith insisted. "I enjoy what I do - I'm totally addicted to it, full on. Some people are into it for the money, but just to be into it to taste that energy, that's the highest level. I like this life; I love it, it's brilliant...

"These questions are a minefield, when you start asking them you bring everything into question - what is it all about?" he mused. "At some of the parties, it is almost like magic, it's close to that. It's conjuring. Now we're getting on to things that I don't really talk about because it sounds crazy to most people…"

Although wars have long attracted adventurers, mercenaries and profiteers, Adrian Fisk said he believed that Keith wasn't just driven by his desire to avoid everyday tedium.

"I think it's a bit like that question where mountaineers are asked why they climb the mountain: because it's there," Fisk said. "I think that was part of Keith's motivation, because it was there and because he could and because he wanted to. And I think he wanted to because he was driven by the challenge of putting on parties in increasingly difficult environments and he was quite political in his own way, and so I think he was motivated by what he saw as great injustice and oppression.

"He has quite clear ideas of what is right and wrong, so that opportunity to go and have a good party is accentuated if he knows it's for the right cause. Of course he is motivated by the adventure. But he went to Bosnia - not without risk - because it was a cause he believed in."

It was on their first trip to Bosnia that Desert Storm met Fish and his friend Ben, who they would later bring back to Britain while the war was still raging. "These kids saw a passage out of there because we were nutty enough to take them," Danny Baxter explained. "A lot of the local kids would dive on you, nick as much chocolate as they could and fuck off. But these kids were a bit smarter than that and they hung around, interpreted for us and helped us out, showed us around, let us stay at their houses so we didn't have to sleep in the truck, made their parents cook for us."

When they made the decision to take Fish and Ben to Britain, some of the aid convoy workers tried to dissuade him. "They were saying: 'Do you know what you're doing? They're refugees, they could get shot at the border!' Which was feasible, because the war was still on then," Danny said. "They could have got tortured, we could have got chucked in prison, God knows, anything could have happened. But I said I didn't mind, I thought it was a good thing to do because he was only 15 and he'd been on the frontline shooting people, off his head on Artane, which is not really what it should be about at that age…"

Ben couldn't get accustomed to his new life in Britain, sitting around playing his nostalgic old tapes of Bosnian music and pining for his homeland, and eventually left again. But the hyperactive Fish learned to DJ and became an integral part of the crew, putting in long sessions behind the turntables when everyone else went to sleep. Even when he settled in Scotland, though, his problems weren't over; according to Keith, his mother was shot dead while visiting a friend in the Bosnian town of Srebrenica, and then his room-mate in the Glasgow hostel where he lived hung himself.

I had met young men like Fish and Ben too, when I was in Bosnia a few months after the ceasefire agreement was signed, in that uncertain time when there was no longer war but no genuine peace either. I came in from Zagreb, driving south with my friend Vanya Balogh through the ravaged landscapes of southern Croatia and northern Bosnia, seeing for the first time the burnt-out villages and shrapnel-scarred homes that I knew only from the disconnected reality of television reports. I found it upsetting, but for Vanya, a Croat who had grown up here in more peaceful times, before Yugoslavia collapsed, it brought back desperate memories of working as a photographer during the conflict in his disintegrating homeland. I remember him talking once about finding piles of bodies in the road and being too disturbed to take pictures, about seeing rockets streaking across the horizon from the balcony of his apartment in Zagreb, about watching a battle from a hilltop as soldiers fired back and forth at each other, and it not seeming to matter who was fighting who, or for what…

We eventually arrived in the northern Bosnian town of Bihać, which at the time was still under curfew at night, pockmarked with shell-holes after a three-year siege during which it had come under repeated bombardment from hilltop artillery positions.

Bihać, of course, had been another UN-declared 'safe haven'. Vanya and I had come to do some reportage along with a small British aid group called the Bosnian Cultural Support Network, which was bringing in boxes of studio equipment and CDs to resupply the local independent station, Radio Bihać. But when we got there, we found people who seemed to have lost hope in hope itself. "We have won the war," said Mirsad, the radio station's 24-year-old music programmer. "But what exactly have we won?"

At the Hotel Park in the dilapidated town centre, we were given free postcards depicting the lush waterfalls and rich wooded hills of the area, and a brochure designed for tourists. But instead of listing local attractions, it offered statistics outlining the extent of the town's destruction: 50 per cent of buildings damaged, another 20 per cent terminally ruined. There were few jobs here and only meagre pay for those who did have work, and nobody could see many optimistic prospects coming their way.

As we chain-smoked the evening away with Mirsad and his friends behind the closed curtains of a little café before the 11pm curfew sent us scurrying for home in the darkness, dodging the rocket craters and nocturnal security patrols, they told us how they would sit here in this same room during the war, smoking cigarettes while shells demolished buildings across the road: "If it was small artillery, we had two seconds to duck under the table; if it was large artillery, we had 20 seconds, and we could finish our cigarettes before we had to duck," one of them said.

"Shakespeare!" exclaimed Mirsad suddenly. "To be or not to be? That is what I would say to myself then, as we waited to die, that was the question." There was also some justified bitterness about people like us who came to sightsee amid the misery of this picturesque little settlement surrounded by magnificent mountain peaks from which it was bombarded into rubble. As I gazed out from a bridge over the sparkling emerald waters of the

River Una that afternoon, Mirsad had remarked: "This is a beautiful town - for you. This place is 90 per cent Bosnians and 10 per cent journalists; they all come to see this amazing country. You should get yourself a T-shirt made: 'I have been to Bosnia.'

"You want to know what I need down here, you want to send me something useful?" he asked. "Send me a BMW."

A luxury car would not necessarily have been out of place in Bihać though, as the town's vehicles told a typical wartime story: the majority were beat-up and rusting, but there were a few shiny new Jeeps and Mercedes, trophies acquired by profiteers who had made fortunes from arms-trading across the frontline, black-market food scams and selling on boxes of Western aid supplies. Keith had seen it in Tuzla, too: aid being stolen and resold to the poor and desperate by illicit entrepreneurs. Meanwhile Pixi, one of the DJs at the Bihać radio station, explained what people from his generation had lost: "When war started, time stopped. People who would have gone to school or college went to fight instead. So we have many educated killers, but not people educated to do anything else."

We spent an evening dancing at the Galaksija club, a kind of seventies time capsule that could have been designed for a Barry White video, with red leather upholstery, Greek friezes and a bizarre sculpture of a robot hoisting a naked woman aloft. The resident DJ, Ance, a Muslim refugee who had been 'ethnically cleansed' from Serb-dominated Banja Luka, told us that he loved house and techno, dreamed of living in Amsterdam and despaired of what he had to do, seven nights a week, to get by in the place where he had ended up, this "village" of Bihać. "My job," he said ironically but completely accurately, "is to play the *Macarena* ten times a night. For me, that is big shit. I try to look to the future. I live for the future."

That night at least, the club attracted a strange mix of young Bosnians - boys with buzz-cuts in hip-hop tracksuits, girls in tight jeans with dark hair and smouldering eyes - and squaddies from the NATO regiments that were stationed near Bihać, dancing in full combat gear with automatic rifles swinging by their sides despite the sign at the entrance that pleaded: "Leave your guns at the door."

Another evening, we were invited to participate in a rock'n'roll talk show on Radio Bihać alongside a member of the cultural aid group and a British DJ, Lawrence Ritchie from the Smokescreen sound-system crew, who were in town to play a free party at Galaksija. The show itself was a lively mix of information, satire and off-the-wall humour, delivered with irreverent verve. But although we found some common ground during our north-south European exchange, we also encountered unnavigable chasms in experience. The presenters, Davor and Steka, asked us about raves, about our opinions of Bosnian rock, about European drug culture. They were particularly fascinated with Ecstasy after reading so much about it. What did it feel like when you took it? Was it legal in western Europe? Could it really kill you? We felt, not for the first time, that we were a long way from home.

In turn we asked them about local bands (there were five or six, but they had limited access to equipment and nowhere to play live), what people did for fun during the siege (they chatted and drank coffee at friends' houses) and whether they found the idea of British sound systems driving hundreds of miles to Bosnia insane (they said they didn't; they were glad that some kind of alternative entertainment had come to town, although they preferred Nirvana to house music). Traditional folk was the dominant sound here, Davor said, and he found it suffocating and regressive: "They should put all those accordions on a big bonfire and burn them!" he raged.

But despite the poverty and the unemployment and the sheer grinding boredom of everyday existence, many young people told us that they had chosen to remain in Bihać. Running away now, after all they had endured, would be to finally accept defeat: "I could leave, but now I have fought for Bosnia, I want to stay here," one said.

All around Bihać that week, I saw European Union propaganda posters that were trying to suggest that post-war Bosnia was now on the road to Brussels. They showed a little boy staring hopefully out from behind a sofa, as if he was just about to come out of hiding, with the feel-good slogan: "The future begins today."

I asked Mirsad if he felt as though he lived in Europe, but he immediately threw the question back at me: "Do *you* think we are in Europe?" I answered yes, geographically, Bosnia is in Europe. "Geographically!" he laughed, with an ironic glare that ended the conversation.

"'Mr Polis... SUCK MY CUNT!'

"It's the girl who, ten minutes previously, was dancing maniacally in front of the speakers, her arms spread-eagled in the strobe. Now she's over the edge and ranting.

"'Suck my cunt, Polis!'

"Her mates are trying to get her to shut up. After all, this is a bust, and you can never tell when policemen - insistent that the party's over yet affable enough until riled - will turn nasty and decide that it's time to fill the van with ravers in handcuffs.

"'I sucked your father's dick, Polis man! Now fuck off!'

"The generator has been switched off and, disguised by total darkness, people start to join in with her, chanting, shouting, raging against the silence, demanding that the music be turned back on.

"Friday night at Junction 23 of the M8, Glasgow city centre. Under the motorway, a triangular wedge of concrete space where roadmenders store their traffic cones: an eerie cavern, traffic rushing in and out of the city on each side, lorries careening overhead triggering a ghostly subsonic boom that

resounds through the damp night air. A fine place for a party,
or so Desert Storm and their Glasgow compatriots Common
Knowledge believed. But, two hours after kick-off, it's over.
'I'd move that gear, son,' a young copper smirks sarcastically,
indicating the slide projector and lights stacked outside the
tunnel, ready for getaway. 'I'm not such a good driver and I
might just run it over when I tow your van away...'"
Report by the author in *Mixmag*, 1996

The threat of arrest, of police seizing vital sound equipment or
vehicles, was a constant worry for those who lived this itinerant
outlaw existence, flitting across borders from illegal rave to
outlaw festival and back. But the middle nineties was also a time
when party and protest intertwined on the British rave scene's
radical fringe, a time when sound-system crews put their liberty
on the line for their beliefs.

The roots of this connection lie deep in the arcane history of
British counterculture, reaching back to the free festivals that
started at Stonehenge in the seventies and the 'new age'
travellers of the early eighties, wandering hippies whose annual
raggedy jaunts across the country in their venerable buses made
them tabloid folk devils. In June 1985, police smashed up a
traveller convoy heading for Stonehenge, launching a summer of
evictions and harassment of hippie encampments that radically
politicised the scene. When some of the travellers joined forces
with urban crusty squatters and psychedelic ravers who saw
acid house parties as technologically-enhanced hippie festivals
in order to stage all-night sound-system sessions at the
Glastonbury festival in 1990, a new alliance was born.

Collectives of ravers and DJs started to buy buses and trucks
as well as records and sound equipment, and began travelling
around the country, staging free raves that lasted for days rather
than hours in rural fields and farmlands across Britain, updating
the travellers' itinerant revels for a new generation. Some of

them, like Mark Harrison of Spiral Tribe, were veterans of Stonehenge as well as acid house clubs like the Haçienda in Manchester, and saw the countryside as a politically-charged arena for a symbolic showdown between the hallucinogen-fuelled rebels and their oppressors: the aristocratic landowners, their police lackeys and the shadowy forces of Control.

After the movement peaked at Castlemorton Common in May 1992, the Conservative government launched new legislation to ensure such an outrage would never be perpetrated again, drafting a law that targeted unlicensed raves as well as other groups of marginal undesirables like squatters and hunt saboteurs. The 1994 Criminal Justice and Public Order Bill proposed to outlaw house and techno - "sounds wholly or predominantly characterised by the emission of a succession of repetitive beats" - when it was played at an illegal party. The outrage about the proposed law became British rave culture's key political moment, as tens of thousands turned out to demonstrate against what they saw as the criminalisation of their generation. Among them, at the 100,000-strong final protest against the impending law that ended in clashes with police in London's Trafalgar Square, were Desert Storm.

Keith's crew were not what one might consider 'political activists' in the orthodox sense - they were in favour of the freedom to party anywhere and at any time, explore the psyche-delic frontiers without harassment, and live their lives their way without too much state interference - but their vaguely-defined anarchist sentiments drew them to the rally in Trafalgar Square in 1994 with their faces painted camouflage and their speakers boiling with techno fury - "firing at the cops with music" as the riot broke out, as Keith remembered it.

With the Labour Party opposition leader Tony Blair backing the anti-rave legislation - a forewarning of the civil-liberties transgressions that would follow after he became prime minister - the demonstrations failed and the law was passed. It cast a shadow over the travelling rave scene, many of whose leaders had already moved on to Europe after Castlemorton to carry on the party abroad, with Spiral Tribe staging the first Teknival in July 1993. But the heightened political awareness coincided with an upsurge in environmental protests against government road-building schemes across Britain which saw hardcore campaigners camping out in trees for months in an attempt to stop what they saw as ecologically-devastating construction projects.

The most remarkable manifestation of this new radical green movement was Reclaim the Streets, a series of outlaw events that fused sound-system techno with environmental activism: a convergence of direct-action politics and hardcore hedonism that took over city streets and even motorways for demonstrations that were a peculiarly British mixture of hippie theatre, crafts festival and outdoor rave. Desert Storm saw them as a logical inheritor of the transformative power of the MDMA-charged summers of love in 1988 and 1989 and the original illegal parties. "It gives you that energy again, that raw fucking energy," Danny explained. "It's electric energy at Reclaim the Streets, it really is, I've never experienced that kind of thing before."

Danny was another wild and complex character, a natural-born misfit who had grown up near Nottingham in the tough working-class village of Ilkeston, which at the time was a haven for right-wing racists who were handy with their fists and didn't much care for this teenage scamp's freakish demeanour, particularly when he was wearing make-up, as he sometimes liked to do. He then drifted around the country, making a living as a travelling salesman and later working on the door at the Haçienda in its acid house glory years, before getting involved in sound systems while living amid the post-apocalyptic concrete crescents of Manchester's condemned and now-demolished Hulme housing estate - until he joined up with Desert Storm.

Danny saw Reclaim the Streets through the prism of the

typically ill-defined hippie-raver's political ideology, as a cheeky poke in the eye for The System: "What it's about is having a mad party in the middle of the street - you're basically telling the establishment to get stuffed in no uncertain terms," he said. But he also recognised the inconsistency of driving a big truck to a demonstration against automotive capitalism: "It's a bit hypocritical actually, we got a couple of people coming up as I'm driving the truck at one mile an hour through the city centre, leaning over and going: 'That looks like a car to me, mate!' But how the fuck are you supposed to get a sound system there? One band carried their instruments, the crowd were supposed to help them but nobody did."

I saw what he was talking about for myself at a summer solstice Reclaim the Streets protest in Bristol in 1997, when a shaven-headed percussion troupe led by a mad-eyed barefoot hippie headed a ramshackle procession of crusty punks, anarchists in Crass T-shirts and fluo-clad ravers along the main shopping drag to occupy a traffic roundabout that served as the hub for drivers entering the West Country city.

Over on the other side, I spotted a black DAF truck which had driven the wrong way up the street and jolted to a halt as policemen struggled to grab the wheel from the driver's hands, before retreating after the keys were slipped to a collaborator in the crowd: Desert Storm had arrived. Keith swung the RDV's concertina side-panels open and they loaded their sound system down onto the tarmac. A frenetic techno beat crashed out as Keith raised his clenched fist to the crowd, screaming victoriously: "Come on!" Reclaim the Streets was now in full effect.

Protesters painted anti-capitalist slogans on the asphalt, squat-punks crouched on the kerb swilling beer from cans, crusties twirled and looned about to the sound systems' groove as a man built a little stone circle out of bricks and children frolicked in the temporarily car-free zone while another rig shuddered with a techno remake of The Ruts' incendiary punk anthem from 1979, the time of protests against the fascist National Front: *Babylon's Burning.*

Billboards advertising Ford cars and a local airport expansion project were defaced and a huge banner quoting anarcho-feminist heroine Emma Goldman was hung from an overhead walkway: "If I can't dance, this isn't my revolution." Keith meanwhile was deep in the mix, playing grungey new tunes that he'd just brought back from a Teknival in Italy. He gripped my hand in a fierce greeting, hyped and adrenalised, burning up with the power of the moment.

My notes that day are a rambling, somewhat intoxicated essay about taking over urban environments which have been colonised by cars and turning them into human spaces for people to interact rather than drive past each other to work or shop, about asking questions about what and who cities are really for, about the liberating charge felt by people taking control of their own environment, if only for one symbolic afternoon. It was an optimistic few hours, but the euphoria didn't last.

After the sound system trucks packed down and moved out in the early evening, diesel fumes blurting and airhorns blaring out a noisy farewell, a group of crusty punks started to goad the police: "Are you ready?" As a helicopter hovered overhead, hundreds of officers edged forward with dogs and horses, batons drawn, ready to clear the area. When they finally charged, the remaining demonstrators had become moody rabble rather than a celebrating mass, and the drunken punks started to hoik beer bottles into the air, one of which immediately smashed into the back of a teenage protester's head, knocking her to the ground with an audible crack of glass on bone. The crowd began to scatter in panic, throwing cans and stones back at the advancing police line.

I had been involved in confrontations with police before, when anti-racist demonstrators tried to shut down fascist bookshops in Nottingham and Welling, and during the miners' and printers' strikes of the eighties, but those had a specific political target while this was just boozy belligerence posturing as 'anarchy'. The day had already been won, but now it was being lost again by a bunch of lager-addled poseurs whose first victim was not The Man, but one of their own.

It had started to rain, and it was time to leave. I later heard that more than 20 people were arrested, and even though Desert Storm seemed at first to have got away, their truck was later impounded and two of them, including a pregnant woman, were briefly but unsuccessfully charged with 'conspiracy to cause a public nuisance'.

> **"You're playing with heavy chemicals, you're playing with heavy vibes - you're in a free zone in Babylon."**
> Sebastian of Spiral Tribe in the documentary film
> *23 Minute Warning*

July 1996, the Czech Republic. We're on the road through Bohemia, on the way to the next Teknival: Czechtek, as it would become known. I still wasn't sure of the exact location; I had called the information line but only heard the piercing squeal of a fax machine at the other end. We were going the right way though; on the road we saw vanloads of techno-skinheads, their faces pierced, their vehicles decorated with the geometric monochrome swirls beloved of Spiral Tribe. And I knew the name of the nearest village: Hostomice, it was on the primitive photo-copied flyer I had picked up a few days earlier in a club in Prague, alongside a tripped-out smiling sun and some sentences in Czech that I couldn't decipher.

Hostomice turned out to be a nondescript provincial hamlet with a dusty, tree-lined main street and little else. A few local hardmen sat on a wall, dressed in shell suits, boozing. Nothing to do out here except glug hooch and psyche out any strangers passing through. A right turn into a country lane, and groups of young Czechs were lugging sleeping bags along the road: the site is just up ahead, they shouted.

Pulling into the huge field, it was obvious that this was much bigger than the Teknival at Vitry-le-François earlier in the year. There were two circus tents, for a start, one of them belonging to the Spirals. Desert Storm weren't on site yet. "They're on their way," offered a baldheaded woman from the Spiral Tribe crew, deep tanned like her comrades after months on the road.

I had read about the first Czech Teknival, two years earlier, in an online dispatch by a raver called Nel Stroud: "On the site in Hostomice is a MiG, a 1940s Russian fighter plane, mounted on a trailer," Stroud wrote. "Military vehicles, with wheels taller than a man, cluster around it. In a four-pronged, ten-foot-high cage hangs a metal creature, bolted and welded together, its head twisted to the sky like a [Francis] Bacon alien scream. In the confusion of night, as the dust rises through lasers, the Mutoids tear back and forth amongst the screaming crowd in a deconstructed car with fire shooting out the windscreen and the exhaust pipe, surrounded by fire-jugglers.

"A particularly hot day evolved through twilight into an electric storm, and all present emerged from various camps and vehicles and danced on a plateau of dust with electricity crackling in the air, and amongst gusts of hot and cold wind the vibes built and built, acid all around, tangible... Rhythms careering forward, piling into the future, bellowing into the sky, and then a voice sampled: 'YOU DON'T KNOW WHAT YOU'RE DEALING WITH.'

"Spiral Tribe will make you paranoid," Stroud concluded, "but then you should be... while standing in front of stacks of bass bins I had the feeling that they were declaring war on the rest of the world."[7]

In 1996, as well as the Spirals, there was an array of vehicles dotted around the field in little circles, and more arriving hour by hour: buses and trucks, psychedelically-decorated wagons with trading signs like Chaos Cafe and COCKtail BAR, BMWs and Mercedes with Vienna registrations and tiny, dirt-encrusted Eastern European crawlers. Most vehicles, however, seemed to have UK plates.

Darkness fell. We took a slug of *slivovice*, Czech plum brandy, bought a couple of beers from a local entrepreneur who had pulled in with a van full of booze, and headed off into the throng. Another man, English this time, offered pills: "They're MDMA, 140 milligrams," he promised. The classic dose - the Godfather of Ecstasy, Californian chemist Alexander Shulgin, would have been proud. "My stuff's got to be good. I go round this circuit all year, and if it's not good it would be a problem, because everyone will see me again at the next site," the man said.

In Spiral Tribe's red-and-blue-striped marquee, the vibe was getting harder. A huge strobe flashed relentlessly, short-circuiting sensory perception, disconnecting mind from body. After a few minutes, I wondered whether my limbs were my own... fucked-up hard style, indeed...

Nel Stroud's dispatch suggested that the Spirals were a spiritual reincarnation of Ken Kesey's Merry Pranksters, but while those legendary psychonauts shone with the positivity and impending liberations of the sixties, "this new lot, they are altogether more fearsome and dark, a nihilistic vision... the dreams of a generation are being expressed by these outlaws, and what dreams, what nightmares!"[8]

The DJs were spinning endless loop beats, tracks that seem to last for half an hour, the only change coming when they ratcheted up the pitch again. Outside, someone had installed a battery of searchlights which played across the skyline. The Spirals had an even more extravagant set-up than in France: well-stocked bar, stall selling T-shirts and tapes - even a currency-exchange service...

I picked up a couple of photocopied leaflets from the stall.

One of them was the usual blather about how Teknivals disrupt our normal timeframe references, cutting us loose into an altered state of social perception. There were a few mentions of ley-lines, UFOs, the Illuminati, mystic earth energies and other lysergic obsessions. But one seemed to be questioning the usual Teknival certainties. "We must awaken from the trance that we are in; ie. the illusion of revolution," it urged.

There was an email address and I sent off a few questions after I returned to Britain, and got a response from someone called Richard, who said he was part of a crew called the Hard Sound Project: "We despise the so-called 'trance' of most current music and the fake spirituality that is sold to people," he wrote. "Too many have got into the habit of not thinking about anything at all and buying into a 'higher state of consciousness' which is merely making some talentless fucker a shitload of money. We try to operate in the true spirit of 'industrial music' (as invented by Throbbing Gristle, Einstürzende Neubauten) as a modern-day blues; taking whatever tools are available to express ourselves."

It was the first time I had heard anyone on the Teknival circuit mentioning Throbbing Gristle, although there was clearly a link, and not only in the music, the machine-gun rattle of sound-system techno that was just as industrial, and occasionally as unsettling, as TG's analogue assaults. Desert Storm's lightning-flash logo also strongly resembled Throbbing Gristle's symbol, although when I mentioned it to Keith once, he said he had never heard of TG. Then there was the obsession with the number 23, which the Spirals shared with TG, William Burroughs and Aleister Crowley. The writer Jon Savage once described TG as a "laboratory", a place where "matters were pored over, researched, put into practice, lived out: the last is quite important". He said that TG were seekers after "truths about the limits of human behaviour that we are encouraged to ignore" - a description that could equally be applied to some of the Spirals' sorties beyond the boundaries of everyday consciousness.[10]

That night I bumped into Simon Lee from United Systems just as he was about to go on the decks on the Ooops! sound system, the only rig on site that was playing jungle rather than frenetic techno and had a black MC on the microphone, hyping up the mood. Simon was radiant with enthusiasm, bouncing up and down on his Fila trainers: "I'm going to rinse out some serious motherfucking techstep!" he yelled. Techstep was an austere and disciplinarian descendant of jungle, with all the ragamuffin ebullience replaced with a digital storm of swarming sub-basslines, horrorcore samples and steam-hammer snares. While it didn't have the narcotising thrill of jungle's shape-shifting rhythms, its dark energy was perfect for a Teknival.

As Simon's set took flight, he played a tune I remembered from the Teknival in France, and suddenly I was up there, in the immaculate zone, the music floating right through me, the excruciating desire, the savage yearning of a spectral girl's voice synching those memories right into the present and making this moment and these words the only things that mattered or had ever mattered.

"Let me be... let me be the one...

"Let me be... let me be the one... to satisfy... your every need..."

I never found out the name of the tune, but knowing what it's called, owning a recording of it, would always be insignificant compared to what I felt in this moment. Indeed, that would have been enough, but there was more, as Simon broke the mix down into a libidinous, rutting groove that shuddered into silence, before a gruff northern accent admonished: "Keep jumping, you bastards!" Everyone around the rig cracked up laughing instantly, bringing us all together out of our individual trances. "Keep jumping, you bastards!" - somehow it felt more human, more real than all those mystical techno slogans.

Lounging by our tent the next day as the beats pounded on relentlessly under the Czech sun, I fell into conversation with

Peter, a Dutch raver from Eindhoven who turned out to be a serious fan of Prince, the funky visionary who had fucked with the parameters of pop, gender and race. Peter had been travelling around Europe, trying to find something better than Ecstasy. A couple of years after his primal encounter with MDMA, he had become disillusioned, like many others, with the predictability of E-plus-techno-equals-rapture. He had explored the finite contours of the experience, didn't want to rush onwards over the edge into oblivion, and was contemplating where to go next. He said that he had never found enough *meaning* to satisfy him in electronic dance music, and was hoping that one day, maybe, his hero might come up with some answers: "If Prince made techno," he mused, "it would be something altogether different, with his imagination..."

My friend Dave Rimmer, who was working in Prague at the time, had also arrived in Hostomice and one night we wandered together aimlessly through the gaggles of dancers and the circles of bodies huddled around bonfires, each little enclave focused on its own vibe, while men in black insect costumes loomed up from behind stacks of speakers, fireworks burst into the sky and motorbikes raced around in crazed circles amid bizarre Cubist inflatables strewn around a bar playing lounge muzak with its neon sign etching out a smoking cowboy.

The site seemed to get larger after dark, more labyrinthine, like the romantic pirate vision of the temporary autonomous zone that Hakim Bey once described: "camps of black tents under the desert stars, interzones, hidden fortified oases along secret caravan routes, 'liberated' bits of jungle and bad-land, no-go areas, black markets, and underground bazaars".[9]

Dave remarked on the dedication of people who were continuously crossing borders, copping hassle from Customs officers and police, running out of money, their rickety vehicles constantly breaking down, all to keep the Teknival show on the road. As he observed in an article that he wrote later: "The whole thing is surprisingly well organised considering it's basically been put together by a bunch of loony anarchist crusties dedicated to staying absolutely shitfaced all summer long."[11]

(The Czech authorities, unlike the British and French, seemed to care little about this annual convocation of lunatics, or at least in the early years of the Teknival at Hostomice. In 2005 however, pitched battles broke out when hundreds of police with tear gas and water cannons moved in to stop that year's Czechtek near the village of Mlynec. The riot became a national scandal as the Czech prime minister, Jiri Paroubek, insisted that the ravers were "not dancing children but dangerous people" with a taste for drugs, alcohol and political violence. He said that it was offensive to compare the police operation to crackdowns on students while the country was under Communist rule, as some Czech media commentators had done. "Any analogy drawn with the current savagery of young anarchists is wrong," he said.)[12]

That afternoon, we had driven into Hostomice to try to buy some supplies because the only sustenance available on site was booze and drugs. The village shop was shut, so we took a seat in the local pub. It was full of ravers from the Teknival and the owner was beaming like an E-head, pulling endless glasses of Staropramen for his captive market. The sole dish on the menu was deep-fried cheese and chips, the staple diet of vegetarians in the carnivorous Czech Republic.

Then it happened. There was a commotion outside; someone had collapsed, a half-naked bloke with a shaved head. An ambulance pulled up and his friends crowded around him, frantic, desperate. As they lifted him onto a stretcher, one of them attempted to give him mouth-to-mouth resuscitation and a paramedic banged on his chest, trying to restart his heart. Then the doors closed and the ambulance pulled away with his friends tearing after it in their beat-up little car. Later I was told that he had died.

I never discovered his name. All through the following week,

I checked the press for any mention of his death, but there was none. He passed, or so it seems, almost without trace. Dave Rimmer learned more about what happened from one of the man's friends, a young woman who was travelling with one of the sound systems and who claimed that she was a trained nurse. He had choked on his own vomit after consuming a "cocktail of drugs", she explained. "I wish I could have saved him," she said. "I wish I could have stopped him dying..." She babbled something about how the sound systems would hold two minutes' silence in his memory, then seemed to forget her dead friend entirely, snapped into another mood and asked Dave: "Hey, do you want to buy any trips?"[13]

Drug-taking at raves is hardly a revelation, but the sheer intensity of the Teknival scene, with its days-long parties and 'on-top non-stop' attitude to both music and pharmaceuticals, had taken recreational narcotics use to a completely different level. LSD, magic mushrooms and the dissociative hallucinogenic Ketamine were the defining drugs here, rather than Ecstasy. Some Teknival acolytes genuinely seemed to believe that lysergic acid, when consumed in heroic doses, could push the human ego to the brink of dissolution and short-circuit years of conditioning, just as the followers of Timothy Leary and Ken Kesey had suggested back in the sixties. "MDMA has its place, but once you've taken it a couple of times, its lessons are learned very quickly and it becomes unnecessary. It has a definite perimeter of experience, and once tried and tested, it doesn't go beyond that," Mark Harrison of Spiral Tribe once told me. "LSD and magic mushrooms have a much more creative influence, not just on raves, but on life, on one's understanding of oneself and the world around."[14]

Ketamine was also ubiquitous, partly because it was cheap and easily available. Its detractors called it 'techno smack' because it sometimes reduced overenthusiastic imbibers to slurring, dribbling blobs of horse-tranquillised flesh lost in the

'K-hole'. But some ravers seemed to love the way it hurled them down into these churning, plasticised wormholes of the mind, warping electronic music into random alien patterns of dislocated sonic signals.

Then there was DMT, dimethyltriptamine, a naturally-occurring psychedelic that induces a short but shatteringly intense trip into phantasmagoria and was prized as a tool for mental catharsis by some of the Teknival scene's most headstrong explorers of inner space. "Everything was like, 'Whoosh! Zoom!' There was power everywhere," one DJ told me after taking it. "There seemed to be people there, or maybe something there, talking to you but not in words, *showing* you feelings and expressions and taking you on this mad high-speed guided tour of this bizarre place that either exists behind everything or doesn't exist at all. It makes you look at yourself, at who you are, and feel your own power."

Of course a Teknival without drugs would have been unthinkable: psychoactive chemicals, like extremist techno music, chaotic sleeping patterns and the rigours of endless impoverished road trips, were a way of creating and occupying a liberated psychic space - a 'free zone in Babylon' - located beyond the norms and values of mainstream behaviour and consciousness. It was just a question of how far you wanted to go: right to the edge, where reality and fantasy blurred into new visions of the moment, or beyond it, into the unknown, where there were no longer any maps to guide you…

"If it's going to happen, it's going to happen."
Private Richard Harvey, Royal Regiment of Scotland

After a couple of summers chasing the Teknival scene across Europe and tracking Desert Storm's idiosyncratic trajectory, I drifted away and gradually fell out of touch with them - until more than a decade later, I read an article in the venerable

Edinburgh newspaper *The Scotsman*, published under the headline: "Royal Regiment of Scotland Sets Off for Afghanistan."

The Scottish troops were departing to fight the Taliban in the turbulent Afghan province of Helmand, the article said. It quoted 28-year-old Private Richard Harvey, who said that recent killings of Scottish troops in Afghanistan preyed on his mind, but he didn't think that he could suffer the same fate... probably. "If it's going to happen, it's going to happen," he said. The newspaper added that he "found it difficult saying goodbye to his three daughters, Vikki, 11, Jennifer, 5, and Emma, 4".

A second soldier, named as Shaun Garrett, aged 17, said that he was "excited" but had no idea what to expect when he got to Afghanistan. I felt uneasy that my country still sent teenagers off to fight and die in lands about which they knew almost nothing - but then I read the comments made by another of the regiment's soldiers.

"I quite believe in the cause politically," this third squaddie said. "I feel our way of life and society are under threat." He said that he had been forced to justify his decision to go and fight to many of his friends, but he felt that the world was "at a bit of a tipping point".

The newspaper named him as "techno musician Keith Robinson", adding that he was "a rave organiser, a member of Desert Storm Sound System band".

It couldn't have been a coincidence or a misprint or some weird newspaper production error: it had to be Keith, the techno rebel, off to fight for the West in this brutal post-colonial conflict.

"I wanted a new challenge," his final quote went, and then I knew for certain that it really was him.[15]

A few months later, I saw a photograph posted on the internet: striking an insouciant pose in a waterlogged bunker, stripped to the waist with an automatic rifle in his hands and a cigarette between his lips, there he was - Keith Robinson, NATO warrior in Afghanistan.

I finally tracked down the mercurial raver-turned-squaddie a couple of years later in Bristol. By this time he had already been promoted to the rank of lance-corporal and was living in a terraced house in the working-class Easton district, its living room littered with party flyers and bits of army kit. His hair was shaved back to a sharp fuzz and dyed brilliant white, and although he was now in his forties, he had as much restless energy as ever.

Desert Storm had reached the end of the line about a decade earlier, he explained, on a travellers' site in southern France where they had pitched up. Times were hard, money was tight, and the rest of the crew decided to quit and head home to Britain, leaving him there alone.

Feeling deserted, he holed up in his caravan as paranoia took hold and he started believing that some of the other travellers were out to get him, plotting to burn him out and steal everything he had. There were vicious dogs and weapons on site too; after all those years of getting away with it, now it seemed that every-thing had finally come on top.

Fearing for his safety, he realised that it was time for him to leave too - and quickly. He retreated to his mother's home in the Scottish Borders, disillusioned and lost, and decided to join the Territorial Army. "It was time for a new start," he said, although the army wasn't initially convinced that it needed an outlaw rave DJ in its ranks: "They didn't just look at me slightly strangely - they thought I was completely off my head!"

He then volunteered for deployments to Afghanistan, where his first tour of duty saw him do eight months in Helmand province - "the dodgiest place on this planet". Deployed at a remote base deep in the Taliban's hunting grounds, he had to face remote-detonated roadside bombs and direct assaults by militant fighters, he recalled, describing scenes that could have come from the Afghan war documentary *Restrepo*. "They were ambushing us every time we went out. They even tried to take the base a couple of times - even I have to admit, that was a bit scary..."

His decision to volunteer for a series of Afghan tours was ideological: he genuinely believed that he was fighting the good fight. By way of illustration, he told me about a skateboard ramp that British troops had constructed for Afghan children, and how little girls would come and skate as they would never have been allowed to do under the Taliban's rule. "I saw this and I thought, 'This is why we went to Afghanistan,'" he said.

But, as so often in the Afghan conflict, there was no happy ending.

"A few weeks ago, I heard another story about this - a man persuaded a boy to become a suicide bomber and go and blow up the whole skateboard ramp and kill everybody there. So that's why we're there too - to stop people like that."

He had obviously taken a lot of grief from techno-scene friends for joining the British Army, but someone who has faced down the Taliban in Helmand is probably not going to be phased by the complaints of a few peaceable ravers. Indeed, he spoke with the same passionate sense of pride about the armed forces as he had done about Desert Storm 15 years earlier. "If we didn't have an army, we wouldn't be having this conversation," he insisted. "Why? Because I wouldn't exist for a start, because I'm black and Hitler would have killed all the blacks."

Now he divided his time between military manoeuvres, DJing at the occasional rave and installing sound systems for nightclubs in Asia, he said. The Teknival crews meanwhile continued to thrash their anarchic way around Europe in an annual merry-go-round which seemed to have established itself as a permanent alternative lifestyle choice.

I spoke to Keith once or twice on the phone over the weeks that followed, but then he disappeared again, seemingly without trace, heading back into whatever foxhole or underground lair that had lured him. I wasn't worried; I knew that he would surface again somewhere at some unexpected time or in some obscure place with a cheeky grin on his face and yet another remarkable tale to tell.

And of course that's exactly what happened: in the summer of 2014, he posted a letter on the internet that he had written to his company captain, resigning from the army. "Over the last few years I have found the juxtaposition between the two characters of LCpl. Robinson and Keef Desertstorm rave organiser harder and harder to reconcile," he wrote. "I realised that I had to choose one path or the other." [16] He had achieved what he wanted while fighting in Afghanistan, he said, but his mission to play music was still unaccomplished.

A few days later, he posted a photograph of a huge stack of sound system speakers that he had set up in a warehouse somewhere on the outer fringes of east London. Its message was clear: Desert Storm was back on the road again.

Chapter Four

At the Court of the Disco King

Yellow dust billowed up from the rocky track, mingling with the exhaled fumes of dozens of cheap cigarettes and the leaded vapours belching from the exhaust pipes: a low-hanging cloud of pungent, airborne grime...

We're going to a disco.

Our scruffy little convoy huffed and chuntered its foul-smelling way up the hill - ancient Soviet Lada saloons with creaking suspensions and rust-latticed paintwork, filthy white minibuses full of sullen-faced parents and wide-eyed infants, the sleek black jeeps of the apparatchiks and the nouveau riche, their expressions inscrutable behind dark-tinted glass - up, up and around the mountain, past the troops with their guns, standing vigil by the roadside, then rolling steeply downwards into some of the most inhospitable territory in this volatile region.

Downwards into South Ossetia. A place where villages had been divided for years by fortified checkpoints and belligerent militiamen. Where Kalashnikovs spat fire as soon as night fell. Where ethnic cleansing was a time-honoured way of seizing power. Where violence has usually been the preferred method of 'conflict resolution'.

We're going to a disco on the frontline.

We're going to dance to Boney M.

I had taken a strange road to get here. After spending years working as a magazine editor and writing a couple of books about cultural resistance movements in former Communist states, I had moved to Tbilisi, the capital of the former Soviet republic of Georgia, to work as the BBC's correspondent in the perennially unpredictable Caucasus region. Georgia itself seemed to exist on a political faultline; it was located on a strategic corridor between the Black Sea and the Caspian, and had been fought over for centuries, repeatedly invaded and occupied by Mongols, Persians, Turks and Russians. Indeed, the country's very existence as an independent state seemed to be something of a miracle. But even at the start of the early twenty-first century, it still had two unresolved conflicts which, when I got there, looked ready to escalate into war at any moment, on the territories of Abkhazia and South Ossetia, self-proclaimed 'independent republics' which had been waging lengthy campaigns, backed by Moscow's cash and military resources, to break away from Georgia forever.

Instead of interviewing cultural renegades, I was now spending my time gathering the opinions of local potentates, oligarchs, refugees, covert intelligence operatives, dissidents, soldiers, aid workers, diplomats and criminals; what would become a familiar cast of characters in a country traumatised by decades of suffering. But stories about music were still much more attractive to me than raw politics, even in a place like the Caucasus, which has always been at the sharp end of history. So when I was at some government press conference somewhere listening to some official saying something about how someday Georgia might join some important Western alliance, and a journalist from one of the local TV channels confided that she had heard that seventies pop veterans Boney M were coming to play in the country, I immediately tuned out the political drone and starting concentrating on what she had to say. I couldn't really believe it at first: Boney M, she said, were coming to play a government-sponsored concert in South Ossetia. A 'Misha gig', she called it. In other words, a propaganda rave for the Georgian president, Mikheil Saakashvili, in the middle of a conflict zone.

I imagined Misha, as everyone called Saakashvili in Georgia, wearing a *Saturday Night Fever*-style white suit, hair slicked back, medallion swinging free, flares flapping in the breeze, twirling and twisting across the stage, his fingers cocked like pistols pointing upwards at the sky in jubilant abandon, the crowd moving with him in tranced-out syncopation, narcotised by the strobes flashing off the mirrorball as it spun, while their leader lip-synched the lyrics to the disco hits. The funky president - Daddy Cool, incarnate - bringing the poor huddled masses of South Ossetia what they never knew they wanted or needed. It had to be an inspired piece of creative madness or a self-destructive excursion into hell. Either way, if it was true, I wanted to be part of it.

A few weeks later, on the morning before the gig, Boney M were giving a press briefing at the Sheraton, which at that time was one of the few luxury hotels in Tbilisi, and it was immediately clear that they had no idea what they'd got themselves into. They may have been one of the few Western pop groups to play in Moscow during the Communist years, a gig apparently approved by Leonid Brezhnev back in 1978, which helped to ensure their continuing popularity all over the former Soviet Union. But they had now got themselves entangled in a complex and malevolent internecine conflict which had been simmering for years, utterly ignored by a world that neither knew nor cared where South Ossetia was, or who killed who there, over what, or why...

A bunch of teenagers were running around the hotel lobby wearing bright yellow T-shirts with exclamation marks printed on them. They were activists for a government-backed 'youth movement' called *Kokoity Fanderast!* - Goodbye Kokoity! - a project aimed at discrediting the rebel South Ossetian president, Eduard Kokoity, a heavy-set former Soviet wrestling champion whose fleshy bulk and surly demeanour appeared to be more suited to employment as a bouncer on the door of a Moscow nightclub than as a political leader. When I interviewed Kokoity once, he was wearing a snug fleshtone T-shirt under his suit jacket, which clung unappetisingly to his fulsome gut at he glared at me across his desk; his vulpine grin more of a threat than a welcome as he spat malice against his Georgian foes and their American sponsors.

The Boney M gig was to be held under the Goodbye Kokoity! banner, although the band seemed to have no idea what the slogan meant, or even who Kokoity was, having simply been told that they would be performing for 'peace'. I asked the lead singer, Marcia Barrett, a large and jovial black woman in her late fifties, what she knew about the conflict in South Ossetia.

"Not much," she admitted. "But because it's a peace festival, I'm really, really honoured to be invited to come and take part."

Peace festival? No idea *at all* about what she had got herself into here...

I asked her if the band were scared about playing a concert in a conflict zone.

"No... *scared*?" she responded, a little nervous for the briefest moment. "Should we be?"

Then she gave a hearty laugh and abruptly switched into showbiz diva mode.

"*No*... we're going to make music! Oh, this is *hot*!" she yelled theatrically. "We're going to let people feel good with our show. We're going to give *gas* on stage, and bring those Boney M hits!"

No idea where she was going. But I knew. I had been there before, and I knew it wasn't a good place at all.

Although South Ossetia later went on to insist that it was a genuinely independent state after being 'liberated' from Georgia by Russian troops during a five-day war in 2008, there isn't really much to the place. The little region is little more than a bunch of orchards and a strategic road leading down from southern Russia, through the Caucasus mountain range, into central Georgia. The 'road of life', the Ossetians call it, although death has travelled that way often enough too. A friend of mine in Tbilisi used to have a Soviet-era children's cartoon map on the wall at his office, with sketched representations of the various regions of Georgia, showing their folklore, traditions and industries. All across the country, there were beaches, factories, churches and ancient monuments, but South Ossetia was only represented by an apple tree and a peasant carrying fruit to market in a home-made knapsack. Little had changed since then, although that hardy peasant would probably now have to negotiate a military checkpoint to get his apples to their buyers.

Around the time of the Boney M show - this was October 2007 - Georgia was staging a new campaign to reassert its rule over South Ossetia, which had not been under the Tbilisi government's control since its first civil war with Georgian forces in the early nineties. Georgia's ill-conceived attempts to take the region back by force in the years that followed had failed miserably. But now the Georgian government was trying out a creative if risky strategy to peacefully undermine bruiser Kokoity's grip on his renegade enclave, essentially by using economic bribery.

South Ossetia had long been a patchwork of ethnicities, living side by side in uneasy coexistence. The ethnic Ossetian villages and the scruffy little 'capital', Tskhinvali, were held by Kokoity. I was once given permission to watch an 'independence day' celebration in Tskhinvali organised by Kokoity's regime - a gloomy farce with pretentions to Soviet pomposity which only emphasised its *Monty Python*-style surrealism. The ramshackle parade made its way down Stalin Street, as the main thoroughfare was appropriately still called, because little appeared to have changed there since the Soviet dictator's death in the fifties. It was led by men on horseback in traditional warrior costumes, waving Ossetian and Russian flags, followed by militia fighters and a troupe of ageing Cossacks. Then a gaggle of young nurses tottered past on high heels, wearing hospital whites and garish make-up, followed by a procession of farmers on their tractors, bakers brandishing loaves of bread, small children driving go-karts, and then, inexplicably, a little truck carrying a table, upon which a dead turkey was proudly displayed. The whole event showed the South Ossetian 'state' for what it really was: a shabby deception which failed to mask the petty despotism and relentless poverty of everyday life, while its slogan, "Indestructible Unity with Russia", said all that needed to be said about the region's claims to independence.

But the paranoid and hostile Kokoity administration and its Russian backers didn't by any means control the whole of South Ossetia. Many other villages in the region, before the 2008 war anyway, were populated by ethnic Georgians who were loyal to the central government in the capital, Tbilisi. Other villages were mixed, Georgians and Ossetians together, intermarrying, miscegenating, fuddling the bloodlines and transgressing the political divides.

In 2006, on the same day as Kokoity was re-elected as 'president' with almost 100 per cent of the vote, the Georgian authorities held rival South Ossetian 'presidential' elections and put up a local Ossetian, Dmitry Sanakoyev, as their favoured candidate. Sanakoyev was a former rebel militiaman who had once fought against the Georgians in the civil war in the early nineties but had later switched sides. A photograph in his autobiography, taken sometime during that ugly little conflict, shows him brandishing a Kalashnikov with the sated pride of a young hunter after his first blood - although he later insisted that he had never actually took anyone's life: "I fired, but thanks to God, I did not kill," he told me. So after Sanakoyev won a rival landslide victory in the 'alternative' presidential elections, tiny South Ossetia - with a population of around 70,000 people, if that - ended up with two men calling themselves its president, installed in headquarters just a few miles apart, within shelling distance of each other.

In Tskhinvali, of course, 'Dima' Sanakoyev was damned as a quisling. "Dima will die! He will be killed!" raged a local pensioner in the town square when I asked him what he thought of the 'alternative president'. The Ossetians claimed that

Sanakoyev had only gone over to the Georgian side because his gambling debts had been paid off for him. "Sanakoyev is simply a scoundrel and a traitor," the entertainingly combative Irina Gagloyeva, spokeswoman for the separatist administration in Tskhinvali, once told me. "He escaped from here in shame. His parents cannot look people in the eyes because of him." Less than a year after the Boney M show, the Ossetians would attempt to kill Sanakoyev with a roadside bomb attack on his convoy.

The Georgian government invested millions of dollars in the Sanakoyev 'presidency', building roads, a petrol station, shops, a cinema and even a hotel in some of the most impoverished territory in the impoverished Caucasus. The idea was to show the recalcitrant Ossetians what they could have if they returned to Georgian rule: cashpoint machines, imported delicacies and the latest Russian blockbusters. "People will pass the [Russian] checkpoint and go dancing. What can the soldiers do to prevent this?" Saakashvili once asked.[1]

The Boney M gig was another part of this soft-power social-engineering experiment: it would illustrate how life could be more peaceful, more prosperous and probably more funky with Misha at the controls; a latterday Midas with all the right tunes.

Back in the lobby of the Sheraton hotel, after the Boney M press briefing, I had a word with Vladimir Sanakoyev, a distant relative of 'alternative president' Dmitry Sanakoyev, and the man who was running the 'Goodbye Kokoity!' campaign for the Georgian government. This genial Sanakoyev had lived in Russia for many years, before returning to South Ossetia, getting involved in politics, and subsequently being expelled at gunpoint by Kokoity's goons, chucked out of a car in no man's land and forbidden to go back to his birthplace. Since then, he had been making ends meet by hosting a talk show on a propa-ganda TV channel set up by the Georgians to target the South Ossetian audience across the frontline. (Years later, he confessed that he'd actually been working for the Russian intelligence services all along, but that is another sleazy little story altogether.)

When I had first met Vladimir Sanakoyev a few months beforehand, he was cracking dirty jokes and toasting the Queen of England for my benefit with a brimming glass of wine. Now he was orchestrating the Boney M show in a coolly determined style.

"How can this concert help to resolve the conflict in South Ossetia?" I asked him in Russian, as he spoke little English.

He responded like the political operator he was, when he was on duty: "The concert is like a message of peace," he insisted. "The world-famous group Boney M is visiting the conflict zone. That means people in the conflict zone want to listen to music, sing songs and dance. That means this concert has great significance."

But why Boney M, of all people? Because their groove has a "Caucasus spirit", he explained, not entirely convincingly. Any other reasons? "Because I like them."

His young activists then crowded around the band, posing in their anti-Kokoity T-shirts for the Georgian television cameras. The Georgians loved it: foreigners - *pop stars*, even - supporting *our* campaign to oust the rebels and get back our historic territory! The disco veterans were making a cameo appearance in a vicious Caucasian drama which they couldn't even hope to comprehend.

The gig was scheduled to take place on a makeshift stage outside the newly-built, government-funded, glass-fronted cinema in Tamarasheni, a small village just a short walk from Kokoity's headquarters in Tskhinvali, if one could have walked that way, which of course was impossible because the rebel militias were dug into their positions on the nearby frontline.

"A sunny day is breaking and the heart is full of hope."
Patriots, a Georgian government propaganda song by rapper Lex-Seni

Georgia is a land of extraordinary beauty, of subtropical beaches and enchanting mountain passes, luscious forests and mysterious spiritual monuments hewed from ancient rock. But for the first two years I was working there, when the prospect of armed conflict with Russia was becoming increasingly likely, in all my travels across the country, I never really managed to see the all the sights that beguile the tourists. Instead it was back and forth, along the raddled asphalt, to and from the conflict zones, to and from the places where people suffered and schemed and dreamed of revenge and retribution. To dour Tskhinvali, where the mutinous Ossetians were bunkered down. To the brutalised grandeur of Sukhumi, the seafront stronghold of the rebel-held zone of Abkhazia, once the playground of the Communist elite, but since then ravaged by years of conflict. Then back to Tbilisi, the capital, where the rhetoric raged ever harder and the conspiracy theories seemed to get wilder by the day.

Just like the Boney M gig, the catalyst for most of these travels was one extraordinary man, the man who came to dominate our lives, by day and sometimes by night; the Pied Piper who led us on his manic dance across the highways and the dirt tracks. A charismatic, unpredictable man who wanted to make impossible dreams come true, and summon from the debris of post-Soviet disorder and corruption a kind of state which had never really existed in Georgia before. A tempestuous conjurer who thrived on the edge of creative chaos as he conducted what one journalist called "government by adrenaline": Mikheil Saakashvili, Georgia's funky president.[2]

Still in his thirties when he came to power, Saakashvili understood the power of culture to help shape new realities. The Boney M concert was just one in a series of experiments with using music as a political tool for state-building, as Georgia's young leader elevated pop propaganda to a level previously unseen in the former Soviet Union - and perhaps anywhere else in the world. Almost every political event in Georgia during his reign was delivered as a multimedia package, with slogans, visuals, and very often a song. According to the cheery chorus of his 2008 presidential election campaign anthem: "Sometimes the sun shines; sometimes the wind blows. Sometimes we have problems; sometimes we're joyful. It doesn't matter if the weather's good or bad - Misha is cool!"

Misha, the wild card with the restless enthusiasm. A few days after I moved to Georgia in 2006, a local colleague briefed me: "You've got to know one thing about Misha - he's like a little boy playing with his favourite toy. That toy is our country." She laughed after she said it, but she wasn't really joking.

Because Misha transformed Georgia, like an ingenious child constructing a phantasmagorical metropolis out of plastic bricks. He styled himself, variously, as a modern equivalent of David the Builder, the great Georgian king who united his country in the twelfth century, or as Mustafa Kemal Atatürk, the creator of modern Turkey, or as David Ben-Gurion, who helped to found the state of Israel. He was the man who would drag Georgia out of its corrupt and decrepit past, set aside the desperate years of civil war, economic breakdown and political turmoil that followed independence in 1991, win back the unruly territories of Abkhazia and South Ossetia, and march onwards with his people into a brighter, more prosperous future. He would fulfill the nation's historic destiny and turn it into a genuinely European country. (Or in the optimistic words of his election campaign song: "We will open the doors to Europe and NATO!")

Misha would build a state, and it would be good. Or at least that's what he promised.

Everywhere in Georgia were the signs and symbols of his rule. The ubiquitous red-and-white national flag, with its five Christian crosses, used to be a medieval standard but was revived by Misha's political party. Once in office, he got rid of Georgia's drab post-independence flag and replaced it with his own, and also changed the national anthem to one that reflected his own agenda. Then there were the ornate fountains which he installed in almost every urban centre, some of which danced in time to the rousing guitar riffs of Blur's *Song 2*, or, fittingly for a man seeking improbable paradises, the *Wizard of Oz* theme song, *Somewhere Over the Rainbow*. Then there were the monuments he ordered to be built, reflecting his impulse towards grand architectural statements, such as the ultra-modern glass bridge that spans the Mtkvari river; a bright, bold structure which clashes uncomfortably with the venerable backdrop of Tbilisi's Old Town. (Its unusual resemblance to an enormous sanitary towel caused some scurrilous wits to name it 'Always Ultra'.)

Then there was the gaudy golden likeness of St. George, the country's patron saint, locked in battle with the mythical dragon, which was installed high on a column above Freedom Square in the centre of Tbilisi, where a likeness of Lenin had once gestured augustly to his Soviet comrades. Inaugurating the new statue, Saakashvili said that it depicted the victory of good over evil; an allegory for his nation, nobly struggling through the generations to vanquish its beastly foes: "St. George will lead a united, strong and honourable Georgia to its ultimate freedom," he promised.

Finally, there was Saakashvili's monument to himself: his extravagant new presidential palace, an architectural tribute to Berlin's Reichstag with neo-classical columns and a big glass dome, made radiant at nightfall by multi-coloured lights; a construction which some sarcastic locals referred to as 'Misha's egg' - a sublimated symbol of manhood which its inhabitant saw as a secular icon of statehood. "This is the biggest governmental building built in Georgia in 2,000 years," he boasted proudly at the palace's opening ceremony. "The Georgians were always fighting and we had no time to build such things. Today we are again involved in a struggle for the existence of our country, but we are fighting with one hand and building with the other hand." With a characteristic lack of understatement, he went on to inform his people that it was the "most perfect, modern palace which has ever been built by anyone anywhere in the modern world".[3]

Saakashvili was personally involved in the more high-profile construction projects, even tinkering with the plans himself, it was rumoured. A local art historian offered me a possible reason, suggesting that the Georgian president, like other former Soviet leaders seeking a hallowed resting place in history, saw himself as the grand architect of a resurgent nation; a man whose orders could transform the landscape around him according to his whims and taste. His choice of architecture, she continued, mirrored his style of governing: "His aim is to change not only laws, but the whole environment according to his desires."

But it wasn't just monuments and fountains which obsessed Misha, it was also lights; everywhere, lights... Saakashvili instigated a rabid fantasia of illumination which made parts of Tbilisi look like an Ibiza discotheque seen through an ecstatic haze, with one main street lit up by night in lurid pink, lime green and electric blue, and the huge red-and-white television tower on Mtatsminda mountain, which overlooks the city, flashing maniacally like some bizarre hybrid of a Christmas tree and a raver's glow-stick.

In many ways, it was understandable. Before Saakashvili came to power, a moribund, kleptocratic Georgian government, led by former Soviet foreign minister Eduard Shevardnadze, couldn't even keep the electricity on. A documentary from 2003, *Power Trip*, illustrated the endemic institutional corruption and mass theft of electricity which characterised the late Shevardnadze era. "People in general lost their hope," one woman says at the start of the film. "Electricity is very much connected with hope in human nature. It's difficult to understand for people living in civilised countries or whatever, how much depends on electricity. It's something very oppressive, you feel so insecure when light goes off."[4] Now, everywhere, illuminated façades and floodlit monuments sent a constant message: *See how far we have come! See how we gave you the gift of light!*

For some, of course, electricity wasn't enough; they wanted more. But others were grateful. One evening, looking down upon Misha's luminous installations from a balcony high above the Old Town, a Georgian friend remarked to me: "The people who say Saakashvili has done nothing for this country are suffering from amnesia. They just don't remember what it was like before. They don't seem to remember how *dark* it was. They don't remember how *cold* it was."

In the years after he was elected president for the first time in 2004, Misha didn't just dominate the political life of Georgia - which became, in effect, a one-party state in which the president wielded almost unlimited power - he also colonised its cultural life. His reach extended to music as well as architecture, as he became the leading patron of government-funded pop, with state funds gathering around him a circle of latterday court musicians who would play not only for his amusement, but also to further his political aims. If the moment required a song, they were ready to rock. Every major institution, including the police and the army, seemed to have its own theme tune. In an impoverished country that could barely support a professional music industry, singing for Saakashvili became one of the few lucrative gigs in town.

The musicians were largely driven by pragmatism, according to Georgian journalist Nico Nergadze: "Pop singers need to be aligned, because that's how they earn their money and get good bookings at big concerts," he explained. "They are so eager to be heard, you can get them to write a song about anything. It's so easy just to buy yourself a song. I know some guys from a kayaking federation, and they paid a songwriter to write one about them.

"So if the president approaches you and says that Georgians need ideological help, we need a song about how Georgia should be united again, the singers are flattered because of the attention, and they have a chance to sing a song that's going to be popular and get a bigger audience, as well as doing something that's seen as good for the country." He paused, then added: "Some of them also genuinely believe in it."

Saakashvili's re-election campaign theme song from 2008, *Misha Magaria (Misha is Cool)*, was one of the prime examples of pop propaganda. It was written by a former singer from a Georgian boy-band who later became a government minister. The lyrics, set to a jaunty little tune with a cheeky squall of Middle Eastern melody, speak of the sun rising, the country flourishing, and the Georgian army leading the way down the highway to Sukhumi, the capital of rebel Abkhazia. "Georgia will become united!" it promised, underlining Saakashvili's repeated insistence that he would soon win back the renegade territory.

An extravagant video for the song was filmed in the lavishly-renovated Italianate hill town of Sighnaghi, one of Saakashvili's showpiece reconstruction projects. In one long, constantly moving shot, it showed a procession of smiley-faced young people joined first by schoolchildren waving Saakashvili's party's flags, then by men in traditional costumes with swords, then by soldiers, dancers and sportsmen, until there was a huge joyous crowd skipping its way through the streets to the jubilant beat of Misha's funky aspirations.

The video would be played on a huge screen to warm up the crowds before his election rallies in the provinces, while voters waited for the sudden blur of black Jeeps which constituted the Saakashvili motorcade to hurtle into their town square, unloading the man who would deliver his message of plenty from a stage mounted on a huge truck equipped with a sound system and a massive video screen. The whole event would then be filmed for an advertising spot which would be broadcast on national television the following day. (When I went to check out Saakashvili's main opponent in the battle for the presidency a few days later, the impecunious oppositionist was making his speech on a street corner using four tinny megaphones mounted on a Lada saloon.)

While some people only attended the rallies out of curiosity - or, if they worked for the state, out of duty to their employer - others were completely bewitched. One elderly man in the dilapidated industrial town of Bolnisi approached me holding an elegantly-framed portrait of Saakashvili, which he hoped he could somehow get signed by his hero, and a page of handwritten verse, which he recited with passion. "Oh, Misha Saakashvili!" he declaimed, waving his arms in frantic emphasis. "The protector of the poor and miserable! You are a rising moon, a piece of the Georgian sun!"

Almost overwhelmed by emotion, the old man continued: "When you think about your country, you have tears in your eyes. Oh God, give a long life to our hope, Misha Saakashvili!" Even after several years in office, Misha's rock'n'roll charisma was obviously still working its magic. Televised rallies depicted Saakashvili surrounded by adoring musicians; at one campaign concert in a Tbilisi suburb, he arrived on stage just at the moment when a veteran pop crooner was presenting his lyrical homage to his president: "You are my hero; I offered you my hand and you will win."[5]

In western Europe, of course, such shamelessly sycophantic grovelling from a musician would cause widespread ridicule. But in some parts of the world, where the democratic process is, let's say, less 'sophisticated', it's almost unremarkable. Saakashvili was hardly the first post-Soviet president to be hymned in song. Back in 2002, a techno-pop hit in Russia praised the virtues of strongman leader Vladimir Putin - Saakashvili's nemesis - with lyrics like this: "I want a man like Putin, full of strength; one like Putin, who doesn't drink; one like Putin, who won't mess me around; one like Putin, who won't run away." Putin was also acclaimed in a song by a rock band called White Eagle, who linked his name with resurgent Russian power and the Grad battlefield missile system: "The coast is clear thanks to Grad; with us are Putin and Stalingrad!"[6]

The authoritarian president of Belarus, Alexander Lukashenko, also commissioned an election campaign song which praised his self-proclaimed virtues and omniscience. *Listen to Your Daddy*, it was called, although its portrayal of Lukashenko - *"When you look at him, you can easily see, who is the master in the house"* - sounded less like an enticement to potential voters than a warning to his opponents.

Outside the former Soviet Union, the information ministry in Zimbabwe was involved in commissioning albums of songs promoting President Robert Mugabe's repressive government, aimed at countering the influence of anti-regime musicians. They apparently got so much airplay that musicians who weren't even being paid to praise Mugabe started to record songs in his honour, in the hope of cashing in. Recordings by outspoken dissidents, meanwhile, were suppressed. "The government's strategy was first to blacklist songs that were against its policies and all those that talked about human rights abuse, corruption and the abuse of power by the establishment. These were to be 'banned' from the airwaves so as to pave way for those songs that preached the 'true gospel'," wrote Zimbabwean journalist Maxwell Sibanda.[7] One radio presenter even fled the country and claimed political asylum in Britain, alleging that he feared for his life after refusing to play the government's propaganda albums on his show.

Saakashvili, of course, was not Putin, Lukashenko or Mugabe, although his regime was rather less liberal than he liked to tell the Western media. Nevertheless, in terms of free speech, the Georgians were living in paradise compared to most of their ex-Soviet brothers and sisters. But the campaign for the 2008 presidential elections certainly wasn't the first time that rock music had helped to advance their leader's political ambitions.

Five years earlier, the 'Rose Revolution' which ousted Eduard

Shevardnadze in 2003 and swept Saakashvili to power was a righteous outburst of popular anger, driven by the sense that Georgia had somehow gone rotten, plundered by amoral exploiters who didn't care that they had turned their beloved nation into a failed state. It was also an uprising whose momentum was at least partly energised by the inspirational power of rock'n'roll: Saakashvili's clique was already using culture as a political weapon even before he came to power. In the run-up to the rigged polls that became the flashpoint for the overthrow of Shevardnadze, a group of young Georgian bands toured the country, urging young people to get out and vote. And in the cold and rainy days after revolutionary protests began outside the Georgian parliament, the bands were there again to lift the spirits of the freezing demonstrators; the 'rain musicians', they were called, as they played on and on through the downpours and the early winter chill.

"We were musicians, so what could we do? Just play for people," said one of them, Vaho Babunashvili, who led the band Soft Eject. "I'm proud to have been there and I'll always be proud to have been there. If you do something like that with your heart and you are not looking on it as a career step, then it makes a big mark on you until the end of your days. I don't care about the people who say the Rose Revolution was wrong or it changed nothing in our lives, because it changed a lot, and changed it in a good way."

Whatever happened afterwards, Babunashvili said he still believed that he was on the right side of the barricades. "Of course we can see there are still a lot of bad things," he admitted, "but this is real life, it's not a cartoon or something, and in life you have good and bad things. It's important which side you are going to be on - the right side or the wrong side. This is important: to make your choice."

The young activists who helped to plot the Rose Revolution had learned well from the uprising three years earlier in the former Yugoslav capital, Belgrade, which overthrew the war-mongering Slobodan Milošević. There rock music had also played a catalytic role in bringing people to the streets, culminating in a 100-day festival called Exit which counted down the days until Milošević was ousted, and in the years afterwards became the Balkan equivalent of Glastonbury. On the day of the Belgrade revolution in October 2000, as urgent electronic beats blasted out from speakers mounted on a truck, protesters muscled their way through police lines, stormed the parliament building and set it ablaze.

"It was like a movie - the parliament on fire, the sound system playing techno, people dancing in the streets, not knowing whether the army would move in," one of Exit's founders, Dušan Kovačević, once told me. "I think it was one of the craziest parties in the history of the world."[8]

Four years later, during the 'Orange Revolution' in the snowbound Ukrainian capital Kiev, history repeated itself. A constant flow of rock bands, folk troubadours and traditional choirs, as well as Eurovision Song Contest winner Ruslana, entertained hundreds of thousands of protesters as they kept up their vigil against falsified elections for three weeks in sub-zero temperatures on the revolutionary square known as the 'Maidan'. "It was a very special experience for a musician to play on that stage at that time," remembered the Ukrainian rock star Oleg Skrypka, who rocked the Maidan with his band VV. "A lot of people were ready to die for the cause. It was like a war, but at the same time it was like the carnival in Rio de Janeiro."[9]

Once Saakashvili came to power in Georgia, many of the dissident musicians became government loyalists, and pop became a tool to strengthen the state: by staging lavishly-funded concerts featuring international stars, the publicity-hungry president sought to show that his country was progressing culturally as well as economically. His administration's booking policy implied a somewhat erratic taste: glamorous Colombian diva Shakira was flown in to sing, as were operatic tenors José Carreras and Placido Domingo, while another propaganda gig was headlined by the mighty Senegalese band-leader Youssou N'Dour. On the downside, there were also appearances by the Canadian soft-rocker Bryan Adams, British novelty-pop hacks Smokie, and *Lady in Red* crooner Chris de Burgh. But nothing, in all those years of strangeness, could match the audacious and ultimately wretched symbolism of the Boney M gig in South Ossetia.

"Is there any nation as happy as we are?"
Happy Nation, a satirical Georgian pop song by Anri Jokhadze

As Georgian snipers gazed down impassively from the roof of the cinema in Tamarasheni where Boney M were about to play, young government activists handed out free beer from plastic bottles and an accordion player squeezeboxed his way through a selection of traditional Georgian folk tunes to warm up the crowd, before patriotic rapper Lex-Seni took to the stage with a rendition of the Goodbye Kokoity! campaign anthem. *Kokoity Fandarast!* is not a good song; in fact, it is possibly the least inspiring protest song ever written, a lame dirge with a fey, rope-skipping rhythm and a feeble schoolyard chorus: hardly an anthem to summon the masses. But nevertheless, there were chants of "Victory!" from the crowd, and then there was Boney M.

But it wasn't, not really. Because it quickly became clear that only one member of the original seventies line-up was still with the band: Marcia Barrett, backed up by three young stand-ins singing along to a pre-recorded backing track. Their disco revue also looked a little dowdy, because they had lost their flamboyant stage costumes somewhere along the way to Georgia.

Barrett had obviously decided that because this was a conflict zone, it would be appropriate to reprise one of the band's more misguided attempts at social commentary, the excruciating *Belfast*, with its naïve lyrics about the 'Troubles' in Northern Ireland. Admittedly, one of its lines - something about "the hate you have for one another's past" - did sound slightly relevant in a place where history has often been manipulated for political advantage, but the crowd hadn't come to be lectured about the need for forgiveness and peaceful reconciliation by a bunch of foreign pop stars. They had come to dance, and they only really started to respond when the band launched into escapist classics like *Rasputin* and *Sunny*.

Then suddenly, as the pre-recorded strings began to vamp out the deathless riff from *Daddy Cool*, there was a stir of excitement in the crowd. "Misha's here! Misha's here!" my photographer friend Alex Klimchuk shouted. The Georgian president had arrived stage-front to savour his cultural triumph over the rebels.

Saakashvili was grinning gleefully and working his body to the beat as excited children clamoured for autographs and tried to sneak through his security cordon to get their photographs taken with their hero. Although Misha wasn't wearing a *Saturday Night Fever* suit or an Afro wig and stack heels, it was clear from the crowd's reaction that there was only one genuine pop star at the show tonight: Georgia's own Daddy Cool.

Acknowledging this fact, Boney M dedicated a second run through *Sunny* to Georgia's number one player, while I managed to negotiate my way past his minders and ask him the only question I could think of which seemed to make any kind of sense: what did he hope to achieve by bringing a bunch of old crooners to this remote, volatile, war-ravaged place?

"Well, you know, this is a kind of disco approach to conflict resolution," Saakashvili shouted back, trying to make himself heard above the hammering rhythm.

"By doing this, we hope that we'll lure out people from their trenches, force them to drop their Kalashnikovs and come here and dance with the others, and understand that nothing is as nice as peace, nothing is as nice as reconciliation.

"This place was only famous for killings, violence and crime," he continued. "Now it's getting some new thing, you know, it's looking much more colourful, much less violent - just normal. And being normal is such a novelty here."

Then the Disco King nodded his head, shuffled his brown suede shoes, and got right back into the groove.

"A disco approach to conflict resolution..." Saakashvili had a prodigious talent for dropping memorable soundbites, and this one was possibly his best. But what did it really mean? Certainly, a day of pop hedonism had to be better than another night of gunfire in South Ossetia. But was it really likely that the Ossetian rebel forces would throw down their weapons and come grooving across the divide to join hands in peace and loving harmony? And could the surreal event that we were witnessing in this obscure village really be described as 'normal'?

There was more to come.

I had been doing some live broadcasts from the concert for the BBC, and shortly after the music finished, my phone started to ring with some unexpected news. I was told by my editor in London that the manager of another original seventies member of Boney M, Liz Mitchell, had called the BBC to complain that the band we had just watched had no right to use the name. It seemed that after the classic line-up split a couple of decades earlier, 'Boney M' had become the subject of legal dispute. Various rival ensembles were touring the world, using the same name and singing the same old hits. Mitchell insisted that hers was the genuine version, and her claims were apparently backed by the German pop svengali, Frank Farian; the producer who first brought Boney M to life all those years ago.

It seemed right, somehow: as so often in the Caucasus, things had turned out to be much more complicated than they first appeared. An open-air disco in a conflict zone, featuring a band which had also become the focus for a bitter, unresolved historical dispute. It was almost funny, but in South Ossetia, laughter often feels inappropriate, somehow sacrilegious; one doesn't want to risk upsetting the ghosts who stalk these haunted roads.

Our taxi driver seemed to sense the mood and as we left, he slotted an old Black Sabbath cassette into his tape deck: Ronnie James Dio singing *Heaven and Hell*: "Well if it seems to be real, it's illusion," Dio wailed. "For every moment of truth, there's confusion…"

As our car hacked its way up the mountain trail out of the village, its headlights picked out the men in combat uniforms at the roadside, still standing guard with their guns, the tips of their cigarettes glowing red and then fading; watching and waiting in the darkness.

"White smoke drifted low across Rustaveli Avenue for the second time in a month. But this time it was not the tear gas fired by riot police as they broke up anti-government protests. These were clouds of dry ice, pumped out from smoke machines on a stage outside the Georgian parliament, as a band of ageing, frizzy-haired British rockers called Smokie chugged through their back-catalogue of seventies hits."
Report by the author in *The Moscow Times*, November 2007

In Georgia, all roads eventually led to Rustaveli Avenue. This elegant boulevard, the capital's main thoroughfare, had been the nexus of Georgian political life for years, dominated by the imposing arched façade of the parliament building. Named after the country's greatest poet, Shota Rustaveli, it is a street which has seen Soviet soldiers massacre nationalist protesters; a street which has seen the fratricidal madness of the Hundred Metres War, when Georgian shelled Georgian from pavement to pavement as the state collapsed around them after independence in the early nineties; a street which has seen the jubilant, unprecedentedly peaceful triumph of Saakashvili's Rose Revolution. Whenever there was turmoil in Georgian society, it was to Rustaveli Avenue that people came to express their discontent.

When I walked along Rustaveli, I often thought back to November 7, 2007: the day of Saakashvili's unexpected, violent crackdown on his political adversaries who were trying to seize power. I thought of the raw panic, the blinding confusion and the desperate sweat; of running hard up the steep cobbled lanes behind the parliament building, with the riot police closing in on us, firing canisters of tear gas. But because memories sometimes become intertwined with other sensations, I also thought of a song - or, more specifically, a video clip for a song.

The November 2007 crackdown put an end to the first mass demonstrations against Saakashvili's rule, which had been led by radical oppositionists who accused him of turning into an autocrat and setting the country on the path to dictatorship. The protests ultimately failed to bring down the government, but they did create their own pop star; a madcap rapper who showed that although the Saakashvili administration might have been able to afford to book Boney M and Shakira, it couldn't always call the tunes. The rapper's name was Utsnobi - 'The Unknown' - alias Giorgi Gachechiladze, a Georgian pop veteran whose brother, a wine merchant turned belligerent opposition leader, would later challenge Saakashvili for the presidency. Vicious, livid, and charged with vengeful intensity, the incendiary video clip for Utsnobi's song *Deda Ena* (*Mother Tongue*) visualised the protesters' rage.

It is possibly one of the angriest pop promo videos ever made, and it opens with a shot of a hooded hangman sitting on a gallows platform, beckoning a child towards him. As the young girl looks up warily at the dangling noose, the hangman grabs the Georgian book that she was holding in her hands and tosses it into a fire. Then he pulls back his hood to reveal himself as a Roman emperor in a blood-red toga. His face exactly resembles that of Mikheil Saakashvili.

Then the beat starts to pump and traditional *duduki* pipes wail out across syncopated hip-hop scratching, and the monstrous Nero begins to cavort lasciviously through his torch-lit colosseum with a group of scantily-clad beauties, giving his thumbs-up to the summary justice dispensed by blind judges as Mickey Mouse jives on a podium nearby. He gorges himself bestially on meat and wine and giggles idiotically at a toilet which spurts water like one of his beloved fountains, while the pages of the Georgian book - the 'Mother Tongue' of the song's title - curl and start to blacken in the flames.

But then the scene changes, and the benighted crowd starts to rise up, holding placards demanding freedom and justice, and as the child rescues the book from the fire, Nero-Misha is suddenly left alone in the arena. Three determined young men face him from the gallows platform, the oppressed masses with their burning torches standing strong behind them, and the noose still dangling, waiting...

It's a cannonade assault on a leader who is portrayed as arrogant, lecherous and intoxicated by power, accused of selling out Georgia's traditions and culture to pernicious Western influences - forsaking the mother tongue for Mickey Mouse. A man who deserves to be hanged, it seems to suggest. It expressed a viewpoint that was held by many Georgian traditionalists and hardline Orthodox Christians, that Saakashvili's embrace of Western values would bring no good to the country; that Western liberalism would corrupt the nation's morality; that Western capitalism would corrode its cherished way of life.

Whatever the merits of Utsnobi's music - and to be honest, there weren't all that many - he was certainly the most creative figure in a Georgian opposition whose idea of putting on a show was to bring their supporters to Rustaveli Avenue and then harangue them through bullhorns for hours on end. In the *Mother Tongue* video, Utsnobi rapped from inside a cage in the imitation colosseum, and these prison bars would eventually become his motif. A couple of years later, in the run-up to yet more opposition protests, he launched a political chat show entitled *Cell Number 5* on a small independent television channel. It was also a kind of reality-TV programme, because the unshaven and increasingly scruffy Utsnobi imprisoned himself in a specially-built prison cell in the studio and promised to remain there in self-imposed incarceration until Saakashvili was ousted.

I went to meet him there once, and found the cell cluttered with satirical puppets of Saakashvili, random irate graffiti and scribbled poems, Orthodox icons and other religious parapher- nalia. But I have to admit that I found it hard to take his hyperbole seriously after he compared Saakashvili to a latterday Adolf Hitler. His evidence was the notorious case of a young banker who was beaten to death by Interior Ministry officials; a murder which was initially covered up but eventually caused huge damage to the Saakashvili government's reputation. But even this, and several other deaths for which Utsnobi blamed the authorities, did not exactly add up to six million. His one hope was for mass resistance - a display of popular passion was what Rose Revolution alumnus Saakashvili would truly understand, he told me: "The only things he's afraid of are a huge amount of people out on the streets and a sequence of events that he'll simply be unable to control." Another revolution on Rustaveli Avenue, in other words.

The programme nevertheless turned Utsnobi into a political celebrity. His arrival at an opposition rally at the national football stadium invoked mass delirium and a display of devotion that no Georgian politician could have hoped to inspire at the time. Tens of thousands of people rose from their seats to cheer as the singer, dressed in iridescent white, was borne aloft on a lap of honour around the arena, and tears flowed as he doffed his trademark urchin's cap to his admirers. After the rally, one phone-in caller to his TV show was ecstatic: "You are not Gia, you are Saint Giorgi!" she gushed, insisting that the star had been sent by God to save the nation. A prominent opposition activist declared: "America had Martin Luther King, Georgia has Gia Gachechiladze."

Utsnobi's prison show also inspired the opposition to blockade the centre of Tbilisi with imitation cells, intended to symbolise the authoritarianism of Saakashvili's rule. Hundreds of these cells, built from steel bars, rope and polythene sheeting, sealed off roads outside parliament, the presidential palace and the state television channel. Some activists even lived in them around the clock, for weeks on end.

But Saakashvili remained aloof, not wanting a repeat of the November 2007 crackdown which had shocked his Western allies and soiled his carefully-manufactured international reputation as a progressive democrat. He didn't even respond when protesters hung placards with obscene slogans on the perimeter fence of his palace, or when they accused him of acting like a 'scared rabbit' and started throwing carrots, cabbages and even a live bunny over the metal gates into the courtyard. In fact, his only reaction was to joke to one interviewer that the vegetables had at least yielded some decent soup, and to show another journalist a novelty watch he was wearing, which was decorated with drawings of rabbits having sex with each other in various positions.

"Yeah, it's a bunny watch," he laughed insouciantly. "So what?"[10]

"Together towards victory! Together to success! Together we will overcome everything! Together we will defeat our enemy!"
Teenagers chanting in a video promoting the Georgian government's 'patriot camps', 2007

What journalists were almost guaranteed during any encounter with Saakashvili wasn't just a personal charm offensive, but the kind of colourful, unguarded quotes which it would be impossible to imagine coming from most other leaders of former Soviet states. Whatever other failings the Georgian leader might have had, he was no grey apparatchik.

Travelling with Misha was always a high, wild ride. He liked to thrill foreign reporters by giving them a seductive glimpse of his turbocharged presidential lifestyle, whirling them away by helicopter or by plane to the other side of the country to show them his latest pet project, or propelling them along the highways at cortex-scrambling velocity in his armed convoy.

A journalist from the *Financial Times* once marvelled about how he had flown over the country on Saakashvili's jet with Charles Aznavour cranked up loud on the sound system, before ending up in an underground bunker below an army base in the mountains, watching military videos with Israeli officers who were training Georgian commandos. "Saakashvili is clearly brilliant at winning friends and influencing people," he concluded.[11] A reporter from *Time* magazine meanwhile enjoyed a hectic week-long jaunt which began on the beach, at the site of a new holiday resort on the edge of rebel Abkhazia in the west of the country, and took him all the way to the vineyard region of Kakheti in the east, in what he described as a display of "virility and political kinetics".[12]

Other journalists had to chase Saakashvili down ski slopes or into subterranean grottos deep in the wilderness, and inevitably came away with a good story to tell, although a group of Polish reporters appeared more disturbed than charmed after they followed his convoy to a checkpoint on the edge of South Ossetia, where rebel gunmen opened fire over their cars.

My first experience of flying 'Air Misha' came in 2006, in the midst of a crisis that started when Georgia arrested four Russian military intelligence officers for spying. (The Kremlin denied the espionage charges, of course, but what else would its military intelligence personnel be doing in enemy territory - visiting art galleries and enjoying a bit of sunbathing?) I was among a group of journalists who were flown from Tbilisi to a military airstrip at Senaki, and then driven onwards by minibus to the Black Sea resort of Batumi. When our vehicle pulled up in the darkness somewhere along the road in the late evening, we thought we had reached our final destination. But it was actually an amusement park deep in the countryside.

As weary-eyed staff switched on the flashing lights and the carousel rides for our entertainment, we were told that this was actually the scene of the first triumph of Saakashvili's presidency, where his supporters faced down a local strongman who ran the area as his personal fiefdom until 2004. The provincial tyrant blew up a bridge here to stop his opponents crossing the river and deposing him, but ultimately a popular uprising forced him to flee to Moscow. What Saakashvili and his aides wanted us to understand, it seemed, was that the warlords and the weapons had now been banished; in their place was a funfair.

It wasn't until two in the morning that I finally got my interview with the president, who told me that it was "insane" to talk about any possibility of armed conflict with Russia. "I don't believe anybody can be crazy enough even to contemplate it," he said.[13]

On the way back, we flew by helicopter to the Senaki base, where the presidential plane was waiting to take us back to Tbilisi. Some of the journalists had to stand throughout the flight because several seats were taken up by Louis Vuitton make-up bags belonging to the president's immaculately-manicured PR entourage, while the plane's gangway was blocked by a heap of guns carelessly piled up by his security detail. On touchdown, there was a fast drive to the prosecutor's office, where the alleged spies were paraded in handcuffs before the cameras, scowling in humiliation like petty criminals, clutching their possessions in crumpled plastic shopping bags.

It had been a fine show, seemingly intended to demonstrate how Georgia's plucky young democrats could stand up to their oppressive ex-Soviet masters in Moscow who were seeking to halt their former colony's advance towards freedom, self-determination, fairy lights and discotheques for all. The message probably wasn't understood in exactly the same way in the Kremlin, however; "our patience is at an end", a Russian official is said to have told an American diplomat.[14] From this point on, armed conflict with Russia was probably inevitable, although most of us didn't realise it at the time.

The first report that I filed for the BBC after arriving in Georgia in 2006 - exactly two years before the war with Russia started - was about an unusual vacation that Saakashvili was taking that summer. He had decided to spend ten days at an army training camp, drilling and yomping with reservist troops. "President Saakashvili says he has the right to take a holiday anywhere he wants," my script began. "But his choice is rather different from the beaches and villas preferred by many national leaders. He'll be joining up with Georgia's military reservists, who he praised as patriots serving the motherland."

It was intended as a somewhat frivolous dispatch about what appeared, at the time, to be little more than an eccentric publicity stunt, and I'm not even sure if it was ever broadcast. But when I read through it again now, I hear the sound of guns being cocked. A few days later, I filed another report about Saakashvili opening a new army base in the west of the country and boasting about building up Georgia's military strength. It was to be just one of many such dispatches, and looking back on them with the benefit of hindsight, their general trajectory is unmistakable.

But the long, nervous escalation towards armed conflict wasn't just foretold by Saakshvili's massive increases in military spending, or the increasingly martial rhetoric of politicians in both Tbilisi and Moscow. It could also be heard in music: the drums of war.

The propaganda-heavy video clip for one Georgian power-ballad from the time, *The Water of Psou*, begins with the singer Nino Badurashvili alighting from a military helicopter in tailored fatigues and a cute little army cap. It shows Georgian soldiers cleaning and priming their weapons, then advancing through subtropical forests and rugged ranges that look like the terrain in the rebel region of Abkhazia, as bombs explode around them and injured comrades fall to the ground. As the music swells up towards the bombastic final chorus, army helicopters swoop low over the stage while Badurashvili throws her military jacket aside to reveal her cleavage, watched intently by ranks of determined troops, as if this is their last sight of womanly beauty before going to war. The camera then cuts away to soldiers proudly unfurling the Georgian flag on the territory that they have presumably just liberated.

The lyrics made the whole scenario clear, to Georgians at least. They called on the country's "heroes" to "drink the water of Psou" - "so that your children will be grateful to you". In other words, the song effectively urges them to capture the River Psou, which forms part of the border between Abkhazia and Russia, and to seize back Abkhazia from the rebels by force. "Drink, joy has no bounds," Badurashvili urges. "Heroes, drink - it is ours!"

It was a declaration of war disguised as a pop song.

Abkhazia was also the subject of perhaps the most extraordinary piece of rock'n'roll propaganda of the Saakashvili era. The song itself is called *Gamarjoba Abkhazeto* - in English, *Hello Abkhazia* - a stirring contemporary anthem built around traditional melodies and tinged with melancholy, with the singer wistfully dreaming about the "blue mountains and white sanatoriums" of the rebel region, as he begs his "old friend" to greet him once more, and to be his homeland again.

But it is the video for the song that makes it so remarkable. Shot in sweet sunshine and featuring an all-star cast of local pop celebrities, it shows a series of glamorous Georgians making ready to travel to Abkhazia; in cars and buses, by train and on a huge cruise liner named 'Unity'; one chic couple are even travelling by yacht, sipping glasses of champagne as they cut through the waters. It also shows refugees from the Abkhaz war jubilantly packing up their belongings and making ready for the journey home to the promised land, as Saakashvili speaks to them from a television screen and little children scamper around with Georgian flags.

It is a brilliant, tragic deception. Sometimes it left me in tears when I watched the clip, after hearing so many times the dreams of those dispossessed by the civil war in Abkhazia in the nineties, those refugee dreams of seeing their beloved city of Sukhumi again; dreams that looked increasingly impossible after Russia recognised Abkhazia as an independent state and started to build garrisons there to ensure that Georgia would never regain control. Once one of my colleagues did a pirate remix of the video, cutting in real footage that we had shot of impoverished refugees living in dilapidated towerblocks in Tbilisi, contrasting the luminous smiles of the video celebrities with the resigned faces of the genuinely dispossessed, those who fear that their life in the limbo of the 'internally displaced person' is an existence that will never change for them, despite all the promises they had heard and wanted to believe for so many years. (This version of the video I can no longer watch, because it says too much.)

During his 2008 presidential re-election campaign, Saakashvili declared that his victory would give people "a ticket on a train which will take us to Sukhumi" - just like in the video. That train would be departing, he claimed, "in the nearest future, I mean in the next few months, I am not saying years".[15] With the recalcitrant leadership of Abkhazia refusing to even talk to him, let alone consider any kind of rapprochement with Georgia, it wasn't exactly clear what he could do to achieve it, although the *Water of Psou* video clearly hinted at one option.

It did not come as a surprise that people in Abkhazia weren't exactly convinced by Georgian government statements that they wanted to be friends again and live together in eternal harmony. I once interviewed the man who wrote the music for Abkhazia's 'national anthem', Valery Chkadua, in the shabby third-floor apartment in Sukhumi where he first came up with the tune during the cold, dark days of isolation which followed the rebels' victory against the Georgian army in 1993. As he ran through the pompous little melody for me on his chronically out-of-tune piano, a faded pair of women's knickers hung incongruously from a chair just behind him. Like the apartment, Chkadua appeared sombre and gloomy, although when I asked him about the idea of reuniting with Georgia, his answer was definitive: "Abkhazia has already chosen its path," he stated.

Even the younger generation of Abkhazians, who had no memories of the war and had grown up without even knowing any Georgians, found it almost impossible to forgive. I once spoke with an Abkhazian rapper called Genry Gumba, a lanky, arrogant youth dressed in the latest Moscow sportswear chic. He told me that his role models were 2Pac and Eminem rather than militia fighters, and said that although he didn't blame Georgians of his own age for the conflict, he couldn't see any possibility of reconciliation.

"Neither I nor anyone else can change what happened. It was all their fault," he explained as we strolled among the palm trees which line Sukhumi's seafront promenade, a place where Georgians are no longer welcome and many of their old homes lie abandoned and derelict, ghost houses of which no one will speak. "We cannot take the first step towards friendship today because we don't know how they'll behave towards us tomorrow. This is how we look at it: we *have* lived without them, we *can* live without them."

The song *Hello Abkhazia* was the winner of an annual competition called 'Patriotebi' - the government's patriotic song contest, a kind of small-scale, propaganda-charged Eurovision. Encouraging patriotism, officials believed, was a form of state-building in a country where national institutions had not functioned properly since independence from the Soviet Union in 1991. It was important, they thought, to turn young people into cheerleaders for their nation in order to make it strong and united, and what better way than through music?

"In the sixties and seventies, it was popular to make good patriotic songs, but after the civil war in Georgia, this trend went down," the culture minister at the time, Papuna Davitaia, explained to me. "That's why our party and government leaders wanted to help our composers make this kind of music." State-sponsored pop promoting a government agenda doesn't exactly reflect the dissident spirit of rock'n'roll, but Davitaia insisted that the contest was simply giving young people what they needed: "I think you can never have enough national pride," he said.

Saakashvili's 'Patriot Camps' were another element of his campaign to instil national pride in the younger generation and bolster his state-building campaign. Each summer, thousands of teenagers were sent to spend a week or so in government-built holiday chalets in the countryside, where they got to play sports, write poems and sing traditional Georgian songs. Apparently, Saakashvili was a frequent visitor to the camps, where he donned the Patriot uniform and threw himself enthusiastically into the games with the teenagers.

The idea of the Patriot Camps, of course, recalls the Soviet-era 'Pioneer' camps, where children spent their summers being instilled with Communist values. Growing up in the Georgian Soviet Socialist Republic, Saakashvili was a Pioneer himself, and was sent to a summer camp in Crimea as a youth, although he fiercely denied that his experience there had in any way influenced his agenda. (After I made such a suggestion in a newspaper column once, he referred to me in one of his televised speeches as an "idiot".)[16] But when I visited one of the camps, and watched the teenagers in their identical Patriot T-shirts performing choreographed dance routines to nationalist anthems, it was hard not to think that the ideology might have changed, but the methods were still similar. I recalled something that the veteran Georgian political analyst Alexander Rondeli once said to me: "Lenin and Stalin are still within us - not with us, but *within* us. This Soviet culture is still inside our heads, and until we finally get rid of it, we cannot be genuinely free."

Perhaps all this martial rhetoric and propaganda should have raised fears that armed conflict was imminent. Of course there were such fears, but even just before the war with Russia broke out in August 2008, few really believed that it would happen. I certainly didn't believe it myself.

A couple of days before the serious fighting began, the Georgian government organised a press trip to ethnic Georgian villages in South Ossetia, to show the international media the proof of rebel aggression. We were introduced to a man who had suffered shrapnel wounds after a rocket-propelled grenade attack and shown around houses and orchards which had been damaged by enemy shelling. Although it looked bad, and the villagers were extremely frightened about what might happen next, the bucolic, sun-lit fields of the Didi Liakhvi gorge did not appear to be about to turn into a battleground.

But a couple of days afterwards, on August 7, 2008, Saakashvili decided to use the rebel attacks as justification to seize the moment, hit back hard and recapture the territory (or, in the cynically disingenuous words of a Georgian army chief's official statement, to "restore constitutional order"). Apparently believing that a military triumph was achievable, Saakashvili ordered an assault on the South Ossetian capital, Tskhinvali, and at around 11.30 that night, his forces launched a shock bombardment of the little town.

But the Russians had 'peacekeeping' troops in Tskhinvali;

Moscow had also been handing out Russian passports to South Ossetian residents for years, and had repeatedly promised to intervene to defend its 'citizens' in the event of any attack. In other words, this was a perfect pretext for the Kremlin to - as Vladimir Putin memorably put it - hang Saakashvili "by the balls". So within a couple of days, Russian tanks were rolling across the border in a lethal display of punitive force, and the Georgian army was in retreat.

This brief but ferocious war left Georgia defeated and humiliated, with its ambitions to regain control over South Ossetia and Abkhazia destroyed, while hundreds of people lay dead and tens of thousands more fled their homes to escape the fighting, creating a whole new generation of refugees. The 'disco approach to conflict resolution' had been abandoned, and people had returned to the old ways: ethnic cleansing and murder. All that went before had been for nothing, a futile waste of money, of hope, and of blood.

Ten months after the Boney M 'peace concert', the village where it took place, Tamarasheni, was looted and torched by marauding South Ossetian irregulars as the Georgian army retreated from the Russian onslaught. The cinema where Boney M had played was trashed, along with all the other expensively-built symbols of the Georgian state, and the ethnic Georgians were driven out in a savage frenzy of revenge for the assault on Tskhinvali. Tamarasheni effectively ceased to exist.

My friend Alex Klimchuk, a Georgian photographer whose images of the Boney M gig accompanied an article I wrote about the event for British newspaper *The Observer*, was shot dead not very far from where the disco veterans had played and where we had once laughed together, enjoying the absurdity of that moment.

Approaching a group of armed men at a checkpoint, Klimchuk and his colleagues mistook them for Georgian soldiers and shouted out a greeting in Georgian: *"Gamarjoba!"* But the troops were Ossetians, and they immediately opened up with their Kalashnikovs. I cried when I heard what had happened, but what difference could my tears make in a place like this, where people had been weeping for generations?

Once the fighting was over, the Ossetians and their Russian protectors rejoiced in victory and mourned their dead with a commemorative concert in Tskhinvali's rocket-scarred town centre. Soldiers watched in combat-weary fascination from their armoured cars while locals waved Russian flags in gratitude and South Ossetia's thuggish 'president' Eduard Kokoity glowed bright with self-satisfaction as Valery Gergiyev, the lead conductor of the London Symphony Orchestra and probably the world's most famous Ossetian, led a performance of symphonies by Shostakovich and Tchaikovsky. "We are here to tell the whole world that we want everyone to know the truth of the terrible events in Tskhinvali," Gergiyev declared.[17] While the melodic tribute sweetened the battle-fouled air of Tskhinvali, clouds of smoke rose over the horizon as Georgian villages burned to the ground.

During the concert, a French reporter slipped away from the Russian military officials who had arranged a press trip to the propaganda concert for the Western media in order to flaunt their triumph for the cameras. Not far from the stage, in a nearby park, the Frenchman made a discovery. He got out his mobile phone and surreptitiously photographed Georgian prisoners who were being held hostage by Ossetian militia fighters, imprisoned in makeshift cells behind rolls of barbed wire; civilians who had probably been detained simply because of their ethnicity.

Georgians locked in cages, while Ossetians celebrated their 'liberation' in harmony: just another desperate Caucasian tragedy, the latest local blood ballad, sung with the irrepressible lust for retribution.

"Come to your senses! What else has to happen?"
Anti-Saakashvili protest song, 2012

Postscript from Tbilisi: four years would pass after the end of this squalid war before the Saakashvili era finally began to draw to its close. Again, it would come with its own soundtrack, but this time the sonic propaganda would be turned back on the regime.

Just before parliamentary elections in Georgia in 2012, covertly-filmed videos of prison guards appearing to brutally assault convicts and rape them with broom handles were released through the internet. The shocking images were then broadcast to the nation by a television channel owned by a billionaire oligarch turned opposition leader, Bidzina Ivanishvili. This new Georgian political messiah had built a futuristic James Bond-style steel-and-glass headquarters on a hill above the capital, kept penguins and zebras at his private zoo, and had named his opposition movement after a song by his albino rapper son Bera, *Georgian Dream*. Now he was using his fortune to get Saakashvili out.

For many people in the country, the prison videos seemed to symbolise the authoritarian tendencies that were barely concealed by the Saakashvili government's libertarian, pro-Western rhetoric. As crowds of youths took to the streets to show their disgust at what they had seen, a group of disaffected independent rock musicians and rappers headed for the studio to cut a protest song: *The System Must be Destroyed*, they called it. "I cannot close my eyes, I cannot stand aside while the system totally shits on our heads," the lyrics raged, while simultane-ously warning anyone who did avert their gaze from the regime's injustices: "Don't be surprised if you get a broom up your ass."

"It was a personal thing for me, because lots of my friends were imprisoned during those years and I knew how bad the situation in the prisons was," said Sergi Gvarjaladze, who sang on the track. "I was scared that if these guys would stay in power, it was going to be terrible."

Released on the internet just days after the prison scandal

broke, the video went viral instantly. "We realised how huge it was the next day when students went out on the streets and started to shout the title of the song and put some of the lyrics on their posters," Gvarjaladze recalled.

Saakashvili's political party was crushed at the polls and driven from office in shame, its dominance of Georgian life brought to an end. The super-rich Ivanishvili was now in control, and a year afterwards, he would install his rapper son's former record label boss as the new prime minister.

The extravagant propaganda shows were now over, and the lights had gone up on this surreal discotheque on the ex-Soviet frontline. Misha was no longer 'cool', and little more than a year later, the Funky President had gone into exile.

Chapter Five

Freakout on the Bosphorus

Saturday 08:00, Taksim Square... Behind the barricades, a folk ballad curled like a wisp of steam from a sound system at the top of the steps leading to Gezi Park, its delicate melody evaporating into the warm air above the gutted hulks of construction diggers and patrol cars that were ranged out like medieval battle trophies around the edges of the rubble-strewn square. Smoke plumed upwards from the overnight bonfires still smouldering in the morning heat as weary-eyed campers roused themselves from their tents, stretched out their limbs, reached for a cigarette, a cup of tea, and got ready to welcome a new day of hope and wonder...

Taksim Square was locked down on all sides, castellated with ramshackle fortifications lashed together out of corrugated iron sheets, crash barriers, discarded pipes, wooden planks and other construction detritus. People could walk in and out freely, but the improvised ramparts sent out the message that invaders would be repelled, by any means necessary. Every possible surface was decorated with graffiti - spraycanned stencils of masked faces and clenched fists and a blizzard of swirling slogans: "Freedom forever", "The old king is dead", "Seize the day", "Rise up!" It was June 2013 and the Istanbul resistance was entering its second weekend.

Near the tents, in front of the blood-red banners that now decked the monument to modern Turkey's founding father, Mustafa Kemal Atatürk, a young couple were posing for an early-morning just-woken memento photograph; the girl standing tall and hard in a flesh-tight miniskirt with ziggurat heels, the boy pulling her close and raising his hand to flash a peace sign to the azure sky: *oh yes, this time is ours...* And after they had finished, a group of headscarved women came and took their place and had their photos taken too, by the rebel flags and the statue of old Atatürk, smiling sweetly for the camera, all in this together, at least for the moment...

In Taksim Square, nothing was as it had been when I was in Istanbul just a few weeks earlier, before the demonstrations erupted. Everything had been reimagined, remade - a Starbucks coffee shop had been seized and repurposed as a pop-up protest café; an overturned police car was being used as an open-air message board, covered with hundreds of little handwritten notes that rustled softly in the morning breeze, while another smashed-up patrol van had been repainted like an oversized child's toy in crazy dayglo colours; around it, teenagers skipped and bounced through an impromptu game of handball.

Inside Gezi Park, the tree-lined space at the heart of the Istanbul resistance, a scene of yet more glorious chaos sprawled out along the pathways. Hundreds of hand-decorated tents, thousands of banners and posters delivering a multitude of messages, from socialist slogans to gay-rights declarations, feminist invocations and environmentalists' rants, black flags, red stars and even football insignia: one banner showed the black-and-white colours of Istanbul team Beşiktaş, but at its centre, woven right into the club's emblem, was the face of Che Guevara.

The week gone by had already seen a remarkable outpouring of do-it-yourself creativity, as if all the repressed vitality of Istanbul's youth had been suddenly released at once. Gezi Park had become a kind of incubator, what one local website called "a laboratory for a new culture of resistance" - constantly developing, spreading, mutating. "It's like punk rock, literally," one Turkish musician told me proudly. As well as the tents and a captured police bus which had been turned into an improvised dormitory, there were dozens of cafes and tea stalls, a couple of photo exhibitions, a stage for bands to play and activists to make speeches, a well-stocked bookshop, a children's play area and even the park's own radio station, Gezi Radio 101.9FM. Within a few days, the area had been transformed into an autonomous, self-policing and virtually self-sufficient commune, right in the middle of Turkey's greatest metropolis.

The T-shirts worn by the protesters told their own stories: peace signs, pictures of Jimi Hendrix, Janis Joplin and John Lennon; the logo of the German anti-fascist football club St. Pauli, Karl Marx with the slogan "I told you so!", and, best of all, a reworking of the Sex Pistols' *God Save the Queen* record sleeve, with the safety-pinned face of the British monarch replaced by the image of the despised Turkish prime minister Recep Tayyip Erdoğan, and the words: "God Save the Sultan."

As night started to fall over the Golden Horn, the park was transformed into a carnival of liberation, reverberating to a cacophony of competing rhythms: sound systems pumping out traditional tunes for whirling circles of dancers, tea stalls blasting psychedelic funk and Turkish rock anthems, troupes of wandering drummers bashing out martial tattoos as they stepped lightly through the crowds, students strumming acoustic guitars, hippies pounding on bongos, elderly women crooning mournful laments and folk groups singing insurrectionary anthems.

But although it certainly looked like fun, this was no game. A few hundred metres down the road, riot policemen stood cradling their automatic rifles as they lounged against their armoured cars, lazing away the hours until they got the call to move in, end the protesters' pranks and take the park back.

I had arrived in Istanbul after getting an urgent email from Serhat Köksal, alias 2/5BZ, the pioneer of politically-charged Turkish electro music. Köksal explained how, a couple of weeks earlier, at the end of May 2013, riot police had staged an early-morning assault on a small tent camp set up by environmentalists who were protesting against prime minister Erdoğan's plan to demolish Gezi Park, which lies adjacent to Taksim Square. In its place, the Turkish premier wanted to build a huge replica of a nineteenth-century Ottoman barracks complete with a shopping mall and a giant new mosque nearby, transforming the unruly hubbub of Taksim into a twisted capitalist-Islamic theme park that encapsulated the governing values of a man who seemed increasingly possessed by the arrogance of an emperor. Like the hubristic Caucasian and Central Asian potentates who order lavish makeovers of their capitals or build entire new cities in far-flung wildernesses, Erdoğan seemed to want to leave his permanent mark on the landscape, to become the grand architect of a new Istanbul, redrawing the skyline according to his whim.

Köksal had been one of the first demonstrators to arrive in Taksim Square that morning in late May after the police moved in to bust the environmentalists' camp. As they charged, he fled through the clouds of tear gas with the other protesters, half-blind and choking, then stumbled and collapsed into a construction trench, smashing the bones in both his arms. He lay there for a while, screaming for help, alone but for an elderly man in a wheelchair who had also tumbled into the trench when the riot squads attacked, until someone finally came to lift them both free.

He told me in his email that he had just come out of surgery which had left him with 24 titanium pins in his arms. But like the 'lady in the red dress' who became one of the visual icons of the Istanbul uprising when she was photographed being pepper-sprayed by a policeman in Taksim Square, Köksal insisted that he did not see himself as a special case: "I am only one of the many injured in the ongoing police attacks in various cities," he wrote. The ongoing protests were a "folk war", he said: "The struggle against the state is a struggle for being human."

The authorities had presumably expected all the peacenik eco-activists to simply pack up timidly and go home after the police smashed their way into Gezi Park, beat them up and burned their

172

tents. But instead, something remarkable happened: thousands of Istanbul citizens, shocked by the cold brutality of the assault, poured into Taksim to vent their disgust, marching in columns across the Bosphorus Bridge from the Asian side of the city as the protests swelled into an all-out resistance movement against a government that many believed was threatening their way of life and culture as well as their freedom.

It quickly turned out that most of the other musicians I knew in Istanbul were out there on the frontline as well as Köksal - indeed, it seemed that everyone I had ever met in the city was mad as hell and had collectively decided that they could not take it anymore. "The park became a symbol but there are many things behind this resistance," I was told by Barkın Engin, guitarist with Replikas, Turkey's most powerful and sonically adventurous rock band. He spoke of restrictions on freedom of speech, theocratically-inspired limits on alcohol and abortion, the creeping privatisation of public spaces: "This resistance is a natural result of the neo-liberal capitalist politics of this authoritarian government and an undemocratic prime minister who thinks he's the nation's father figure and uses religion to gain popularity," he said.

Köksal had all but predicted this uprising a year earlier when we first met near his home on the Asian side of the city. We sat in a bar in Kadıköy where he had once sipped beers with the late BBC DJ John Peel, who often played 2/5BZ tracks on his radio shows; Köksal had spoken darkly about an increasingly authoritarian country in which the interior ministry used anti-terrorism legislation to enforce obedience, critical journalists were prosecuted and jailed, hundreds of workers met violent deaths on perilously unregulated construction sites, while the state had become intoxicated by neo-liberal fervour and was selling off public assets to fuel the 'economic miracle' overseen for a decade by Erdoğan's Islamic-conservative Justice and Development Party. "The climate is getting more oppressive in the last years, sincerely critical and alternative organisations, journalists, places, artists, formations are under enormous pressure," Köksal had said. And he had warned that a backlash must come. As an anti-capitalist multimedia activist, Köksal had long been seeking to awaken the spirits of resistance with his music. Folding Burroughsian cut-ups of political speeches and clips from old Turkish movie soundtracks into jackhammer art-attack beats, he created electronic collages that recalled the fearful intensity of early-eighties Cabaret Voltaire or the seething unease of Mark Stewart's Maffia and Adrian Sherwood's Tackhead.

His last recording before he was injured in Taksim Square was a powerful mix called *Istanbul Courthousestep*, inspired by the building of a massive new 'justice palace' in the city - a bloated symbol of a state gone crazy for both construction and prosecution, he explained. The spookily prescient artwork for the mix depicted a group of seditionaries dressed like Pussy Riot in brightly-coloured balaclavas, raising their middle fingers and clenched fists as they cavorted across an architect's model of the monstrous new construction on the Istanbul shoreline. A bitter rage was rising, it seemed to suggest.

It turned out to be another prediction fulfilled: a few months later, in June 2013, with that rage already exploding, there was a real-life showdown outside the opulent new 'justice palace' when police rounded up scores of lawyers because they were supporting the Taksim Square protesters.... and the day afterwards, hundreds of lawyers rallied outside the courthouse again, chanting in unison: "Everywhere Taksim! Everywhere resistance!"

"Pepper spray is a Beşiktaş fan's perfume."
Beşiktaş football club supporter, June 2013

Saturday 19:00, Beşiktaş... Red flares belched smoke from a balcony overlooking the eagle statue at the centre of the waterfront Beşiktaş neighbourhood where thousands of football fans had gathered to drink beer in the evening sunshine; trading jokes, clinking bottles, chanting slogans in a mood of lawless abandon. Here, they controlled the streets... But there was no match on tonight; the fans had come together for a different reason - to march on the city centre and join the resistance in Taksim Square. Many of them flew flags bearing the silhouette of the Beşiktaş eagle; even more raised anarchist banners aloft.

These were the infamous Çarşı, the left-wing, anti-racist Beşiktaş FC ultras whose symbol is the encircled 'A', the anarchists' logo, and whose slogans include the punkish motto: "Çarşı against everything!" A Turkish documentary about the Çarşı movement, which grew out of Beşiktaş's working-class bazaar area, was titled *Asi Ruh - Rebel Spirit*. As soon as Taksim erupted, they got stuck in to the action; a video shot during the earliest days of the protests showed Çarşı ultras hot-wiring a bulldozer and then using it to clear away police water-cannon trucks. "We're experienced with tear gas, you know? That's why we were able to be in the front lines with our banners. We eat tear gas at least two times a week [at football matches]," one of them boasted to a journalist. "Pepper spray is a Beşiktaş fan's perfume."[1]

Serhat Köksal told me that in the early days of the resistance, the Çarşı had passed on their terrace wisdoms to inexperienced protesters who had never come up against tear gas or water cannon before: "The Çarşı came and taught them how to put up barricades," he said admiringly. "They learned everything from the Çarşı - these guys, they *know* how to fight the police!"

Riot policemen had been circling around Beşiktaş for hours already that afternoon as the fans gathered, toting gas guns as well as shields and batons. But the mood was exuberant as the chanting Çarşı started to march upwards through the city streets towards Taksim Square, raising their beer bottles in the air again and again in satirical toasts to the teetotal Erdoğan.

"Shoulder to shoulder against fascism!" they yelled, and from the balconies above, middle-aged women bashed out urban gamelan rhythms on their saucepans in approval. By the time they reached Taksim, it became clear that fans of the city's bitter rival clubs Fenerbahçe and Galatasaray had also marched to the square that evening. But when they came together, there were remarkable scenes of previously warring ultras hugging and kissing each other, old enmities exorcised, at least for the moment, through the alchemy of resistance, like those mythic tales of hooligan reconciliation-through-Ecstasy during the acid house 'summer of love' in Britain. A banner was hung from the barricades, combining all three clubs' logos and the unprecedented slogan: "Istanbul United - since May 31, 2013."

I had walked down through the narrow backstreets of Beşiktaş to the Çarşı rally from the home of my friend Ulaş Şalgam, a creative impresario who was managing some of Istanbul's most interesting alternative rock bands, although she had put the music business on hold for a couple of weeks because she was too caught up in the protests.

"I never thought this would happen," she told me. "Actually I was even talking to my friends about leaving Turkey to live somewhere else. What connects you to life is hope, hope that life will be better, but I left my hope in the past, I didn't see any possibility that something could happen, something collective and public. I was feeling sad, nervous and hopeless.

"When I was young, I was going to demonstrations, I had that hope that something might change, but then I lost it. I was just living in my small community, my small life, with my friends. But when this happened, I got my hope back," she said.

Şalgam joined the protests after she found out that one of her friends had been hit in the head by a gas canister fired by the riot police. "I saw her picture in a newspaper with blood coming down her face, and so I went to the streets, me and my friends, we all went onto the streets.

176

"I felt that there might be hope if we came together and shouted the same thing against the government. I felt that really strongly. It was a really pure feeling, to stop this government destroying the park. I felt I should be there."

The crackdown released deeply-buried emotions in Istanbul's progressive youth, she said, feelings that their own territory was under threat: "Taksim is a place where people who are different can meet. Erdoğan wants to change it into a more Islamic, traditional place that is for 'normal' people, not for the ones who are aliens, like us."

The area around the square had long been on the frontline of cultural battles between liberals and traditionalists in the city, Turkish journalist Çınar Kiper noted: "Its countless bars, nightclubs, bookstores and galleries stand as testament that there are Turks who enjoy more of life than simply shuttling between work and prayer. As the centrepiece of Turkey's window to the world, the area has been at the forefront of the country's image wars for years, with more religious elements wanting to dress it in mosques and Islamic architecture to show where it really belongs."[2]

The outrage over the planned redevelopment of Taksim channelled resentments about Erdoğan's paternalistic hectoring, his perennial references to Koranic teachings, his moral lectures about the "sacred institution" of the family and his urgings for women to stay at home and have more children, his stated desire to raise a "conservative and democratic generation" of "religious youth"... his government's increased funding for mosques and Islamic schools...

But the resistance was not just about attempts to force Turkey's secular state to take on a more Islamic identity, Şalgam insisted: "This is not about religion, this is about human rights. And it is not about politics - political parties should not try to use this for their advantage. I don't want to see any party flags or posters in Gezi Park. This is a civil movement."

She said that she was fearful about an uncompromising speech that Erdoğan had just made at a rally at the airport, vowing to push through the plan to tear up Gezi Park. He was applauded by thousands of fervent followers, chanting "God is great!" and threatening to oust the Taksim protesters with their fists and boots: "Let's go, let's smash them up!"

She rummaged through the contents of her bag, checking that everything she might need was still there: face mask, goggles and vinegar to soothe the fierce sting of the tear gas; the standard protection kit that many people took everywhere during those days in Istanbul. "Yes, I'm going to keep carrying them with me," she smiled. "Because we don't know, how will it end? Will the police come in the morning again? What will he do? His speech at the airport - it was like he was offering a civil war..."

There had already been an outpouring of new songs directly informed by the protests, she told me, but the one that had resonated most deeply was pop-rock band Duman's *Eyvallah*, with its lyrics about police brutality, batons and pepper spray, and its defiant message that proclaimed: "We are still free."

The protest sympathisers who hammered out rhythms using kitchen utensils while marchers filed past in the streets below had also inspired a band called Kardeş Türküler to write a tinkling acoustic tribute entitled *The Sound of Pots and Pans*: "What happened to our city?" its lyrics demanded. "What woe, what grief, what gas is this?"

One of the most popular Taksim Square anthems on YouTube meanwhile was called *Everyday I'm Çapuling*, a collage of news clips of the initial police crackdown and its aftermath, including a protester in a gas mask moonwalking behind the barricades, all cut to LMFAO's boisterous pop hit *Party Rock Anthem*. *Everyday I'm Çapuling* was a satirical poke at Erdoğan, who notoriously described the Taksim demonstrators as *çapulcar* - marauders or looters. "We cannot leave the streets for anarchists and terrorists to roam," he had warned. The protesters had happily picked up this intended insult and turned it into a badge of honour: in Gezi Park, there was a 'çapulcu café', a 'çapulcu TV lounge', even a 'çapulcu barber' and a 'çapulcu hotel' where protesters could bring their own bedrolls and doss down for the night under its canopies.

Like other resistance movements over the previous decade in places like Georgia and Ukraine, where rock bands had helped to sustain revolutionary passions during weeks of struggle, music had become a crucial part of the internal feedback loop of the Turkish uprising, calling forth the dissident spirits of the metropolis. While it was hardly remarkable that liberal-minded rockers were supporting the Taksim cause, what was interesting was that many Istanbul bands were not only more politically aware but also much more overtly anti-capitalist than their western European counterparts, creating an instant cultural infrastructure for the Gezi Park occupation.

Turkey already had a tradition of revolutionary songs dating back to the politically turbulent sixties and seventies, and now the canon was being updated. "Music helps create a sense of solidarity," one Istanbul rocker explained. "It spreads the feeling and the idea and it encourages the people who are on the streets."

But during the first police assault at the end of May, music had no role to play. "When they were firing tear gas at us, it didn't matter if you were a musician - you were just a human trying to breathe," I was told by Gökçe Gürçay, the drummer with the folk-rock band Gevende, who had played live at the protest camp in Gezi Park. Another musician also recalled similar memories of those first days on the streets: "No eating, no sleeping, no music, no sex..."

Like Şalgam, Gürçay said that he had been considering whether to emigrate before the protests began. "One month ago, if you asked me, I would have said there was no hope for change," he explained. "One month ago, we were talking about which country we should move to. Now we see that there is a future here."

"Everything is dark, there is no humanity..."
Damn This World, Turkish *arabesk* song by Orhan Gencebay

In the early morning of September 12, 1980, Turkey's national security council made a solemn announcement on state television: the army had seized power. Parliament was dismissed, the cabinet dissolved, all political parties banned and their leaders arrested. A state of emergency was imposed and no one was allowed to leave the country. After years of bloody violence between leftists and right-wingers which had resulted in thousands of deaths, Turkey's generals had decided that it was time to restore order. It was necessary, stated the communiqué announcing the takeover, "to preserve the integrity of the country, to restore national unity and togetherness, to avert a possible civil war, to re-establish the authority of the state and to eliminate all the factors that prevent the normal functioning of the democratic order".

The price of stability was extortionate. In the aftermath of the coup, 650,000 people were arrested, 230,000 put on trial, more than 500 sentenced to death and 50 ultimately executed, while a further 170 were tortured to death, according to a Turkish parliamentary investigation.

Turkish photographer Kadir Can has published a remarkable book of pictures from the period that led to the coup, *Akil Tutulmasi (The Eclipse of Wisdom)*. Can's stark images show helmeted police clubbing demonstrators, water cannon trucks dousing angry crowds, bloodied victims heading home on ferryboats, buildings decked with multicoloured banners and walls decorated with anti-government graffiti, the shells of burned-out cars and bodies lying dead in the streets. His shot of panicked protesters fleeing a police onslaught in Taksim Square is strongly reminiscent of the Gezi Park uprising 23 years later, although the seventies protesters' placards are more traditionally political, their jeans more flared and moustaches bushier.

The 1980 coup, and the three years of military rule that followed it, cast a long shadow over the generation that was growing up at that time, too young to fully understand what was going on but dramatically affected by the cultural changes that the generals brought with them.

In 2012, I travelled to Istanbul to interview Replikas about the new album they had just recorded, *Biz Burada Yok İken* (*When We Were Not Here*), a collection of reinterpretations of vintage Turkish psychedelic rock songs that were originally produced during an incredible outburst of creativity in the country in the late sixties and seventies, before the coup, when musicians combined traditional melodies and instruments with the electric vitality of peak-period Western rock'n'roll.

This 'Anadolu Pop' movement began when restrictions eased and artistic freedom flourished in the years that followed a previous military takeover in 1960, but came to a crushing end when the generals seized control over the state again in 1980. After the 1980 coup, some musicians fled into exile, some were jailed, songs and films were banned, and the Turkish rock scene never really recovered.

"The coup was a tragedy not only for music but for all culture," explained Replikas' electronics and keyboard player Burak Tamer. "Lots of writers and film-makers and academics were also affected. Some disappeared."

Bassist Selçuk Artut recalled how his parents even got rid of their record collection, fearing possible persecution in the new climate of cultural conservatism that followed the generals' takeover: "People were worrying, 'If I listen to these records, will they put me in prison?'" "Books too, if they caught you with certain books, you didn't know what might happen, they could put you in prison or torture you," added drummer Orçun

Baştürk.

"While we were kids in the nineties, we were not aware of the music that happened in the sixties and seventies because it was being hidden by the authorities because of its political connotations. After the military coup, all this music disappeared, all the records were on dusty shelves somewhere," continued Artut.

"Later on when we started as a band, we were playing mainly Anglo-Saxon music, and then we realised that something else happened in Turkey that has a great value, which was this Anatolian pop period."

Replikas' sound was initially shaped by bands like Sonic Youth, Nirvana, Can, Einstürzende Neubauten and other post-punk and industrial bands that they discovered in the nineties, when Western alternative music largely circulated around Istanbul from hand to hand on pirated cassettes. But finding abandoned Turkish classics in secondhand shops was a revelation: "The Anatolian pop movement actually helped us to discover our own cultural identity. It was like a gateway for us," said guitarist Barkın Engin.

It was Engin who had first introduced me to the abundant delights of Anadolu Pop and Turkish psychedelic rock a couple of years earlier, when we met for the first time in a café just off Taksim Square. "You should check these people out," he said, scribbling down a list of what to me, at the time, were strange names indeed: Moğollar, Üç Hürel, Bunalimlar, Cem Karaca, Barış Manço... The only name that I recognised on his list was Erkin Koray, Turkey's original psychedelic explorer, who claims to have played the first ever rock concert in the country back in 1957, when he led an amateur band doing covers of Elvis Presley and Fats Domino.

Koray went on to invent the electric bağlama - an amplified version of the traditional Turkish stringed instrument - which he deployed to exhilarating effect on a series of sixties and seventies recordings that meshed Anatolian sonic motifs with blazing fusillades of psych-rock guitar. He maintained his indomitable commitment to the freak cause for decades, despite being attacked in the street several times during the sixties for being a longhair. "I'm still lost in amazement how I am still alive," he once said.

The Anadolu Pop era produced innumerable amazing singles and a series of extraordinary albums - Barış Manço's space-dusted, synth-spangled *2023*, Selda Bağcan's searing, passionate *Selda*, Ersen and Dadaşlar's psych-pop stomp *Dünden Bugüne*, Mustafa Özkent's acid-funk freakout *Gençlik Ile Elele*, amongst others - but because of the intemperate political climate of the times, it was inevitable that its singers and players became drawn into activism or were compelled to declare which side they were on, as left battled right in the bloody struggle for power in seventies Turkey.

Selda Bağcan wrote a series of bitterly beautiful songs castigating corrupt politicians for condemning the masses to poverty and desperation, while left-wing rocker Cem Karaca, one of the cultural heroes of the post-1968 generation in Turkey, railed against social injustice, exploitation and the cruelties of capitalism. The honey-voiced Ersen, however, came out for the right, even performing at military parties and police balls, making him a hate figure for many liberal Turkish rock fans for years afterwards.

When the military seized power in 1980, the glory years of Anadolu Pop came to an abrupt end. Bağcan's passport was seized and she was jailed on three separate occasions in the years after the coup. Karaca, who was hiding in Germany at the time of the takeover to avoid the threat of prosecution, was charged with inciting terror and stripped of his citizenship, and had to remain in exile until the civilian government that eventually replaced the generals amnestied him and allowed him to return seven years later. Another left-wing singer, Edip Akbayram, was attacked and threatened with death. Naturally, their opportunities to record or play live diminished significantly. But Barış Manço, who had managed to avoid any political associations, remained successful for years to come, cherished for his peace-loving philosophy and his family-oriented television show as well as his widely-cherished recordings. When he died in 1999, tens of thousands of people turned out to mourn a man who had been a crucial figure in Turkish pop culture for more than three decades.

The influential Istanbul DJ Barış K, whose mixes and re-edits of Turkish psych-funk helped to nourish a revival of interest in Anadolu Pop some 30 years after the coup, once told me that the military takeover was a watershed; what he remembered as the end of a period of cultural freedom. "The whole social structure changed. I remember my father sold all his records, my mother started wearing this headscarf," he recalled. "When society changed, people stopped listening to wild music. Before it was lyrics like, 'I will create my own destiny!' Then people started listening to arabesk, with lyrics like, 'Oh God, why did you do this to me?'"

The melancholic sound known as arabesk, with its lyrics bemoaning cruel fate, broken lives and unrealised dreams, became increasingly popular in the post-coup years among Istanbul's urban poor, those who lived in illegally-built shanties around the rapidly-growing city: the authentic sound of the ghetto. "It portrays a world of complex and turbulent emotions peopled by lovers doomed to solitude and a violent end. It describes a decaying city in which poverty-stricken migrant workers are exploited and abused, and calls on its listeners to pour another glass of raki, light another cigarette, and curse fate and the world," musicologist Martin Stokes explained.[3]

Some of the middle-class intellectuals who made up the city's cultural elite found arabesk vulgar, kitsch and unspeakably common. As the eighties progressed, it was also banned from state television by the culture ministry on the grounds that it was morally corrupting, although its popularity remained undiminished. It was unconsciously subversive because it "articulated popular despondency", British journalist Tim Kelsey has suggested: "The *arabesk* said that something had gone very wrong indeed with Atatürk's republic. That is why the government took it so seriously."[4]

In the beginning at least, arabesk had a vital political edge, agreed Serhat Köksal, who sampled some of its melodies for 2/5BZ's agit-prop electro soundscapes. The music's troubled soul fitted right into his sonic tapestry of dissent, he insisted: "When it first appeared, arabesk was an honest expression of people's pain and rebellion." The political character of the genre changed, however, when it became commercialised and was even adopted by populist politicians trawling for votes, as Turkey became increasingly dominated by the eighties-era free-market principles known as Thatcherism in Britain and Reaganomics in the US: "Some arabesk stars were glorified as stories of upward mobility, as an example of spreading the hope that 'you can do it too'," Köksal explained. "Today, the injustices of the economy, and the pain and suffering in the lives of people are even more aggravated," he continued. "Arabesk is less and less an expression of these difficult lives and the voice of the urban poor. Most of the well-known figures of arabesk adapted well to the changing economic conditions of the post-eighties. And now, they are not really distant from the interests and the likes of the new power elite."

As well as Anadolu Pop and arabesk, older influences also came into play as contemporary Turkish rock bands sought to trace their country's nonconformist musical lineage back through time. Replikas for example delved backwards to explore the mystic troubadours and wandering 'truth-tellers' known as *aşıki*, and had found echoes of their own tranced-out rock'n'roll in the ritualistic music of the religious sect known as the Bektaşi. "It's very minimalistic, very trance-like, like some electronic music, with the same loop repeating over and over again," Barkın Engin explained. "In the Bektaşi rituals, with repetition, you can reach a state of higher consciousness."

The Bektaşi are a Sufi mystic order who take their own idiosyncratic view of Muslim customs and don't abstain from pork or alcohol. There are a series of sly Bektaşi jokes based on this unconventional relationship with Islam; the kind of subversive humour that would not have been out of place in Gezi Park in 2013.

A Bektaşi goes into a mosque, one of them begins. He starts to pray: "Oh Allah, give me a bottle of raki!"

A devout Muslim overhears him and exclaims: "Don't you have anything else to ask God for? You know very well that raki is not allowed!"

"What should I ask for, then?" responds the Bektaşi.

"Well," says the other worshipper, "you could start by asking for Allah's mercy."

The Bektaşi snaps back: "I've already got Allah's mercy - what I don't have is a nice bottle of raki..."

"Yes, I am drunk - but I will be sober tomorrow..."
Quote attributed to Winston Churchill

Saturday 24:00, Taksim Square... By midnight, the square had been gripped by hedonistic frenzy, music and laughter reverberating from every corner, crowds drifting this way and that, seemingly at random, a melee of protesters, sightseers and canny street traders who had adapted their wares to fit the insurrectionary mood. "Booze, booze, booze, booze, *booooooooze!*" yelled one of the scores of hawkers who were selling tins of beer from ice-packed buckets; supping ale had become a symbolic act of resistance, it seemed, another jab at Erdoğan, who in his latest speech had condemned the secular republic's beloved founder Atatürk as a "lush".

The pavement vendors were also offering everything a protester might need when the next crackdown finally came: respirator masks, goggles, construction worker's hard hats and bandanas decorated with the skull and crossbones, as well as cans of spraypaint for those who wanted to add their own messages to the graffiti-spattered walls. Hundreds of Guy Fawkes facemasks were laid out across the flagstones in sprawling rows - the same design that had been adopted as a symbol by the anti-capitalist Occupy protesters, copied from Alan Moore's *V for Vendetta* graphic novels. Hawkers were also doing a lucrative trade in 'Everyday I'm Çapuling' T-shirts, printed up quickly to cash in on the *çapulcu* craze, reminding me of the instant commodification of the Orange Revolution in 2004 in Kiev, when commemorative orange-themed merchandise was on sale just days after protesters seized the Ukrainian capital's main square.

In every corner tonight, there was a different party: someone had set up a laser system and beams of neon-green light were strafing the Atatürk memorial while protesters who had climbed up onto the monument were pumping their limbs to Turkish disco tunes; a few metres away, a street musician tried to compete by thrashing out distorted garage-band chords on an amplified banjo, while an elderly troubadour coaxed unearthly wails from his *ney* and circles of dancers swayed to the percussive rumble of a drum troupe...

"Taksim is liberated and all sorts of weird energies are pouring out," I wrote in my notebook that night as I moved through the celebrating throng. Chinese lanterns floated gracefully into the sky, rising above the pungent smoke from the kebab merchants' barbecues, and the air was thick with voices - activists making political speeches, traders yelling their pitches, people shouting to their friends, children giggling, protesters singing... it was hard, sometimes, to remember that this was a political demonstration rather than a street festival. As dawn broke the next morning, the music was still pounding...

Sunday 15:00, Taksim Square... I met up with Replikas again the following afternoon, in a café overlooking the square. They had also been gassed by the riot police in the early days of the protests, they told me. "Except for Selçuk, none of us did military service, but I think that now we have enough training - I've never run so much in the last years as I've run from the pepper gas," grinned Barkın Engin. The government had spent millions of dollars buying gas for the police to fire at the protesters, he said: "There is a saying at the moment: for the first time in the Turkish republic, our taxes are really being spent on the people..."

Laughter played a crucial role, those days in Taksim Square: laughing at the politicians seemed somehow to drain their power, puncturing their certainties and making them shrivel like pricked balloons, their speeches reduced to comical glossolalia. Like the youth movements involved in ousting authoritarian leaders in former Communist states in the early years of the twenty-first century, demonstrators had realised that humour was a potent weapon. As far as I heard, none of the Turkish protesters had been studying the classic peaceful-resistance manual by US academic Gene Sharp, *From Dictatorship to Democracy*, a rebel's handbook which was originally developed to help subvert military rule in Burma and later used to help inform the strategies behind uprisings in Eastern Europe and the Arab world. But the Gezi Park masses were, even if unwittingly, deploying some of Sharp's insurrectionary concepts.

Serhat Köksal had told me that deftly-targeted jokes were a traditional "reflex of resistance" in Turkey: "As Turkish humourist Aziz Nesin once put it: 'Throughout history, popular humour and humour that is on the side of the public has struggled with oppression and malice, through making fun of the dominant classes, dictators and bad governors,'" he said. Now placards around Gezi Park mocked Erdoğan's pious pronounce-ments, his moral lectures, his distaste for alcohol. One young protester's poster satirised Erdoğan's call for Turkish women to have more children: "Do you really want two more like me?" it demanded.

American writer Thomas Goltz reported seeing a man holding up a placard quoting Winston Churchill's retort to a woman who criticised him for being inebriated, but with its slogan redirected at Erdoğan: "Yes, I am drunk - but I will be sober tomorrow. You, in contrast, are now ugly and will be ugly forever."[5] Other posters depicted penguins wearing gas masks, mocking CNN's Turkish affiliate, which on the day of the first crackdown on May 31 had screened a nature documentary about Antarctica instead of covering what was happening on the streets of Istanbul. (The mainstream media, largely controlled by government-friendly tycoons, initially ignored the protests; another TV channel, whose headquarters was just a short walk from Gezi Park, instead broadcast a studio discussion about schizophrenia - "an apt metaphor for the state of journalism in Turkey", one commentator noted.)[6]

But Replikas said they were ambiguous about the festive atmosphere in the square, as if people were trying to convince themselves that the crackdown might never come by dancing a frantic tango of denial: "At the moment it is like a carnival but people are celebrating too much, perhaps; we have to think carefully about what will happen, what should be the next step," said Orçun Baştürk.

Despite the visceral physicality of their music, Replikas are a decidedly intellectual bunch. Engin, for instance, has taught the history of electronic composition at the Istanbul conservatory, while Artut has written a book theorising how new media technology has altered our perception of reality. Some of the band are also involved in avant-garde side-projects which could be described as 'sound art'. So before I met them, I think I was expecting some kind of coolly academic analysis of what was going on in the city. What I was not prepared for was sheer *fury*.

"This is a dictatorship in progress," insisted Burak Tamer. "It's an authoritarian government that restricts people's rights so they are not free any more, and that is not a democratic regime. The prime minister says you can't meet in parks and squares. So what are these places for, if people can't meet and interact there - what are they for?" he demanded angrily.

"Thousands of people have been through Gezi Park during the week. The prime minister says there are just a few 'marginal' people, hooligans or looters, but how can they all be 'marginal'?" asked Baştürk. "What the government is doing is dividing people, and if you don't take their side, you are 'marginal'. That is not democracy."

Some people however were right behind their moustachioed premier Erdoğan when it came to the *çapulcar*. In a taxi later that day, the driver seized the opportunity to vent his frustration about the Taksim 'marginals', who he clearly thought were just a mob of wanton wreckers: "Protest - bad for economy," he grumbled to me. "Looters - bad for tourism, bad for hotels, bad for taxi drivers." When I mentioned the possibility of another police crackdown in Taksim, he retorted with easy malice: "Good! Bye-bye protest!" A series of attacks on demonstrators by people wielding sticks or knives also showed that there were people who were ready to take up arms and do the riot police's work for them, out of belief in their own moral superiority or just for the love of Erdoğan - or the love of violence…

But among those who were involved in the resistance, there was an almost cosmic sense of being on the same wavelength: a harmonic convergence of righteous energies. The greatest achievement of the protests, Replikas argued, was this expansion of dissident consciousness. They described it as a "great awakening".

"It's hard to predict what's going to happen next but I have to say that we never pushed our limits before like that, as a public, we never went this far," suggested Baştürk. "There is a feeling of freedom, people have no fear of anything anymore. We don't know what will happen in the end, but that consciousness will exist for a long time."

"Everything pretends to be something, but everything is something else."
Berna Göl of Istanbul band Kim Ki O

Crossing the Bosphorus on a gloomy arabesk evening, the twilight ferryboat gliding through the sleeting rain, past the shadowy stone digits of the mosques and the neon signs murmuring indecipherable messages from the façades of distant office blocks; a lone muezzin echoing off the purple water, his voice harmonising with the cries of scavenging seabirds and the mournful clang of the tramcars' bells as they patrol the waterfront tracks, the foghorns of the tankers groaning into the October mist...

It was 2010 and I was on my way across the Bosphorus to Kadıköy on the Asian shore to meet Berna Göl and Ekin Sanaç, the two young women who made up the Turkish electro duo Kim Ki O. We spoke about a lot of things that evening, but many of them only really made sense to me much later, in 2013. If I had really understood what they were saying, if I had known how to read the signals, I might have picked up on the sense of introverted dissatisfaction and festering unease that was eddying beneath the surface but would only surge upwards into plain sight three years later, in Taksim Square.

Göl and Sanaç led me from the ferry port to a crepuscular shopping arcade, one of the places which had helped to nurture Istanbul's alternative rock scene in the nineties, they said. Back then, this narrow tiled passage lined with record shops and book stalls had been a kind of bohemian enclave where young Turks would come to buy bootleg cassette copies of Western alternative rock albums which were all but unavailable elsewhere in the country. The air was thick with smoke: tobacco, occasionally cannabis. Göl and Sanaç were still at school, and the two teenage girls would come down in their uniforms to buy punk rock tapes: Sex Pistols, Nirvana, Ramones, Sonic Youth...

"It was a very emotional time for us," Göl recalled. "It was also very special, because it was so hard to get the music." There was no downloading and no file-sharing back then: everything had to be sought out, genuinely discovered through sheer determination; each new acquisition was a minor victory in an arduous campaign of self-emancipation, and all the more treasured because it was hard-won.

Sometimes the police would raid the arcade, Göl said, blocking both entrances so nobody could flee and searching everyone inside for illicit substances. She was detained during a bust once, but because she was just a schoolgirl in her uniform, the police let her go and sent her home to her parents. It never stopped her going back, though.

Later, drinking peppermint tea and eating sweet pistachio cakes in a nearby café, Göl explained why punk rock, of all musics, had gripped her imagination as a teenage girl growing up in a Muslim country: "It was all about the feeling," she said. "It was the first thing that I heard that made me feel something that I'd never felt before."

She met Sanaç when they were both attending a prestigious American private school in the city - a place where they felt that they never really fitted in. "There was a disconnection, and music played a big part in discovering ourselves," Sanaç recalled.

Music offered a way for them to define an outsider identity for themselves and liberate a psychic space in which they could thrive. "Looking back now, maybe a part of it that we were imagining we were living in a different city, in a different culture," Göl said. "We wanted to assume, maybe unconsciously, that we were living somewhere else. Going to an American school meant we learned the rules and social codes of a culture that we would never be living in, practically. So the problems in our daily lives didn't fit with the things we would be learning in class. There was this huge gap."

Punk also illuminated connections to feminist theory and avant-garde art, helping them create an internal world unconstrained by the difficulties of growing up female and nonconformist in a society where Islam doesn't exactly dominate daily life, but where its cultural traditions still to some extent shape morality and behaviour.

"There are these certain codes," said Göl when I asked her if there were invisible restrictions on what was possible for a woman in Istanbul. "There are always these unspoken, hidden conservative notions."

"We feel like we live here but we're not living the life we're supposed to," added Sanaç. "We have this feeling of not belonging here, not belonging there - so where do we belong?"

Earlier that day, I had experienced an unexpected Istanbul epiphany. I was playing a Replikas track, *Ruh-Feza*, in my freezing room, wrapped up in a woollen blanket against the October chill, when the heavily-amplified call to prayer tore through the mist from a sound system hooked up to the mosque across the road. For one pure moment, the soulful vuvuzela of the muezzin's wail combined in dissonant anti-harmony with the fearsome guitar riff - the spiritual and the secular grappling with each other, coalescing briefly, tearing themselves apart then coming together again for some kind of feverish atonal consummation as the muezzin reached his pious climax and the guitar feedback howled its feral response.

It was a sonic clash of cultural identities, something that Barkın Engin of Replikas had told me that he valued: "I think living here has an effect. You cannot ignore it. Turkey does not consist of a single culture; there is not something called a 'Turkish person', actually. It is not an identity. It does not exist. It's a combination. Some fascists will claim that's not true, but they're not right."

Later that evening, in the terrace bar at the Peyote club in the pulsing backstreets of the Beyoğlu nightlife zone, with the DJ spinning electro and vintage Krautrock tunes, it was hard to believe that the country was being run by an Islamic political party. Moody, crop-haired girls in polo-necks smouldered darkly over shots of raki, while straggle-bearded hipster boys hooked down bottle after foaming bottle of beer as night rushed onwards towards dawn. When Kim Ki O came on stage, the audience was much more disturbed by the menacing growl of Göl's depth-charge basslines than by the fact that two young women were rocking the dancefloor.

But the worry was always there, some of the Peyote clubbers told me, that the ruling party might start to push its religious agenda harder, that fanatical men would begin to use political power for cultural oppression. A few weeks earlier, in September 2010, Islamist mobs armed with sticks, knives and bottles had attacked people who were drinking in the street outside art galleries in the Tophane district, smashing windows and beating up onlookers, furious that bourgeois boozers were flaunting their infidel sins in *their* neighbourhood.

Beneath Istanbul's sheen of stability and sophistication, there was often a distinct sense of uncertainty about the future, something that Göl and Sanaç alluded to repeatedly when we talked. Their emotions about their own city seemed complex and uneasy, especially in 2010, long before the Taksim resistance erupted.

"Here everything pretends to be something, but everything is something else," Göl had said. "It feels very beautiful when you look at the view, but then when you look more clearly, you see all the garbage thrown in the water."

Sunday 18:00, Karaköy… It was now June 2013 and I was meeting up with Göl and Sanaç again, this time on the European side of the Bosphorus. As we chatted in a café next to the ferry terminal, hundreds of protesters poured off the boats pulling in from the Asian shore, chanting, clapping, banging drums and blowing whistles, all heading for their big night out on Taksim Square. Both Göl and Sanaç seemed jubilant, charged up with hope; as if this was what they had been waiting for, even if they didn't realise it before.

They told me that during the couple of years since we last met, they had been living under dark clouds - seeing only the garbage in the water, perhaps. "We were so depressed, all of us, that we didn't even know we were depressed. This was beyond feeling desperate, it had become this thing that kept all of us so silent and was eating us from the inside," said Göl.

"We felt invisible, we felt that we weren't meant to be ourselves," added Sanaç. "We were being threatened in the streets, we weren't safe anywhere - in a cab, on a bus or walking by yourself in the dark, you felt hatred."

"I was always thinking, who is going to pay for this, for this feeling of lack of safety and trust in the system, who will pay for this anxiety, this depression, this not having control over anything?" asked Göl. Now the time had come.

They had just released a new album, *Grounds*, with lyrics that were "very much about the depression that was going on before these protests", said Sanaç. Coincidentally, a video clip for one of the tracks had been shot in Taksim not long before the uprising, climaxing with footage of the square exploding. Another of the songs conjured fantasies of escape using a looped sample of Richey Edwards, the guitarist from the Manic Street Preachers who vanished in 1995. Edwards' disconnected voice ends the song with a wistful expression of his urge to flight, repeating over and over again: "Go and live with my dogs somewhere..."

The crackdown on Gezi Park finally unleashed the passions that had been repressed for so long, said Sanaç: "It was very emotional and actually quite magical, how it started. After all the hopelessness and powerlessness we had been feeling for so long, at that moment there was nothing else we could do but go to the streets. It was a moment that connected everyone."

"When it first started, there was so much violence, but a different feeling also started, it was as if everyone around us got rid of this never-ending depression in their lives," continued Göl. "Even though so much is happening, we feel like we can breathe now."

Whatever happened next, some kind of victory had already been won, they agreed; like Replikas, they said that this was an "awakening".

"It's not about Erdoğan anymore, it's bigger than that, more important that that now," insisted Göl. "And we don't think this will stop because people got the virus of questioning authority, questioning the media, and it won't go away that easily. These last few days... people are different now."

"Were we going to kneel down in front of these people?"
Recep Tayyip Erdoğan, Turkish prime minister, June 2013

Sunday 21:00, Gezi Park... It was deep into the evening when they finally came, with their gas guns and armoured cars, to end the fleeting reveries of liberation. In a frantic last stand, protesters linked arms at the entrance to Gezi Park, trying to stop the onslaught, but they were shoved aside by the riot shields as white-helmeted officers came tearing through the trees amid the swirls of gas and blurts of pepper spray, dragging young campers screaming from their tents. Some fought back, setting fire to barricades and hurling missiles, but police forced them away into the side-streets around Taksim where they were trapped and gassed and clubbed down. The Gezi Park 'wishing tree', which had been decked with scores of individual handwritten notes telling of the protesters' dreams, was incinerated.

"Something this beautiful has to be destroyed," I had written in my notebook in Gezi Park one night, just a week earlier, as I watched the sheer joy on the faces of these young idealists revelling in the temporary Eden they had created for themselves. "It cannot be permitted to last."

The raid came little more than an hour after Erdoğan issued the last of an increasingly stern series of threats to send in the security forces to clear the protest camp. He had been rallying thousands of his supporters around the country, attempting to demonstrate that he was not only still in control, but as much of a popular hero as ever.

Police had already seized back Taksim Square a few days earlier, fighting running battles with hardcore protesters until they finally cleared the area and reopened it to traffic. Erdoğan mocked his critics pitilessly: "They say the prime minister is rough. So what was going to happen here? Were we going to kneel down in front of these people?" he had demanded after the operation to take the square had begun. "If you call this roughness, I'm sorry, but Tayyip Erdoğan won't change."[7] Eleven people were killed and more than 8,000 injured during the weeks of protest.

Now Erdoğan blamed "terrorists, anarchists and rioters" for ignoring his warnings and holding out in Gezi Park, those same old 'marginals', who he insisted were being backed by unnamed 'foreign interests' - the classic paranoiac rhetoric of the demagogue who suddenly realises that not everyone is going to stay in line, but can't explain to himself why they refuse to accept his beneficent rule.

By the morning of June 16, 2013, all the tents had been trashed, the banners destroyed and the posters torn down. An aerial view over Gezi Park showed nothing: no life, unless the sparrows and pigeons were to be counted. The steps leading to the park, which had been decorated with chaotic but tender affection during the 18-day occupation, were now abnormally pristine. Erdoğan had said that once the park was cleared out, everyone could enjoy a stroll there. But nobody was strolling that day.

A few hours later, at 6pm, a solitary man came and stood in Taksim Square. He said nothing and did nothing, just stood there. Others joined him, just to stand there too; first a handful, then several hundred. There was no chanting, no shouting, no clapping, no music. They just stood in silence, keeping close to one other, tiny figures like architect's models amid the dominant expanse of the square, until the police came to move them on. That night, in the nearby streets, a journalist reported hearing young people improvising Turkish lyrics to the melody of a song by The Doors: *The End*.[8] But the standing man's wordless message was clear: no, it's not, not yet.

"This is just the beginning!"
Protester in Istanbul, the day after the Gezi Park crackdown

Sunday 17:00, Gezi Park... It was now July 2013, a couple of weeks after the crackdown: the park was still there, but when I walked through it again, it was as if the protest camp had just been a collective daydream which had passed as quickly as it began. There were no speeches, no music, just the soft bubbling of fountains and the laughter of children playing, as people sat around on blankets in the shade of the trees, relaxing into a lazy summer afternoon in the open air. The flowerbeds had been replanted with new blooms and there were no masks or goggles on sale anymore; instead the street vendors were offering up watermelons and pairs of cheap socks. Even the graffiti in Taksim Square had been painted out; the ecstasies and agonies of the recent past wiped clean away. Only one corner of Gezi Park was still haunted by memories of the resistance: a small shrine to those who died, a temporary memorial adorned with flowers and candles and decked with Turkish flags.

The park had been saved from Erdoğan's bulldozers after a court ruling had cancelled the construction project, giving a belated, unexpected victory to the *çapulcar*. But on the other side of Taksim Square, the water-cannon trucks and armoured cars were still parked up, along with buses full of riot police on standby, waiting patiently in the July heat for their next order to gas their fellow citizens...

I met up with Serhat Köksal again that day in Yoğurtçu Park in Kadıköy, where the trees were draped with multi-coloured banners and satirical posters and the sound system was blaring out old Turkish revolutionary songs: the Gezi vibe transplanted. It was just one of many parks around the city where protesters had set down new roots after the Gezi camp was evicted, Köksal told me: "This is open democracy. Everyone comes here every evening, everyone cares about each other, everyone helps each other." There was a cool determination to the young people who were hanging out at Yoğurtçu, like they were recharging themselves before heading back to the frontline. I remembered a passage from journalist Tim Kelsey's book about Turkey, even though it had been written more than 15 years earlier: "There is tremendous energy and passion in the young Turks, a creativity that will help ensure the country has a much less stagnant future than its present."[9]

Köksal's shattered arms were still strapped up after his operation and he was painfully trying to regain the mobility he had lost a month earlier during the crackdown. But that hadn't stopped him from cutting a raw demo of a new track that sampled the voice of a protester who, in an outburst of kamikaze rage the day after the final crackdown in Gezi Park, had stripped naked and marched alone towards the police lines.

Gesticulating obscenely and cursing the authorities for meddling in his life, as if he suddenly had the chance to take vengeance for all the wrongs that had ever been done to him, the naked protester started yelling about cops and religion and oppression and all the other things that seemed to have reached such a boiling point in his brain that he had no option but to confront his tormentors - without weapons, without back-up, even without his clothes: "Will Tayyip interfere with my dick? Will he mess with this?" he demanded, pointing at his penis and admonishing the police: "This is just the beginning! We will carry on the struggle!"

Köksal had hooked up this bare-arsed rant to a gyroscopic Turkish funk-guitar loop that dropped fast and hard into a punishing dubstep bassline, hurling the man's savage recriminations straight in your face. It was rough-hewn and ugly, but more than any other new music I heard from Istanbul during those heady weeks, it seemed to encapsulate the bloody-minded defiance, the Dadaist absurdism, the anarchic improvisation of that moment; taking the sonic signals emitted by the resistance and feeding them back through the echo-chamber imagination of Köksal, a veteran dissident whose dreams of a genuine uprising had finally come true.

"It hasn't finished, of course; it is just starting," Köksal turned to assure me as we sat there under the lengthening shadows of the park that evening, unconsciously echoing the words of his naked muse.

"This is just the beginning..."

Chapter Six

Moscow Doesn't Believe in Tears

The surge throws us all backwards in a wild cascading wave of human bodies, arms and legs twisted, faces smeared up against chests, necks crushed under armpits, friend and foe entwined in panicked flight: a few young protesters, a couple of press photographers, a family of terrified Korean tourists, a florid-faced priest wielding a huge crucifix like a cosh, a brace of skinheads with fascist logos on their T-shirts, all staggering back before the onrushing battalion of riot police, forcing us across the road and away from Red Square.

In the crowd, somewhere around this brutish heaving mass of cops, sightseers, reporters, Orthodox clerics and Nazis screaming for the blood of gay rights demonstrators, were Yekaterina Samutsevich and Nadezhda Tolokonnikova, although like most people at this point - it was May 2011 - I had never heard of them. But within a year, they had become notorious as the feminist guerrilla heroines of Pussy Riot, the most incendiary art-punk collective of their time, arrested and subjected to an absurd Soviet-style show trial for publicly cursing out the strongman leader of the biggest country in the world.

All the elements were already in place for an outburst of seditious rage on the Moscow streets: an intolerant regime that concentrated power and wealth in its own hands and allowed the corrupt to flourish while jailing those who dared to oppose it, a pliant police force ready to use extreme force if its masters were challenged, and a docile media that lauded its rulers while independent journalists who exposed their transgressions were beaten and murdered. It would just take a spark to set it all off, and when Vladimir Putin declared in September 2011 that he, and not his iPad-wielding, Deep Purple-loving, ostensibly more 'liberal' sidekick Dmitry Medvedev, would be the regime's candidate for the Russian presidency in the next year's election, setting the scene for perhaps another 12 years of authoritarian rule by the former KGB officer, the fury broke loose.

The initially anonymous Pussy Riot were to become global symbols of that fury as tens of thousands of protesters took to the streets of the Russian capital in the winter of 2011 for the first time in two decades. It was a role that the women sought out and embraced, but it would never have happened if the time wasn't right. Protest songs launched into a somnolent void will never make much impact, but the city was roiling with insurrectionary passions and desperate for iconic champions who would dramatise this spontaneous upsurge of resistance on the biggest stage possible. "We wanted to change it all. We wanted to create something that had never existed in Russia before," Samutsevich told me later. "It was... *necessary*."

The three Pussy Riot members who would later be arrested were highly educated and media-savvy, and all in their twenties; typical activists of the contemporary Russian protest movement. Samutsevich, then 29, had worked as a computer programmer developing software for nuclear submarines before quitting to attend a photography college, while Maria Alyokhina, 23, had studied journalism and was a committed environmental activist. Nadezhda Tolokonnikova, the youngest at 22, was reading philosophy at Moscow State University. The two younger women were also both mothers of small children. Unlikely heroes, as Tolokonnikova would tell their trial later: "We are jokers, jesters, holy fools."

The idea to start Pussy Riot was hatched when Samutsevich, Tolokonnikova and her husband Pyotr Verzilov were members of the political art collective Voina ('War'). Voina was best known for cheeky stunts like painting a giant penis on a bridge near the St. Petersburg headquarters of the Russian security services, projecting a skull and crossbones onto the government building in Moscow and having public sex in a biology museum to 'celebrate' the election of Dmitry Medvedev as president in 2008 (among the writhing bodies were Verzilov and a heavily pregnant Tolokonnikova). "After each action, Russian cops start a new criminal case against the group. In those cases they call us vandals, hooligans and pornographers. We are proud to be called that," Voina activist Alexei Plutser-Sarno once explained.[1]

In a ramshackle precursor to Pussy Riot in 2009, some Voina activists, including Samutsevich and Tolokonnikova, smuggled microphones and amplifiers into the trial of a gallery curator who had staged a 'Forbidden Art' exhibition of controversial images which had been banned by Russian museums. Billing themselves as a 'band' called Cock in the Ass, they let rip with a punky thrash called *All Cops Are Bastards*. "The after-party is in the district police station!" Verzilov announced to the courtroom before they began.

In another hint of things to come, the curator was ultimately convicted of inciting religious and ethnic hatred. Voina was then ruptured by a poisonous internal split, with some of its leaders accusing Verzilov and Tolokonnikova of betrayal, plagiarism and fraud, describing them as obsessed with self-promotion and publicity. The couple were expelled from the group. But Verzilov insisted that the allegations were all lies; according to his version of events, members of what he called the 'Moscow wing' of Voina decided to go their own way, and then went on to launch an even more provocative art project - this time with added guitars.

Pussy Riot were never really a 'band' at all, at least not in the conventional rock'n'roll sense. But without the musical element, they would never have attracted the same kind of notoriety or global acclaim, with the powerful media voices that fame allows. Their initial performances established the tone for what was to follow. Before the Russian parliamentary elections in December 2011, they let rip from atop a scaffolding in a metro station and from the roofs of trolleybuses with a song called *Release the*

Cobblestones, a plea to voters to rally in protest instead of going to the polling stations: "Your ballots will be used as toilet paper by the presidential administration," the lyrics warned. They then staged a brief gig outside a detention centre where activists arrested for taking part in demonstrations about the elections were being held. The song - *Death to Prison, Freedom to Protests* - drew rapturous applause from the detainees locked in their cells.

Then, in January 2012, came the performance that brought them international acclaim. The arena they chose was charged with symbolic power: Red Square, Russia's best-known address. Outside the Kremlin walls, with the grand towers swathed in frost and with snow falling on the crazy-coloured domes of St. Basil's Cathedral behind them, eight women in vividly-shaded balaclavas, mini-dresses and heavy winter boots clambered up onto a platform in the middle of the square, waving a purple feminist flag and setting off a smoke bomb as they thrashed their way through a song whose title is sometimes translated as *Putin Got Scared,* but is more correctly if less politely rendered as *Putin Pissed Himself.*

Its lyrics were a compendium of their obsessions: Orthodox Church phallocracy and a savage political regime that "censors dreams" and "eats brains". This was a rabid invocation, summoning the masses to come out onto the streets and occupy Red Square: "Revolt in Russia - the charisma of protest! Revolt in Russia, Putin pissed himself! Revolt in Russia - we exist! Revolt in Russia - riot, riot!"

The platform they chose in Red Square - a stone podium known as Lobnoye Mesto - was symbolic because it had been the scene of an even more courageous protest by dissidents against the Soviet invasion of Czechoslovakia in 1968. For a few brief minutes, they managed to hold up banners demanding freedom before they were arrested and sentenced to long years in prison colonies and psychiatric clinics.

Pussy Riot had a much easier time of it. They weren't very

well-known in January 2012, so the advantage of surprise meant that they were even able to charge through their song twice before the police arrived and arrested them for minor public order offences.

Putin Pissed Himself was inspired by the first major illegal opposition protest in Moscow a month earlier, which had ended in clashes with riot police. The women were thrilled by this public showdown; their revolutionary fantasies, it seemed, were becoming real. "We saw how troops were moving around Moscow, there were helicopters in the sky, the military was put on alert. The regime just wet its pants on that day," one of them explained later.[2]

The parliamentary elections inevitably gave victory to Putin's party, but they sparked yet more protests that drew tens of thousands more Muscovites onto the wintry streets as the presidential vote approached. It was a remarkable moment, Samutsevich recalled: "The situation got of control because authorities did not count on it happening; something happened that they were not expecting. That is why that time was somehow special."

At the start of 2012, the women's identities were still unknown. My colleague in Moscow at the time, Anna Malpas, who covered Pussy Riot for the French news agency AFP, interviewed two of them just before the Red Square gig. The vibe was distinctly bohemian, Malpas remembered: "They met me in the metro and they had scarves covering part of their faces. They took me to this apartment block cellar where some kind of photographer was living and we had tea, and they put on their balaclavas to talk to me. They didn't give their real names, but as it turned out, it was Samutsevich and Tolokonnikova," she recalled.

"I thought they were very sweet, they almost reminded me of the kind of girls I went to school with - they were kind of rebellious but also very well-educated, talking about Judith Butler and things like that. When people say they're stupid, it really annoys me." Indeed, the women often seemed more comfortable talking to journalists about feminist authors like Butler, Simone de Beauvoir and Andrea Dworkin or radical art groups like the Guerrilla Girls than discussing music.

One of their major advantages, Tolokonnikova told Malpas, was that they were never likely to be harshly prosecuted because Russia's institutional prejudices ensured that a court would never give a woman a long prison sentence for demonstrating. "It is sexism, but of course it does work to our advantage," she said.[3]

But just a month after they established their notoriety in Red Square came the event that ultimately led to their jailing: their performance at Moscow's Cathedral of Christ the Saviour on February 21, 2012. It may have only lasted for less than a minute and was only witnessed first-hand by a tiny number of people, but it was to become the most politically explosive rock'n'roll gig in years.

Alyokhina, Samutsevich and Tolokonnikova, along with a few other women who were never identified or detained, entered the cathedral that day wearing their winter coats and scarves. They stripped down to reveal lurid purple, yellow, orange and blue balaclavas and garishly-coloured dresses and tights, then climbed the steps to the altar and shrilled out what they called their *Punk Prayer*, bowing down and crossing themselves in mock obeisance before kicking their legs up like a deranged chorus line and punching the air as they raged about a money-grubbing priesthood that "praises rotten dictators" and whose "chief saint is the head of the KGB".

"Holy shit! Holy shit!" screamed the women at the altar over and over again, while the other band members in the aisles thrashed away at guitars as the song hurtled to its climax: "Virgin Mary, mother of God, drive Putin away!" It was a hot flash of righteous anger, delivered at a time of high optimism for the new Russian opposition, in what would turn out to be the last days of its innocent hopefulness.

By the end of that minute at the altar, their lives had changed forever, even though they didn't realise it at first. "God will punish you, mark my words!" one of the worshippers shouted as they were hustled out by security guards. And so began a process that would yet again expose the black-hearted intolerance at the core of the Putin regime and shine a harsh interrogating light on the way that the country dealt with its twenty-first-century dissidents.

Ironically, days before the cathedral 'gig', they had given an interview in which they insisted that they had no fear of arrest. "With tens of thousands of people routinely taking to the streets, the state will think twice before trying to fabricate a criminal case and putting us away," one of them insisted.[4]

The state, of course, did not think twice.

"A column of rebels heads towards the Kremlin..."
Pussy Riot, *Putin Pissed Himself*

Moscow, one year after the Pussy Riot arrests: a young woman saunters casually through the exit doors of Kuztnetsky Most metro station in the city centre, unnoticed by the pavement smokers, street hawkers and beat cops trolling around the forecourt. Across the road, the reedy voice of Madonna comes keening out of a kebab shop, singing about something special being destroyed.

By this time, Yekaterina Samutsevich was no longer the anonymous activist who had once hid her identity behind a pseudonym and her face behind a balaclava. The Pussy Riot trial, which saw Samutsevich and her two bandmates Alyokhina and Tolokonnikova convicted of 'hooliganism motivated by religious hatred', had removed her protective disguise forever.

"Of course it's cool when you're hiding, no one knows who you are and you can say whatever you think, of course this image had its magic," Samutsevich told me after we had made our way to a nearby café. Not that she was exactly trying to fade into the background; on this warm spring afternoon, she was wearing a pink hoodie with a CND logo and bright orange jeans, and happily consented to having her photograph taken with a shaven-headed admirer who approached her in the middle of our conversation. She was still one of the best-known punk rockers in the city even if she hadn't taken to a stage for over 12 months.

The magic of Pussy Riot's immaculate pop-art costumes, as Samutsevich suggested, was that they were liberating cloaks of anonymity that transformed ordinary young women into feminist superheroes. As soon as they put on the balaclavas, they turned into avenging angels, electric flashes of neon colour, surreal punk-rock apparitions screaming out their message with the fierce abandon of the untouchable.

Without her balaclava however, Samutsevich looked like many other young Moscow liberals, talking shyly but intensely about art, feminism and the politics of culture while repeatedly tugging on her asymmetrical forelock as if she could pull it down and use it as some kind of defensive visor. There was no arrogance, no punkish aggression, just quietly defiant sincerity. By this time, Alyokhina and Tolokonnikova had been sent to remote prison colonies to serve two-year jail terms, but Samutsevich's prison sentence had been suspended on appeal and she had been freed on probation, on the grounds that she was grabbed by a security guard before she could strap her guitar around her neck and start playing during the cathedral gig.

She still seemed astonished about the savage reaction to that brief performance a year earlier. "It was surprising, even when there was some talk that they could launch criminal proceedings... we simply couldn't believe it until it happened," she said. They had prepared as they had done for previous actions, she continued, only worrying about whether all the technical equipment would work and whether the logistics had been sorted properly and whether they would be stopped before they got to their 'stage'. "Doing this is a dangerous thing, because everything is unpredictable, anything might happen and of course we chose a time when there were fewer people in the cathedral and there was no service, and everything was supposed to be more or less quiet," she explained.

The idea of jail time was never even considered - after all, hadn't they got away with no more than petty fines after their previous guerrilla gigs on top of trolleybuses, outside the detention centre and in Red Square? "Every time when we perform, every time we understand that we might violate something - you don't need to be a lawyer to understand that you are violating something. Here we were not violating anything, so we couldn't have predicted this," she said.

"We could have expected that there would be a discussion online and that there would be a lot of cruel comments - and there were actually - but we obviously did not expect a criminal case and all this media campaign across the entire country and around the world."

The group's methodology, grounded in contemporary art practice, was to stage a performance to a pre-recorded sound-track with the music produced by an anonymous female collaborator and the vocals screamed into microphones by the Pussy Riot women themselves. They would then videotape the event and edit and release it as an online multimedia package afterwards. As at previous actions, a small-scale clandestine operation had been mounted to bring journalists to the cathedral in February 2012 without actually telling them in advance where it would be, explained Tolokonnikova's husband and Pussy Riot's occasional spokesman, the fast-talking art activist Pyotr Verzilov, when I met him the following day outside another metro station.

Clad in skinny jeans and sporting a wispy hipster beard, Verzilov, who met Tolokonnikova while they were both studying philosophy at Moscow State University, glanced around briefly, checking for surveillance before we headed down underground into the metro. "From time to time you see people following you, cars following you, your phone is tapped. It's the same for anyone who does any kind of serious political activity in Russia," he explained.

Verzilov played an important role in the Pussy Riot campaign, dealing with logistics for the performances and handling interview requests. As we rattled through the subterranean tunnels towards the city centre, he told me how the gigs were usually organised. "The performances were very simple - guitars, banners, girls, balaclavas," he explained, shouting to make himself heard over the clamour of the speeding train. "We didn't just invite any outsider or spectator. We worked within a close group of friends, some of whom are members of the media."

Some of these 'friends' however were not immediately convinced by the cathedral gig, said Anna Malpas: "The action was so short that my only thought was, 'Well, that was a complete failure to be honest,'" she recalled. "I couldn't really hear what they were singing, just the chorus - 'Holy shit...'"

The international news agencies that feed the global media didn't even file much copy about the event. "It didn't get much coverage that day because the women didn't get detained, and from a journalist's point of view, if you write a story about a protest, it's normally when there are some arrests," Malpas explained.

"At the time, it wasn't obvious what a big story it would be. But when I went out of the church, there were three women standing there and they were quite upset. I said to them, 'What did you think of the action?', and they got really angry, and one of them was crying."

The Pussy Riot women initially managed to get away after the cathedral gig and went into hiding for several days before they were eventually detained, but Malpas, like some of the other journalists who were there, was 'invited' to the police station afterwards and questioned rather desultorily what she knew about the group. It didn't seem that the police were taking it all that seriously, at least at first, she recalled. The only sign, she said, that the situation could have more significance than first appeared was the presence of a shadowy figure she had seen at some of the opposition protests in Moscow: "He wasn't a police officer but he was very chummy with the police. I've asked him who he is before and he wouldn't tell me; that's all I know about him..."

"I wanna riot, a riot of my own!"
The Clash, *White Riot*

Pussy Riot were arrested for the cathedral performance the day before Putin was re-elected as president in March 2012 - after they had uploaded the video to the internet and the media reports started to flow. Like hundreds of thousands of others, I also saw it first online and was thrilled by its raw power.

The footage transported me back to my pre-teen bedroom in Nottingham, where I first heard *White Riot* by The Clash tearing out of a little transistor radio back in 1977; so hard and sharp, it seemed, that it would blow the tiny speakers right out of their plastic casing. Punk's year-zero stance - a symbolic obliteration of the past which left only the future to look towards - was the catalyst that led me, like many others, forwards to the new discoveries of the post-punk era, not only musical but political too: from Rock Against Racism gigs and demonstrations against the right-wing National Front, to campaigns for social justice and cultural liberation...

White Riot was written after Joe Strummer and Paul Simonon witnessed black youths clashing with police at London's Notting Hill Carnival in the summer of 1976, amid the poison clouds of racism and police harassment of Afro-Caribbeans that hung over everyday British life throughout the seventies. The song was a call to arms, "on high alert from the opening police siren to the final burglar alarm", as journalist Dorian Lynskey wrote in his history of protest music, *33 Revolutions Per Minute*, with the millennial dread of Strummer's beloved roots reggae channelled into the militant urgency of punk.[5] The Clash, at least in their early years, approached their work as if they were shooting an agit-prop documentary, with Strummer's lyrics casting a searching eye over his own confusions and dilemmas as much as the injustices that he observed around him.

And in 2012 - again - it was time for punk, in Moscow anyway: a blast of pure righteous venom, a howl of protest racing along on a surge of carefree noise, a ranter's street-corner manifesto screamed out fast and loud before the cops come to take you away; the only rational response to the madness of the times.

After Voina's art pranks attracted international interest, forming a punk band was the next logical step, recalled Samutsevich: punk might have been played out as a radical force in the West, but in Russia, it still seemed full of anarchic possibilities. And with Moscow erupting in noisy protest, any artistic intervention had to be *fierce*. "You need to express yourself honestly, openly and emotionally intensely," she explained. "In public places, if you just appear and talk quietly and sing quietly, this simply won't be understood. In this situation you need to be fully honest, fully emotional. Music has a certain magic, an honesty, because all the other forms of getting a message across which are currently used at protests, for example giving a speech from the stage, do not have this kind of honesty that punk rock has."

Or as Tolokonnikova put it, rather more eloquently, during their trial: "We were searching for real sincerity and simplicity, and we found these qualities in the holy foolishness of punk."

Samutsevich said that a crucial influence was the US band Bikini Kill, part of the Riot Grrrl feminist punk movement which recharged the genre with fresh enmity against the American religious right in the early nineties. Other members of Pussy Riot have also mentioned inspirations as diverse as New York art-rockers Sonic Youth and various lesser-known British punk shouters like the Angelic Upstarts and "working-class boot-boy" rockers the Cockney Rejects. They even sampled the opening guitar riff from the Cockney Rejects' *I'm Not a Fool* for one of their first songs, *Kill the Sexist*, and the Angelic Upstarts' *Police Oppression* for another, *Release the Cobblestones*.

Tolokonnikova would later tell me that she believed that UK punk's expositions of police brutality and miscarriages of justice in the seventies had actually helped to make Britain a better place by speaking truth to power. "I'm 100 per cent sure that this punk rock tradition played a very important role in developing civil society in Great Britain and it helped the country to get a non-corrupted and fairer police system," she insisted.

She cited Sham 69, a laddish bunch who rose up with the second wave of punk and were briefly known for impassioned rabble-rousers like *If the Kids are United*. Tolokonnikova best remembers Sham's song *George Davis is Innocent*, which highlighted the wrongful jailing of a minicab driver for armed robbery. "This kind of campaign to defend human rights and to defend the presumption of innocence inspired me a lot," she explained. "Here in Russia, the presumption of innocence doesn't exist."

Not every critic was convinced of Pussy Riot's musical talents. A writer for the Associated Press news agency dismissed their sound as "simple riffs and scream-like singing"; perhaps he had never listened to much hardcore punk before.[6] The astute Michael Idov, editor of Russian *GQ*, noted however that judging Pussy Riot on artistic merit "would be like chiding the Yippies because Pigasus the Immortal, the pig they ran for president in 1968, was not a viable candidate".[7] The first time they even attempted anything other than all-out thrash was on a track released in 2013 called *Like in a Red Prison*, which began with a loping post-punk rattle of drums and bass before accelerating into the usual screechy racket. "We are not aimed at the music industry or selling CDs or anything like that," explained Samutsevich - a wise decision, because consumers may have proved hard to come by: this was music for riots and rebellions, not 'greatest hits' compilations.

What Pussy Riot were not, they insisted, was a contemporary version of the Sex Pistols. They dismissed Johnny Rotten and his band as fakes and poseurs on the grounds that their record label boss, Virgin mogul Richard Branson, paid to hire a boat to stage their notorious cruise-gig on the River Thames during Queen Elizabeth's silver jubilee in 1977; a promotional stunt that ended in violence.

"It's difficult to find an element of protest when you perform on a boat that you have paid for; on the contrary, it's a type of commercial performance," one Pussy Riot member said. The women repeatedly vowed never to play a legal concert. "We didn't rent and are not going to rent anything; we come and take over platforms that don't belong to us and use them for free."[8]

At the time though, in the late seventies, the Pistols' boat trip wasn't as tame as Pussy Riot may have believed from the distance of years passed. The summer of 1977 was a tense and uncertain time for anyone involved in punk, which was being denounced by right-wing newspapers and politicians as a serious moral threat to Britain's youth. At the time of the boat trip, the Pistols were banned from every venue in the country, blacklisted by radio stations and under constant threat of physical assault from moral vigilantes (Rotten was attacked several times). They had just released *God Save the Queen*, a full-frontal attack on the monarch at a time when an obedient nation was supposed to be celebrating 25 happy years as her loyal 'subjects'.

Journalist Jon Savage was on board the boat that day on the Thames, and he remembers the mood as claustrophobic, cloaked in paranoia. But when it sailed past the Houses of Parliament and the Pistols launched into *Anarchy in the UK*, the heavy mood eased, Savage wrote: "It's like they've been uncaged - the frustration in not being able to play bursts into total energy and attack." Other journalists on board said that when the boat finally docked, policemen who had been on duty all day at the Jubilee celebrations stormed on, frustrated and raging for a fight. Pistols manager Malcolm McLaren baited them, calling them "fascist bastards", and in the scuffle that followed, he took a beating and 11 people were detained, charged with obstructing the police, threatening behaviour and assault. Afterwards, Savage sensed a dread mood rising again. Now, he mused, "if you look anything like a Sex Pistol, or a 'punk rocker', you're likely to get pulled in [by the police]... Things have gotten more serious."[9]

But despite Rotten's lyrics touting anarchy and damning the monarchy, this was not a band with a serious political agenda. Nor was Britain, even in the greyest days of the seventies, much like Russia 35 years later. Indeed, the British authorities put much more effort into legislation to crush the rave scene than they ever did into targeting punks.

Politically, Pussy Riot were simply more *hardcore*. They became notorious for hurling obscenities at one of the world's toughest leaders, while the Pistols initially hit the headlines for swearing at a television presenter during a live broadcast. The balaclava-clad women were perhaps more like an idea reputedly proposed in the early seventies by Christopher Gray, one of the members of King Mob, a British counterpart of the Situationists, who is said to have suggested creating an utterly revolting and cacophonous pop group. Or as Dorian Lynskey has suggested, maybe they also resembled Crass, the early-eighties anarchist punk collective who lived in a commune in rural Essex and specialised in rabid sloganeering set to martial drumbeats. With their use of pseudonyms, all-black uniforms, John Heartfield-influenced political collage artwork and their immaculate graphic logo (part Union Jack, part swastika, part Celtic symbol and part CND logo, but at the same time none of these), Crass essentially used punk as a medium for political activism. Their incendiary musical retort to the 1982 Falklands War - a track that asked prime minister Margaret Thatcher the question: "how does it feel to be the mother of one thousand dead?" - sparked media outrage in the atmosphere of nationalist triumphalism that surrounded Britain's military victory over Argentina.

But whatever the Sex Pistols or even Crass might have said in their lyrics or interviews or on stage, neither of them was prosecuted for it, and by the twenty-first century, it was hard to imagine any Western pop musician being jailed for public dissent; 'rebel' rockers and 'outlaw' rappers were more likely to get lucrative sponsorship deals than jail terms. The old-school South Bronx rapper KRS-One, for instance, whose recorded musings on police brutality were no less inflammatory than those of Pussy Riot, accepted a commissioned to rework Gil Scott-Heron's agit-prop classic *The Revolution Will Not Be Televised* as an advertisement for Nike basketball shoes ("the revolution is about basketball, and basketball is the truth"). The former ghetto testifier promised critics that he was not 'selling out', but then recorded a Christmas song for another Nike television advert in which he appeared as Santa with a rapping reindeer...

Even those who stayed true to their original causes were never in serious danger from the authorities. American Riot Grrrl singer Kathleen Hanna, of Bikini Kill and Le Tigre, made the point directly: "When my band Le Tigre wore STOP BUSH dresses and spoke out against racism, homophobia and sexism, we feared not getting a fair shake in both the music industry and the underground scene, but never jail," Hanna wrote during the Pussy Riot trial. "Bikini Kill suffered jeers, violence and hate campaigns against us, but we never even thought about going to prison for our beliefs."[10]

"I want a man like Putin, full of strength."
Russian pop-propaganda song, 2002

For a moment, it seemed, the strongman was weeping. Scaled up surreally huge on a massive video screen in a square not far from the Kremlin, the camera lingered on his face, red-raw in the biting wind, as a tear trickled slowly from the corner of one eye. Vladimir Putin was crying - or at least that's how it looked to me for a few moments until I calculated the possibilities of this man crying real tears.

He was emotional nonetheless, at this rally two days after his re-election as president in March 2012, announcing his victory to a crowd of tens of thousands of admirers who had been bussed in and marshalled into pre-ordained ranks facing the video wall. Russian techno-pop blared out over the surrounding streets - "Vsyo budyet khorosho!" ("Everything will be good!"), the lyrics of one of the songs insisted - as officials handed out banners with pre-printed slogans like "Russia-Stability-Putin" for the crowd to hold aloft in celebration. But no one was dancing; few were even smiling. When I tried to ask some of these 'spontaneous well-wishers' what had brought them into the city on this bitter evening, whether they were excited that their hero was officially back in the Kremlin's top spot - as if he hadn't been in control all the way through his marionette Medvedev's 'presidency' - none of them wanted to talk; they all referred me to their appointed group leader, who refused to tell me anything more than what was printed on the placard he was holding: "We are for Putin. We are for stability."

This was a different Putin from the one I had first seen up close a couple of years earlier, the happy warrior roaring through the Crimean city of Sevastopol, swathed in black with his eyes masked by dark shades, piloting a Harley Davidson three-wheeler at the head of a thousand-strong convoy of Russian bikers. That was another trip altogether, but this one was no fun

- no fun at all. "I promised that we would win and we have won!" Putin shouted to the regimented, flag-waving crowd. "Glory to Russia!"

Coincidentally, Russian state television had shown the classic Soviet-era film *Moscow Doesn't Believe in Tears* on polling day, so it was no surprise that when 20,000 demonstrators gathered in Pushkin Square for a post-election rally the day after Putin inadvertently switched on his waterworks, many of them carried home-made placards that satirised his apparent emotional lapse.

"When Putin was announced as the future president, he cried. But with this placard I am holding, I wanted to say that we don't believe in his tears or his victory," I was told by one of them, a student called Polina Petrunya.

As I squeezed my way through the crowd, the sheer chaotic randomness of the Russian protest movement quickly became clear: a motley crew of liberals, communists, anarchists, even people waving the skull-and-crossbones flag of the pro-filesharing Pirate Party. Unlike the meticulously-choreographed Putin rally the day before, most of the oppositionists' placards were hand-made and bore slogans that they had thought up themselves. "Thieves must be in jail!" some of them shouted - a deliberate echo of the Russian leader's well-known phrase about imprisoned anti-Kremlin oligarch Mikhail Khodorkovsky.

Some protesters also seemed to be in shock at the scale of Putin's overwhelming victory, although they surely must have expected it. "This isn't fair! They have cheated Russia!" I was told by Alina Koseva, a young woman who had travelled over 900 miles from Orenburg to join the demonstration. "I want a revolution," declared her friend, Aleksey Garo.

As the rally ended and most of the protesters dispersed into the freezing night, policemen at the nearest metro station watched with disbelief as the platform echoed to the previously unthinkable sound of hundreds of passengers chanting: "Putin - thief! Putin - thief!"

But the police quickly exacted bloody retribution: when a few radicals refused to go home after the demonstration's officially-sanctioned time was up, riot squads moved in to crack heads and shove bodies into meat wagons. Inevitably, convictions for insurrectionary affray followed. What else could they have expected? In the former Soviet Union, repressive regimes rarely show much mercy to their dissident children, as Pussy Riot were to find out.

Before Putin was re-elected, there was a brief period of wild optimism that the educated middle class would stand up and demand its rights, and maybe even get them. But I had seen such dreams shattered before, in countries that the newspapers rarely write about unless something seriously horrific has happened - in the twilight states of Azerbaijan and Belarus, the kind of places where journalists and bloggers are jailed for speaking the truth while the corrupt live free and thrive. In both places, in 2005 and 2006, the authorities allowed demonstrators to take to the streets for a few days after rigged elections, then brutally clubbed them down and sent them off to prison.

"Out of the bars and into the streets!"
San Francisco gay rights demonstrators' chant, 1977

Under the harsh Moscow sun, the darkness at three o'clock. Near Red Square, there were groups of daytrippers queuing for the Kremlin tour, lovers waiting expectantly for their loves, crocodile lines of children on school jaunts... but under the picture-postcard towers, lines of policemen with batons, and circling around them, gangs of thugs and neo-Nazis; some hooded and masked, or swollen up with steroids, booze and perverted anger, some with T-shirts bearing images of fists, crosses, swords and wolves, and slogans like 'Glory to Russia' and 'God is With Us'.

A few were dressed up in full combat camouflage, or holding

huge crucifixes aloft. One group of believers was singing religious laments, mournfully, with hate in their souls, while burly men in black prowled around murmuring into handsets. In the nearby streets, trucks disgorged thousands of riot police and at the gates of Red Square, ambulances stood waiting to pick up the casualties, for today it was Moscow Pride, and there would be blood…

"Beat the pederasts!" a chant went up. "Down with Sodom!" One man furiously ripped up a picture of Elton John. Then suddenly, somewhere in the crowd, I saw a rainbow Gay Pride flag raised, and then just as quickly snatched down, as police, fascists and religious fanatics charged forward, fists and batons raised, and the few courageous activists who had tried to show their colours were set upon, seized and dragged away. Hundreds more riot police charged after them to clear the area, shoving us all backwards. It all happened within a few chaotic minutes, and Moscow Pride 2011 was over before it ever really started.

Even before the Pussy Riot arrests - and the many detentions and prosecutions that would follow them after Putin returned to the presidency - the annual attempts to stage a Gay Pride rally in Moscow had showed how political challenges to state-sponsored morality would be dealt with. "This is Russia, my dear," a bystander remarked to one of the journalists who was watching the police charge. "What did you expect?"

Some of the Gay Pride protesters managed to regroup near the mayor's office not far away, but there were lines of riot police there too, already waiting, some of them trading jokes with the skinheads and the fascists. An elderly woman started to rant for the cameras, or anyone else who was willing to listen: "The pederasts and drug addicts are killing Russia," she shrieked. "They do it for money! They smoke grass! People, what are you doing?" she demanded. "The country is dying!"

As the sun kept beating down on this street without shadows, a lone activist, her hair dyed shrieking red and her peasant skirt flaring wildly, launched herself into the middle of the road in a desperate attempt to make the briefest of stands before she was grabbed by the cops. As they manhandled her body away, she turned her head and flashed the most radiant of smiles for the press photographers: a glorious moment of defiance in the face of impossible odds.

Soon the protesters had all been seized or had fled, and only the police and the thugs were left. A weasel-faced boy wearing desert fatigues hugged his girlfriend as they posed for the cameras, grinning broadly. Today, they felt victorious; they had the 'deviants' on the run. For them, today was not Gay Pride, it was Fascist Pride.

"There are so few people who are prepared to fight for their rights in Russia in general. It's always been like that in Russian history. People sit in their kitchens and complain but don't dare to do anything else," Moscow Pride's idiosyncratic organiser, Nikolai Alekseyev, the founder of the Gay Russia campaign group, had told me the day before as we walked through the city centre to the Pride headquarters.

Alexeyev was limping after an accident during a televised debate the previous day; he had bashed his leg while storming off the set in anger after audience members and the show's host described homosexuals as extremists and perverts. Still, he looked immaculate in a sharply-cut grey suit, pink shirt and striped tie. Lounging around the apartment on sofas and in armchairs was his little crew of activists. They had come to Moscow from all over the country, from its deepest and most intolerant corners, from as far away as the conflict-ravaged Muslim republic of Dagestan in the Caucasus.

"Moscow and St. Petersburg is one story, the rest of the country is another story," Alekseyev said after we sat down to talk. "All the rest of the country, there is nothing, no one is able to express themselves, no one is able to do what they want. It's like two different worlds."

Alekseyev said that he had become an activist after he was prevented from writing his thesis on sexual minority rights while studying at Moscow State University: "After that I understood that I could not change the situation by writing - I had to do something more public and political," he explained.

"It obviously makes me a target, for sure. Sometimes I am scared. I'm a target and you never know when an idiot might attack when you're walking in the streets," he continued, presciently as it turned out - a couple of years later he was assaulted while getting on a train by masked men who shouted homophobic insults, hit him and told him to get out of Russia.

"If something happens, what can I do about it?" he told me (and indeed, his attackers were never arrested). "I'm doing what I think is right, what is good for human rights and democracy in this country. If everyone only thinks about his own security, we will go backwards to a totalitarian state and we will never change anything in this country."

A journalist from the liberal newspaper *Novaya Gazeta*, Yelena Kostyuchenko, wrote something similar in an impassioned, confessional blog post just before the 2011 Moscow Pride: "I believe our country deserves something better... Russia will change. It is already changing. And it this is going to happen, you bastards, even if you smash my head in with a baseball bat today," she wrote. By the end of the day, Kostyuchenko was in hospital, as she had predicted, being treated for head injuries after being assaulted by fascists.

"Like Harvey Milk said, you have to come out," Alekseyev continued. "No one has come out here who could be an example and break the taboo. I am openly saying on TV that I am gay. But no one else is saying this, that's the problem."

Alekseyev had become the public face of gay rights in Russia because of his courageous willingness to speak the unspeakable on live television. But he was a controversial, tempestuous, sometimes contradictory character, often getting involved in furious public rows on social networks, accusing others of ingratitude, betrayal and malicious lies, pledging patriotic support for Putin's annexation of Crimea and ranting against hypocritical Americans, the perfidious West and what he called "the Jewish mafia". He denied being anti-Semitic, recalling with pride how his grandfather died fighting the Nazis in World War Two, but not everyone was convinced.

Some other Russian campaigners meanwhile accused him of being a publicity-seeking scandal-monger whose attempts to hold Pride rallies undermined the cause by encouraging a homophobic crackdown. But despite everything, as Alekseyev pointed out himself, if lesbians and gays had not taken to the streets, from the Stonewall Riots in 1969 onwards, few rights would have been won. There was never any likelihood of unforced concessions from politicians like former Moscow mayor Yuri Luzhkov, who described Gay Pride as "the work of Satan", or Putin, who said that homosexuality was fuelling Russia's demographic meltdown, or from the Russian Orthodox Church, which considered it not only a sickness but a mortal threat to traditional values.

"It's a cycle: if you come out you will be attacked by society, by the regime, by the political system. If you don't, you are not able to change this society and its attitudes," Alekseyev said. As we talked, he wound himself up into another rage about the injustice all around him, but then calmed slightly and slipped into a more reflective mood: "I've been trying to find hope for years but I haven't found it yet," he said quietly. "If we have the same situation now as it was in 2006 when Moscow Pride started, I think that hope in this country is dying out."

The following year, the Moscow authorities banned Gay Pride marches for a century, and in 2013, parliament introduced a law criminalising 'homosexual propaganda'. Of course Russia was not as brutal as Uganda, where homosexuality was punishable by life imprisonment, or Iran, where the ultimate penalty was death. But it was hard not to agree with Alekseyev that hope was in short supply.

After Moscow Pride was crushed that afternoon in 2011, I went to sit in a nearby café to get my thoughts down on paper. When I read back through my notes later, I was struck by this line: "Are civil rights impossible in a country where Nazis roam free and peaceful protesters are hunted down and beaten?" Indeed, gays and liberals both seemed to have been cast in the role of enemies of the Russian state; convenient hate figures that the authorities could use to bolster their conservative credentials and provide justification for further assaults on civil liberties.

I later learned that almost 20 protesters were detained that day, among them the pre-Pussy Riot Tolokonnikova and Samutsevich. Tolokonnikova subsequently wrote in an article that the gay-rights campaigners were treated as if they were involved in an act of "cognitive terrorism". Perhaps hinting at what she would help to instigate over the coming months, she concluded her report by warning: "A huge gender shock is coming."[11]

"Oh, my thieving, criminal life - my proud, merry life!"
Russian 'chanson' ballad

As I continued scribbling my impressions down in my notebook, orchestral strings shivered through the air and an ecstatic synthesizer melody spiralled upwards from the café speakers: it was the Salsoul remake of *Ain't No Mountain High Enough* by Inner Life, a gay anthem from the glory days of New York disco. It seemed peculiar to hear such a joyous reminder of the disco high-life here, just a couple of streets from where fascists had been trying to kick homosexuals to a pulp half an hour earlier. But then again, that night, people would queue up as usual at Moscow's gay clubs to dance and drug the night away, ignored if not accepted. While they swirled across the dancefloors, those who had stood up for their rights would be salving their cuts and bruises.

There may have been gay clubs in metropolitan Russia and singers acting 'gay' on national television, but if you wanted to understand the more socially-acceptable side of mainstream pop morality in the country at the start of the millennium, you needed to watch videos by silicone-enhanced dolly-bird troupes like the now-defunct VIA Gra, or listen to the menacing growlers of *blatnaya pesnya* - 'criminal songs' - the outright opposite of Pussy Riot's feminist agit-punk.

Part of the Russian genre known as 'chanson', *blatnaya pesnya* developed out of ballads sung in the country's brutal gulags and post-Soviet prison colonies, often reflecting the outlaw values of the 'thieves in law' - mafiosi with their own criminal codes and hierarchies. For all its vodka-drenched sentimentality about jailhouse camaraderie, the loving brotherhood of thieves and the unwavering affection for one's mother, this was some of the least gay music in the world.

I first heard it back in 2004 in the Ukrainian city of Zaporizhia, where some musician friends were augmenting their unsteady career as an electro-pop band by working in a bootlegging studio. Hundreds of pirated cassettes were piled up around the room, waiting to be trucked out for sale, while the copying machines whirred constantly, purloining sound and transferring it to cheap tapes. Among the stacks of bootlegs were albums by Western stars like Eminem and Depeche Mode, but the ones that caught my eye had lurid covers decorated with photos of menacing thugs scowling at the camera, holding up fists decorated with tattoos and monstrous jewel-encrusted rings, crouched down on sodium-lit pavements, their lascivious eyes trained on the exposed vaginas of knickerless hookers in PVC miniskirts.

My friends, gentle souls as they were, frowned in disbelief when I asked to hear some of these tapes: this was not their music, but the sound of a perilous criminal underworld of which they wanted no part, and which maybe, in their role as hosts, they didn't even want me to know about. They were just copying the vile stuff, earning a living. But when they finally agreed to play some of the tapes, their unrefined power could not be denied.

I couldn't understand what they were singing about because I knew no Russian at that time, but the terrifying croons that emerged from these brutes' mouths were remarkable: boar-like grunts of fury, roars of obscene lust and melancholic laments tinged with the threat of violence, often delivered in the kind of ominous rasping groan that would shake a Westerner's timid heart if he heard it coming up behind him in a strange city late at night.

When I was in Moscow several months later, I mentioned to a couple of Russian music journalists that criminal *chanson* seemed to have quite a lot in common with American gangsta rap: the outlaw mentality, the jailhouse codes, the determination to 'get paid or die tryin'', the insistence on some unwritten code of 'respect' policed by the possibility of violent retribution. They were horrified: "But rap is *cool*, this Russian criminal music is *terrible*," one 'intellectual' yelped in abject revulsion that these mobster litanies could be compared to the 'urban poetry' of Tupac Shakur or Biggie Smalls.

Veteran Russian rock critic Art Troitsky says he has more time for criminal *chanson* than a lot of other writers, but even he believes the comparison with hip hop is misplaced: while American rappers want to get out of the ghetto, the *chansonniers* are content to accept their roles in the corrupt reality of contemporary Russia, where theft can be legal as long as it's backed by the state, he said.

"I think that *Russkiy chanson* is an interesting phenomenon, unlike most intelligent Russian people who say this is an absolute nightmare, and it's *genuinely* Russian, this is for sure," Troitsky told me. "But at the same time there's absolutely no attitude of protest or change - it's very conformist. It's conformist in this kind of underdog, low-life way, but it's still conformist."

Chanson star Mikhail Krug, a sentimental chronicler of underworld mores, embodied many of the values implicit in *blatnaya pesnya*. Although he never actually served time in jail himself, his lyrical heroes were thieves and gangsters. The portly, moustachioed bard also despised gays and feminists and was a member of a political party led by the hardline nationalist MP Vladimir Zhirinovsky. One of his videos showed him tenderly serenading two intricately-tattooed, half-naked convicts in their cell, while perhaps his most famous song, *Vladimirsky Tsentral*, was reportedly written in honour of two gangland bosses in his hometown of Tver.

Another of Krug's lyrics effectively predicted his own violent demise: "Come to my house, my doors are open; I'll sing you a song of fate and parting, of joyous life and ridiculous death," he once crooned. When criminals did actually come to his house in Tver at around midnight in June 2002, hoping perhaps to find expensive trinkets like the diamond ring that he was reportedly given by one Russian mafia don, they did indeed find his doors open. First they attacked his mother-in-law, and then opened fire on Krug and his wife.

The bard died of gunshot wounds in hospital the next day and his lavish funeral saw a huge gathering of tearful fans and glowering crime lords mourning over his open coffin, along with political potentates like Zhirinovsky and Tver's city governor. But a plan to erect a commemorative statue in his hometown ran into opposition, with representatives of the local cultural elite complaining that the idolisation of criminality was an indication of a deep sickness within Russian society.

The monument, depicting a smiling Krug sitting on a park bench with his guitar, was eventually built. But not long after-wards, a group of robbers, who were perhaps lacking in the tear-stained honour-amongst-thieves romanticism that filled some of

Krug's songs, made off with his instrument.

In a country where people like Krug are folk heroes with political connections, however, it would not have been difficult to predict that a band like Pussy Riot would be given a hard time.

"With every execution, the stench of rotten ash; with every long prison sentence, a wet dream."

Pussy Riot, *Putin Lights up the Fires*

Not long after Putin returned to the presidency, the Pussy Riot case went to court. The show trial that followed was a grand farce, a theatre of the absurd seemingly played for laughs but in fact deadly serious, accelerating with queasy inevitability towards its conclusion: convictions and jail sentences. As Pyotr Verzilov pointed out, the conviction rate in Russian court cases was close to 100 per cent, and once the state had made its stand so forcefully, it was never likely to back down: "It was basically no surprise that Putin would make these girls pay the price," he said.

The prosecution was meant to send out a message, insisted Samutsevich: "Whoever criticises Putin and his authority should expect very strict punishment; of course that is why it was done." The actual trial was nothing more than a theatrical sham - a "decoration", she said. "It's clear that the case was completely fabricated... there were these 'victims', very strange ones, clearly selected."

Some of the 'victims' who claimed to have been traumatised by the *Punk Prayer* - either by actually witnessing it at the cathedral or simply by watching the footage on the internet - did appear to be very peculiar indeed, a mixture of genuine if naïve believers and cynical zealots who wanted to see heretics burn at the stake.

One woman complained about the women's "vulgar" mini-dresses, their "devilish jerking" and foul-mouthed blaspheming which had caused her "huge moral damage". Asked by Tolokonnikova whether 'feminist' was a rude word, the witness replied: "In a church, yes." Another said that he was so disturbed by the cathedral performance that he cried afterwards, and insisted that although the women had apologised at the start of the trial if they had offended Orthodox Christians, they had not shown the necessary "repentance". He identified himself as part of a nationalist organisation that arranged "military-patriotic training" for young people. It also emerged that he had testified against an art curator over an exhibition of dissident works that was judged to have 'offended the faithful' - the same trial in 2009 at which Voina activists did their proto-Pussy Riot guerrilla-punk performance under the name Cock in the Ass.

A third witness, apparently called as an 'expert' because he had watched the video of the church show online and read an interview with the women, said that he could tell from what he had seen that they were all going to hell; a place which, he said, was "as real as the Moscow metro".[12]

The prosecutors attempted to focus on religion rather than politics, to show that the performance was anti-Christian rather than anti-Putin. But something unexpected happened as the case unfolded. The three women locked in the courtroom's bulletproof glass cage, who began the proceedings as the accused, stealthily managed to reverse the polarity and effectively put the Russian state on trial; this was their biggest stage yet, and they used it well. Indeed the proceedings could have resembled an absurd Situationist prank organised to give the authorities as much opportunity as possible to make themselves look like fools, if it wasn't for the fact that the defendants were going to jail whatever happened.

The three women's closing speeches at the trial were a righteous tour de force. Eloquent, dignified and deeply moving, they quoted Dostoyevsky and Solzhenitsyn, consciously placing themselves in the lineage of cultural figures targeted for prose-cution by the Moscow authorities. They didn't beg for mercy, wail for forgiveness or soften their stance in an attempt to gain the court's sympathy; instead they remained hardcore to the end.

"In a closing statement, the defendant is expected to repent, express regret for her deeds or enumerate attenuating circumstances. In my case, as in the case of my colleagues in the group, this is completely unnecessary," Samutsevich told the court.

"On the one hand, we expect a guilty verdict. Compared to the judicial machine, we are nobodies and we have lost," she continued. "On the other hand, we have won. The whole world now sees that the criminal case against us has been fabricated. The system cannot conceal the repressive nature of this trial. Once again, the world sees Russia differently than the way Putin tries to present it."

In her speech, Alyokhina alluded to the Soviet show trial of writer Joseph Brodsky in 1964, when his works were dismissed as "so-called" poems by the judge. "For me, this trial is a 'so-called' trial," Alyokhina said. "I am not afraid of you, I am not afraid of falsehood or poorly-disguised deception or of the verdict of this 'so-called' court. All that I can be deprived of is my 'so-called' freedom. This is the only kind that exists in Russia," she concluded, her voice crackling with emotion.

Tolokonnikova also invoked the terrors of Communist persecution: "Katya, Masha and I may be in prison, in a cage, but I do not consider us to be defeated," she said. "Just as the dissidents were not defeated - although they disappeared into mental institutions and prisons, they pronounced their verdict upon the regime."

She ended her speech with a quote from a Pussy Riot song: "Come on, taste freedom with us!"

The verdict was handed down on August 17, 2012. Outside the courtroom in Moscow, hundreds gathered to hear the three woman's fate, some of them chanting: "Free Pussy Riot!" and "Russia without Putin!" The BBC and CNN set up live feeds, broadcasting the seamy reality of Russian justice across the globe. Former world chess champion turned opposition activist Garry

Kasparov was dragged away by riot police just after giving an interview; he was just one of scores of people detained that day. An attempt to stage a guerrilla performance from a nearby rooftop was thwarted, but near the court, someone managed to blast out a new Pussy Riot track called *Putin Lights up the Fires*; its lyrics vowing: "You can't nail us up in a coffin!"

Inside the packed trial chamber, it was humid and sweaty but Tolokonnikova lit up the room with her insouciant bad-girl smirk, clenched-fist salute and T-shirt decorated with the revolutionary slogan "No Pasaran!" All three smiled ironically as judge Marina Syrova explained that they had "plotted to undermine the social order" and outrage "religious-minded citizens" while wearing "inappropriate clothing" during the *Punk Prayer*.

After taking several hours to read out the entire judgement, she announced the sentence: "Two years' deprivation of liberty in a penal colony."

The three young women in the glass cage started to laugh.

"They got what they asked for," Putin commented later, although it was clear that he had got what he asked for too. He got the convictions he wanted for the three young punks who had dared to badmouth him so publicly, while also showing his leniency by saying that "they should not be judged too harshly" and so ensuring that the sentences were just two years instead of the expected seven, although his magnanimity was perhaps not interpreted in a way he might have liked.

The conviction drew criticism from world leaders like US president Barack Obama and German chancellor Angela Merkel, and statements of outrage from pop stars like Madonna and Paul McCartney. But inside Russia, the reaction was very different. Around half the population saw the women as crude blasphemers, not as political activists trying to make a point about the unseemly relations between church and state, a public-opinion survey suggested. As Samutsevich put it: "They think that we are some kind of creepy criminals, hooligans who were having sex there at the altar."

But this was not surprising in a country in which the Orthodox Church, with the Russian leader's backing, was growing in power and influence. Novelist and opposition activist Boris Akunin traced the rise of the clerics back to the start of Putin's rule: "When I was little [in the Soviet era], there was no God. At all," he wrote. "In the Yeltsin years, God was already God, but still not a state one, not an official one... God completely returned to the position that he lost after 1917 in the first decade of the twenty-first century, under Vladimir Putin. And now, if you write 'THERE IS NO GOD!' in a blog, someone or other from among the faithful, most likely, will feel that his feelings are offended, launch a court case and win."[13]

The church, increasingly confident in its strength, made its position clear: feminism and punk were "demonic manifestations", insisted one senior Russian Orthodox cleric, while church leader Patriarch Kirill warned that "liberal society will lead to legal chaos and then the apocalypse". Before the presidential elections, Kirill had also advised that Putin's rule was "a miracle from God".[14]

This message was picked up by hardline extremist groups, Orthodox vigilantes who acted as the shock troops of the religious resurgence and regularly showed up to use their muscle whenever there was an 'outrage' in progress, whether it be the Pussy Riot trial or Moscow Pride. "There is a plan in place to destroy both church and state," warned one white-bearded fanatic wearing a T-shirt decorated with a bizarre mixture of religious and militaristic motifs, a member of an extremist group who called themselves the 'Carriers of the Cross' who were interviewed in the documentary film *Pussy Riot: A Punk Prayer*.[15]

Another of the gruesome crusaders interviewed in the documentary described Tolokonnikova as "a demon with a brain". His face was familiar: I had seen exactly the same man and his twisted pals ranting about 'pederasts' at Moscow Pride in

2011. "In the sixteenth century, they would've hanged them," one of his comrades told the film-makers as they drove to an anti-Pussy Riot 'prayer gathering' called by the Russian Patriarch. "They would've burned them," insisted another. A third man went on to suggest that the best Russian translation of Pussy Riot was "deranged vaginas". His T-shirt was covered with pictures of skulls, a crucifix and the slogan: "Orthodoxy or death."[16]

Samutsevich however told me she believed that these "religious fascists" were just another part of a show staged by the authorities. "They are called when it's needed, they are temporary actors," she said, dismissing the Orthodox extremists as walk-on cameos in a much graver drama: "This is sort of a role, a performance. It is all calculated to create a complete misunderstanding of the situation. Well, yes, and aggression, of course..."

But the hysteria about Pussy Riot, even if stoked by relentlessly negative coverage on state television, had a serious impact inside the country. While protests in support of the band were held across Europe - and Madonna sang *Like a Virgin* at her concert in Moscow with 'Pussy Riot' scrawled on her back - most Russian musicians either didn't want or didn't dare to speak out, apart from a few pop divas who ranted about the women's unladylike behaviour. Art Troitsky, who wrote the first history of rock music in the former Soviet Union, *Back in the USSR*, said this was hardly a surprise.

Troitsky's book relates how punk rock was seen as a hooligan's racket when it first filtered through to the Soviet Union, with newspapers publishing articles detailing the punks' "unsavoury appearance and disgraceful manners". As Troitsky recalled in the book: "The only thing anyone knew about punks was that they were 'fascists'."[17]

As long as they weren't openly critical, rock musicians were not usually subjected to the harshest forms of repression by the Communist authorities, explained Troitsky, who ran Russia's first rock'n'roll disco at a café at Moscow State University in 1972 and helped to stage a series of major festivals across the Soviet empire in the seventies and eighties. But bands accused of having a 'decadent mentality' or being 'ideologically harmful' found it hard to get gigs, he wrote.

More than two decades after the collapse of the Communist regime, Troitsky told me that most musicians in contemporary Russia were afraid to support the 'ideologically harmful' Pussy Riot in case they were deprived of their own livelihoods. Some rockers, like Soviet-era veterans Boris Grebenshikov and Yuri Shevchuk, did sign an open letter complaining that "the criminal case against Pussy Riot compromises the Russian judicial system and undermines confidence in the institutions of power in general".[18] But other stars, like the sexually-ambiguous indie heroine Zemfira, remained silent.

On the contemporary Russian music scene, Troitsky said, most major pop acts relied on playing at lucrative corporate promotional parties - *korporativi* - to earn a lot of their income, and could not be seen to be creating any kind of political controversy. Commercial self-censorship had replaced the dead hand of the Soviet bureaucrat.

"You have to have good relations with the state to be on that corporate party circuit because one of the goals of these parties is to please the big bosses, so if you are the head of a bank and you celebrate its anniversary, of course you invite people from the president's administration, the government, the city council and so on," Troitsky explained.

"So financially, pop stars and some of the top rock stars benefit enormously from their friendship with the state. There are plenty of Western stars who also participate in this vicious practice, especially these old stars from the seventies and eighties, nostalgia bands, they probably earn a lot of their money in Russia," he added with a grimace.

I met up with Troitsky at the Moscow studios of TV Dozhd, an internet broadcaster based at Red October, a former chocolate factory which had been turned into a creative hub for critical media outlets and hipster art projects; a nerve centre for the immaculately-dressed disaffected of the Russian capital. He had just done a live interview with wealthy socialite turned opposition journalist Kseniya Sobchak.

"In Russia, all TV stations except for one - this one - are fully controlled by the state," he noted. "So if pop artists want to have airtime on TV, they must be friendly with the state. Which doesn't necessarily mean they have to brown-nose - although a lot of Russian pop stars do exactly that - at least, and this is a must, they can't be critical."

Not all Russian pop stars were Putin's quislings, he pointed out, citing rapper Noize MC, whose song *Mercedes S666* raged against a Russian oil company executive who got away with killing two women in a car crash, and veteran rockers DDT, whose singer Yuri Shevchuk personally confronted Putin over free speech, corruption and police brutality at a televised meeting in 2010.

Troitsky said that he had tried to organise a Pussy Riot benefit concert in Moscow, but because of the atmosphere of trepidation that surrounded the women's prosecution, it proved to be impossible. "I faced a situation where no venue would dare hold it," he explained. "A couple of clubs said they would try to do it but immediately, because the phones were bugged, they started to receive calls saying, 'Do it at your peril.'"

Pussy Riot was a perfect punk name; a sweet elision of taboos, a provocative intermingling of sex and insurrection. Along with their immaculate pop-art image - fierce young women in primary-coloured balaclavas, the guerrilla concerts in risky locations - it certainly boosted the amount of coverage they received in the West, where their culture-rebel symbolism was greedily consumed. American writer Sarah Kendzior once suggested that the Western media wilfully misinterpreted them as "manic pixie dream dissidents", lusting over "sultry sex symbol" Tolokonnikova and never treating them as serious feminist cultural activists.[19]

Some Western-based Moscow-watchers also complained that Pussy Riot were just a trivial side-show, a tawdry distraction from the oppression of 'real' (in other words, traditionally political) opposition figures in Putin's Russia. "Human rights in Russia are a serious concern beyond the plight of some shock artists, yet that concern has been completely lost in the frenzy over some budding celebrity prisoners," suggested Joshua Foust in an opinion column for America's Public Broadcasting Service.[20]

Others were harsher still: "There are really serious critics of Vladimir Putin in Russia who deserve our attention much more than these three misguided young feminist rock musicians who have desecrated a cathedral," author Robert Service grumbled to the BBC.[21] Simon Jenkins, a columnist for Britain's *Guardian* newspaper, suggested that the women would have got similar treatment in London: "If a rock group invaded Westminster Abbey and gravely insulted a religious or ethnic minority before the high altar, we all know that ministers would howl for 'exemplary punishment' and judges would oblige."[22]

Even the rising star of the new Russian opposition, anti-corruption blogger Alexei Navalny, described the church gig as "despicable", although he also said that the women shouldn't be jailed for mere "stupidity".[23]

The regime, however, would make little distinction: 'silly' punks or 'serious' activists, they all got arrested anyway.

"The surest defence against Evil is extreme individualism, originality of thinking, whimsicality, even - if you will - eccentricity."
Russian-born poet Joseph Brodsky, who was jailed by the Soviet authorities in the sixties

Amidst the outburst of conflicting reactions to the Pussy Riot verdict, one thing was not in doubt: the trial was a publicity disaster for the Putin administration, outside Russia at least. "The Russian authorities took a marginal act of arty protest and, through sheer cruelty, made it into an international cause," as journalist Michael Idov put it. "In covering the trial live, CNN and the BBC have broadcast what essentially amounts to long infomercials against investing in, visiting and generally dealing with Russia."[24]

This, Verzilov insisted, was Pussy Riot's triumph: "I don't think Putin personally sees it as a PR disaster, but if you talk to someone from some American state like Arizona who barely knows anything about Russia, the only two things they would know, apart from the usual bears and vodka, would be Putin and Pussy Riot," he suggested. "It has shaken the regime in the terms that neither Putin nor his policymakers thought that the case of these women could cause such major attention."

The two jailed women remained defiant even though they were refused parole. Tolokonnikova's appeal for early release was rejected after complaints from prison officials about her failure to "repent". Some of the reasons cited fell way beyond the realm of satire: reportedly, she hadn't participated in jailhouse activities such as the 'Miss Charm Prison Camp 14' beauty contest.

Verzilov recalled how an official once approached his wife after a parole hearing and asked: "'After you're released, do you plan to continue your involvement in politics?' She replied, 'Yes, of course.' And the man said, 'Well, you're going to be coming back here again...'"

In a letter sent from jail, Tolokonnikova spoke of "slave labour" conditions in the prison camp's workshops where the women sewed uniforms; of death threats, arbitrary punishments, random beatings, filthy quarters, foul rations... even the 'No Pasaran!' T-shirt she had worn in court was stolen by a guard carrying out a search, she told me later. Both she and Alyokhina went on hunger strike and ended up in prison hospitals.

It soon became clear that their convictions were just the start of a post-election clean-up operation as Putin simultaneously pursued a harsh conservative moral agenda and smashed his fist down on the fledgling dissident-liberal movement. The Pussy Riot prosecution became the first in a series of similar trials: Navalny was sentenced to house arrest; other protesters were jailed for 'plotting mass unrest'; gay rights activists were harassed and detained; Kasparov went into self-imposed exile; human rights groups were hit by a series of raids. "Probably our trial was a sort of precedent," Samutsevich mused - and indeed, in June 2013, the Russian parliament voted in new legislation criminalising blasphemy; a kind of 'Pussy Riot law' that envisaged sentences of up to three years in jail for 'offending religious feelings'. I recalled the young punk I saw on the Moscow metro after I interviewed Samutsevich. Scrawled on her bag were the words: "DESTROY WHAT DESTROYS YOU." This, now, seemed to be Putin's motto.

"Nothing is preventing us from putting on the balaclavas again," Samutsevich insisted. But with their telephones tapped and their movements under surveillance, she admitted that it would be much tougher to set up musical guerrilla sorties undetected. "It's a very difficult situation because they know what we are, they more or less know about who we are, they studied all our [published] materials, they approximately know how we think and where approximately would we like to perform; they know all about it."

Samutsevich claimed that the authorities' "pathological reaction" to the opposition movement was a sign of fear: Putin was still scared, and the battle for freedom was not lost, she said. "Nothing lasts forever. Everything can change, the main thing is to choose the strategy correctly - examine the enemy and then choose the strategy, and fight." It sounded good at the time, but in the months that followed, such optimism started to lose its

238

shine.

When Alyokhina and Tolokonnikova were finally freed from jail under a general amnesty in December 2013, they emerged into a different Russia, a country where the political climate had turned as frosty as a Siberian prison colony. The demonstrators of March 2012 were being tried and jailed, new laws had been passed to criminalise dissent, while shrill propaganda about the interfering West resounded across the state TV networks as an increasingly dominant Putin geared up to seize Crimea from Ukraine. The Russian leader vowed grimly in his Crimea annexation speech that he would also deal with his internal enemies, who he described as a "disparate bunch of national traitors". In these circumstances, the amnesty of the two women could hardly be seen as a victory; instead, it simply showed exactly who held the keys to the prison gates.

When I met Alyokhina and Tolokonnikova in a Moscow pizza restaurant a couple of months after they were freed, they had already been attacked twice, once by young thugs at a McDonald's burger joint in Nizhny Novgorod and another time by Cossacks during the Winter Olympics in Sochi, where they were attempting to film a video for a new song called *Putin Will Teach You to Love the Motherland*. They continued trying to screech out the lyrics through yelps of pain while the Cossacks lashed at them with bullwhips as if they were heretics in need of a flogging.

"It's very hard to feel safe when there are so many attacks," said Tolokonnikova, still only 24 years old, clad in black leather jacket and boots, as magnetically charismatic as she had appeared in court. She said that she believed that the authorities were responsible for the harassment, bugging their phones and tipping off local 'patriotic' goons about their movements: "Any region we go to, just after we arrive and step off the train, the same things happen. It's obvious that this is a well-planned action."

She insisted that being in prison had made her tougher and more disciplined. "You are face to face, non-stop, with an administration that is ready to destroy you morally and physically. And basically you have to make a decision every day, every minute: either you stay true to your beliefs, your opinions and yourself, and stand up against them, or you choose to be silent. You don't have any other option - there is no third way, you don't have a place to hide, to escape and forget about everything. So prison in some ways can make you stronger, but in most cases, especially if you are a woman, it can break you."

Their incarceration had also clarified exactly what kind of country they were living in. "I saw the state from within, I saw this totalitarian machine as it is," Tolokonnikova said directly after her release. "Russia is built on the model of a penal colony."[25]

But although they were sent to prison as cultural provocateurs, they came out as jail-hardened political activists. Their first step after their release was to announce that they were setting up an organisation to campaign on behalf of Russian prisoners, called *Zona Prava* - 'Zone of Rights'.

"Obviously, when you have this kind of personal experience, when you survived it all and now you are free, it's hard to forget about other people who are still there. When we were leaving jail, other prisoners asked us not to leave them behind and not to forget them," Tolokonnikova explained.

"We want those people who are now silent to finally raise their voices, because the things that are happening behind the walls of prison colonies are so dreadful that we think society must know about it," added Alyokhina.

By this time, they were global celebrities who had been lauded in a book-length biography and a documentary film that was nominated for an Oscar. On a visit to New York, they were paraded on stage as the main attraction at an Amnesty International concert, dined with Madonna and posed for photos with luminaries like Yoko Ono and Hillary Clinton. Critics moaned that they had been dazzled by stardust, transformed into a Western liberal wet dream rather than a political force with any relevance in their home country.

But after the two women's release, what exactly was Pussy Riot anymore - and indeed, who was it? A few weeks later, some media gleefully published an open letter announcing that Alyokhina and Tolokonnikova were no longer part of the group. The letter - apparently from some of the other, still-anonymous Pussy Riot activists who had evaded capture after the cathedral performance - said that Alyokhina and Tolokonnikova had "completely forgotten about the aspirations and ideals of our group" and insisted that it was "no secret that Masha and Nadya are no longer members... and will no longer take part in radical actionism".

The letter promised that the anonymous feminist art collective would continue without them. "Yes, we have lost two friends, two ideological team-mates, but the world has acquired two brave human rights defenders," it stated. "Unfortunately we cannot congratulate them in person because they refuse to have any contact with us. But we appreciate their choice and sincerely wish them well in their new career." Towards the end, it emphasised yet again: "They are no longer Pussy Riot."

Alyokhina dismissed the letter as "very strange", although she didn't exactly call it a fake. "We couldn't understand it because Pussy Riot is not a band from which you can dismiss people. This is not a court to judge who is a member and who is not," she argued.

But genuine or not, it did contain some uncomfortable truth: now they were no longer anonymous, and had served hard time for their cause, Alyokhina and Tolokonnikova could no longer be the carefree cultural activists they had once been. Whatever Pussy Riot was to become, it could never again be what it was.

Before I left the restaurant and the two women launched into another interview with another foreign journalist before heading to the airport for another overseas appearance, I asked Tolokonnikova if there was still any chance - in the words of the *Punk Prayer* that had sent her to prison - that people like her could "drive Putin out".

"Sooner or later, of course there will be a chance," she responded immediately, flashing the same insubordinate glare that had illuminated the Moscow courtroom.

"Even in Soviet times, when the situation was worse than now, even then there were dissidents who spread information under total isolation," she insisted. "They had hope, and the fact that we had such brave people in the past gives us the motivation to live and move forward. I think we should remain hopeful and never give up."

Nadezhda means 'hope', and hope dies last, or so the Russians sometimes like to say. And whether Pussy Riot are ultimately judged to have succeeded or failed, they managed to show yet again how music can raise hopes and invoke righteous spirits in the darkest of times. Whatever they did next, the extraordinary spectacle of these balaclava-clad young women who dared to howl their defiance from the squares and the churches, the streets and the metro stations of Moscow would remain an inspiration for a long time to come.

Acknowledgements

This book is for Alex Collin, as he sets out on his own incredible journey.

Thanks for support, advice and much-needed assistance of various kinds during the research and writing of this book are due to Bill Adler, Selçuk Artut, Vanya Balogh, Orçun Baştürk, Helena Bedwell, Shalva Bibilashvili, Slobodan Brkić, Frank Broughton, Nino Chimakadze, Eka Chitanava, Max Daly, Sarah J. Edwards, Barkın Engin, Adrian Fisk, Malgosha Gago, Berna Göl, Sergi Gvarjaladze, Malu Halasa, Alexander Ivanov, Serhat Köksal, Alexander Kvatashidze, Jürgen Laarman, Eddy Lawrence, Vladimir Lozinski, Dorian Lynskey, Anna Malpas, Milica Mančić, Jolyn Matsumoro, Justyna Mielnikiewicz, Mariam Naskidashvili, Jo-Ann Nina, Mark Olden, Gordan Paunović, Mike Power, Dave Rimmer, Paul Rimple, Keith Robinson, Susanne Simon-Paunović, Ulaş Şalgam, Ekin Sanaç, Anton Singurov, Burak Tamer, Sven von Thülen, Wolfgang Tillmans, Pyotr Verzilov,Olga Volodina and Irvine Welsh.

Thanks also to Tariq Goddard and all at Zero Books; to my agent, Matthew Hamilton at Aitken Alexander, and to my various editors over the years, particularly Chris Bohn at *The Wire*, Allan Campbell at *CUT*, Caspar Llewellyn-Smith at *The Guardian* and *The Observer*, Avril Mair at *i-D*, Dom Phillips at *Mixmag*, Helen Seeney at Deutsche Welle and Stuart Williams at AFP, for commissioning reports that sent me on some of the travels documented in this book.

Special thanks are due to Magda Nowakowska for believing in this book when it seemed like it might never happen, and to Monika Lajhner for generously providing the perfect writer's retreat by the Danube.

Finally, as ever, love to Audrey, Richard and Will Collin and to all the extended Collin clan.

Notes

Chapter One

1. Jeff Chang, *Can't Stop Won't Stop*, Ebury Press, London, 2007
2. *NME*, October 17, 1987
3. *Melody Maker*, November 28, 1987
4. *Q*, January 1988
5. Amiri Baraka, Black Art, 1965
6. *Prophets of Rage*, dir. James Hale, 2011
7. *The Guardian*, October 6, 2009
8. *Playboy*, May 1971
9. Simon Reynolds, *Bring the Noise*, Faber & Faber, London, 2007
10. *Melody Maker*, June 6, 1992
11. Chang, ibid.
12. *Washington Times*, May 22, 1989
13. *LA Weekly*, 1989
14. Meet the Press, NBC, April 13, 1997 (transcript via The Final Call website)
15. Professor Griff, *Analytixz: 20 Years of Conversations and Enterviews with Public Enemy's Minister of Information*, RATHSI Publishing, Atlanta, 2009
16. Reynolds, ibid.
17. *Village Voice*, July 19, 1988
18. Chang, ibid.
19. *Prophets of Rage*, ibid.
20. *Fight the Power: Rap, Race and Reality*, Chuck D with Yusuf Jah, Payback Press, London, 1997
21. Chuck D with Yusuf Jah, ibid.
22. Chuck D with Yusuf Jah, ibid.
23. *Los Angeles Times*, January 1, 1992

Chapter Two

1. *i-D*, September 1992
2. *i-D*, ibid.
3. Danielle de Picciotto, *The Beauty of Transgression*, Die Gestalten Verlag, Berlin, 2011
4. de Picciotto, ibid.
5. Otto Friedrich, *Before the Deluge*, Michael Joseph, London, 1974
6. *Völkischer Beobachter*, 1928, quoted in Brian Ladd, *The Ghosts of Berlin*, University of Chicago Press, Chicago, 1997
7. Friedrich, ibid.
8. Brian Ladd, *The Ghosts of Berlin*, University of Chicago Press, Chicago, 1997
9. Sean Nye, *Love Parade, Please Not Again: A Berlin Cultural History*, published in *Echo* Volume 9, Issue 1, Fall 2009
10. *i-D*, September 1992
11. *Real Scenes: Berlin*, Resident Advisor website, December 2011
12. Harry Kessler, *Tagebucher 1918-1937*, quoted in Ladd, ibid.
13. *Wings of Desire*, dir. Wim Wenders, 1987
14. Felix Denk and Sven von Thülen, *Der Klang Der Familie*, Suhrkamp Verlag, Berlin, 2012
15. *i-D*, September1996
16. *Pozor*, 1996
17. Jürgen Laarmann, *The Techno Principle*, published in *Localizer 1.0*, Die Gestalten Verlag, Berlin, 1995
18. Laarmann, ibid.
19. *i-D*, September 1995
20. *i-D*, September 1996
21. Hakim Bey quoted in Steve Beard, *Aftershocks: The End of Style Culture*, Wallflower Press, London, 2002
22. *i-D*, September 1996
23. *Pozor*, 1996
24. *Pozor*, 1996
25. *i-D*, September 1996

26. David Clay Large, *Berlin: A Modern History*, Allen Lane, London, 2001
27. *The Observer*, July 18, 2001
28. *Frankfurter Allgemeine Zeitung*, July 20, 2001
29. *Party, Love and Profit: The Rhythms of the Love Parade*, published in *Dancecult: Journal of Electronic Dance Music Culture*, Vol. 2 No. 1, 2011
30. *i-D*, September 1996
31. *Pozor*, 1996
32. Markus Löffel website, no date given
33. Low Spirit website, July 2010
34. de Picciotto, ibid.
35. Fuck Parade website, 2006
36. Reuters, February 21, 2007
37. *Party, Love and Profit: The Rhythms of the Love Parade*, ibid.
38. *The Economist*, July 29, 2010
39. *Die Tageszeitung*, July 25, 2010
40. *Der Spiegel*, August 2, 2010
41. *Der Spiegel*, July 26, 2010
42. *Bild*, July 30, 2010
43. Reuters, July 29, 2010
44. Reuters, July 31, 2010
45. *Der Spiegel*, August 2, 2010
46. *The Guardian*, July 25, 2010

Chapter Three
1. Matthew Collin, *Altered State*, Serpent's Tail, London, 1997
2. Wayward Tales blog, unknown date
3. Dom Phillips, *Superstar DJs - Here We Go!*, Ebury Press, London, 2009
4. *New York Times*, December 20, 2008
5. *Storming Sarajevo*, dirs. Simon Davies and Kevin Jarvis, from the *World Traveller Adventures* DVD compilation, 2004
6. Fred and Judy Vermorel, *Sex Pistols: The Inside Story*,

Omnibus Press, London, 2011.
7. Underground website, unknown date
8. Underground website, ibid.
9. Sleeve notes to *Heathen Earth* by Throbbing Gristle (reissue), 1990
10. Hakim Bey, *T.A.Z.*, Autonomedia, New York, 1991
11. *Pozor*, 1996
12. BBC News, August 2, 2005
13. *Pozor*, 1996

Chapter Four

1. *Süddeutsches Zeitung*, April 3, 2007
2. *Time*, October 18, 2009
3. Civil Georgia website, July 11, 2009
4. *Power Trip*, dir. Paul Devlin, 2003
5. Civil Georgia website, December 1, 2007
6. *Kommersant*, November 22, 2007
7. *Complete Control: Music and Propaganda in Zimbabwe*, Freemuse website, September 20, 2004
8. Matthew Collin, *The Time of the Rebels*, Serpent's Tail, London, 2007
9. Collin, ibid.
10. *The Independent*, July 5, 2009
11. *Financial Times*, April 26, 2008
12. *Time*, October 18, 2009
13. BBC News, October 2, 2006
14. *The Guardian*, December 1, 2010
15. Civil Georgia, December 1, 2007
16. Rustavi-2 TV, September 6, 2006
17. Rossiya TV, August 21, 2008

Chapter Five

1. *Vice*, June 17, 2013
2. *The Atlantic*, June 5, 2013

3. Martin Stokes, *The Arabesk Debate: Music and Musicians in Modern Turkey*, Clarendon Press, Oxford, 1992
4. Tim Kelsey, *Dervish: Travels in Modern Turkey*, Penguin, London, 1996
5. Thomas Goltz, *The Gezi Park Uprising, the Taste of Tear-Gas and Compressed Pepper Spray*, essay posted on Facebook, June 12, 2013
6. *New York Times*, July 21, 2013
7. Reuters, June 11, 2013
8. Hugh Pope, Facebook post, June 16, 2013
9. Kelsey, ibid.

Chapter Six
1. *The Quietus*, August 16, 2013
2. *Financial Times*, March 16, 2012
3. AFP, January 26, 2012
4. *Vice*, March 2012
5. Dorian Lynskey, *33 Revolutions Per Minute*, Faber & Faber, London, 2010
6. Associated Press, August 20, 2012
7. *New York Times*, August 7, 2012
8. *St. Petersburg Times*, February 1, 2012
9. *Sounds*, June 1977
10. Kathleen Hanna website, August 7, 2012
11. *Konturi*, May 30, 2011
12. *The New Republic*, August 17, 2012
13. *Bolshoy Gorod*, April 10, 2013
14. *London Review of Books*, August 16, 2012
15. *Pussy Riot: A Punk Prayer*, dir. Maxim Pozdorovkin and Mike Lerner, HBO, 2013
16. *Pussy Riot: A Punk Prayer*, ibid.
17. Artemy Troitsky, *Back in the USSR*, Omnibus, Winchester, 1987
18. Ekho Moskvi website, June 27, 2012

19. *The Atlantic,* August 20, 2012
20. PBS website, August 23, 2012
21. BBC Radio 4, August 17, 2012
22. *The Guardian,* August 21, 2012
23. Bloomberg News, August 21, 2012
24. *The Guardian,* August 17, 2012
25. TV Dozhd, December 23, 2013

ZERO BOOKS

If this book has helped you to clarify an idea, solve a problem or extend your knowledge, you may like to read more titles from Zero Books. Recent bestsellers are:

Capitalist Realism Is there no alternative?
Mark Fisher
An analysis of the ways in which capitalism has presented itself as the only realistic political-economic system.
Paperback: November 27, 2009 978-1-84694-317-1 $14.95 £7.99.
eBook: July 1, 2012 978-1-78099-734-6 $9.99 £6.99.

Tqhe Wandering Who? A study of Jewish identity politics
Gilad Atzmon
An explosive unique crucial book tackling the issues of Jewish Identity Politics and ideology and their global influence.
Paperback: September 30, 2011 978-1-84694-875-6 $14.95 £8.99.
eBook: September 30, 2011 978-1-84694-876-3 $9.99 £6.99.

Clampdown Pop-cultural wars on class and gender
Rhian E. Jones
Class and gender in Britpop and after, and why 'chav' is a feminist issue.
Paperback: March 29, 2013 978-1-78099-708-7 $14.95 £9.99.
eBook: March 29, 2013 978-1-78099-707-0 $7.99 £4.99.

The Quadruple Object
Graham Harman
Uses a pack of playing cards to present Harman's metaphysical system of fourfold objects, including human access, Heidegger's indirect causation, panpsychism and ontography.
Paperback: July 29, 2011 978-1-84694-700-1 $16.95 £9.99.

Weird Realism Lovecraft and Philosophy
Graham Harman
As Hölderlin was to Martin Heidegger and Mallarmé to Jacques
Derrida, so is H.P. Lovecraft to the Speculative Realist philoso-
phers.
Paperback: September 28, 2012 978-1-78099-252-5 $24.95 £14.99.
eBook: September 28, 2012 978-1-78099-907-4 $9.99 £6.99.

Sweetening the Pill or How We Got Hooked on Hormonal Birth
Control
Holly Grigg-Spall
Is it really true? Has contraception liberated or oppressed
women?
Paperback: September 27, 2013 978-1-78099-607-3 $22.95 £12.99.
eBook: September 27, 2013 978-1-78099-608-0 $9.99 £6.99.

Why Are We The Good Guys? Reclaiming Your Mind From The
Delusions Of Propaganda
David Cromwell
A provocative challenge to the standard ideology that Western
power is a benevolent force in the world.
Paperback: September 28, 2012 978-1-78099-365-2 $26.95 £15.99.
eBook: September 28, 2012 978-1-78099-366-9 $9.99 £6.99.

The Truth about Art Reclaiming quality
Patrick Doorly
The book traces the multiple meanings of art to their various
sources, and equips the reader to choose between them.
Paperback: August 30, 2013 978-1-78099-841-1 $32.95 £19.99.

Bells and Whistles More Speculative Realism
Graham Harman
In this diverse collection of sixteen essays, lectures, and inter-
views Graham Harman lucidly explains the principles of

Speculative Realism, including his own object-oriented philosophy.
Paperback: November 29, 2013 978-1-78279-038-9 $26.95 £15.99.
eBook: November 29, 2013 978-1-78279-037-2 $9.99 £6.99.

Towards Speculative Realism: Essays and Lectures Essays and Lectures
Graham Harman
These writings chart Harman's rise from Chicago sportswriter to co founder of one of Europe's most promising philosophical movements: Speculative Realism.
Paperback: November 26, 2010 978-1-84694-394-2 $16.95 £9.99.
eBook: January 1, 1970 978-1-84694-603-5 $9.99 £6.99.

Meat Market Female flesh under capitalism
Laurie Penny
A feminist dissection of women's bodies as the fleshy fulcrum of capitalist cannibalism, whereby women are both consumers and consumed.
Paperback: April 29, 2011 978-1-84694-521-2 $12.95 £6.99.
eBook: May 21, 2012 978-1-84694-782-7 $9.99 £6.99.

Translating Anarchy The Anarchism of Occupy Wall Street
Mark Bray
An insider's account of the anarchists who ignited Occupy Wall Street.
Paperback: September 27, 2013 978-1-78279-126-3 $26.95 £15.99.
eBook: September 27, 2013 978-1-78279-125-6 $6.99 £4.99.

One Dimensional Woman
Nina Power
Exposes the dark heart of contemporary cultural life by examining pornography, consumer capitalism and the ideology of women's work.

Paperback: November 27, 2009 978-1-84694-241-9 $14.95 £7.99.
eBook: July 1, 2012 978-1-78099-737-7 $9.99 £6.99.

Dead Man Working
Carl Cederstrom, Peter Fleming
An analysis of the dead man working and the way in which capital is now colonizing life itself.
Paperback: May 25, 2012 978-1-78099-156-6 $14.95 £9.99.
eBook: June 27, 2012 978-1-78099-157-3 $9.99 £6.99.

Unpatriotic History of the Second World War
James Heartfield
The Second World War was not the Good War of legend. James Heartfield explains that both Allies and Axis powers fought for the same goals - territory, markets and natural resources.
Paperback: September 28, 2012 978-1-78099-378-2 $42.95 £23.99.
eBook: September 28, 2012 978-1-78099-379-9 $9.99 £6.99.

Find more titles at www.zero-books.net

Contemporary culture has eliminated both the concept of the public and the figure of the intellectual. Former public spaces – both physical and cultural – are now either derelict or colonized by advertising. A cretinous anti-intellectualism presides, cheerled by expensively educated hacks in the pay of multinational corporations who reassure their bored readers that there is no need to rouse themselves from their interpassive stupor. The informal censorship internalized and propagated by the cultural workers of late capitalism generates a banal conformity that the propaganda chiefs of Stalinism could only ever have dreamt of imposing. Zer0 Books knows that another kind of discourse – intellectual without being academic, popular without being populist – is not only possible: it is already flourishing, in the regions beyond the striplit malls of so-called mass media and the neurotically bureaucratic halls of the academy. Zer0 is committed to the idea of publishing as a making public of the intellectual. It is convinced that in the unthinking, blandly consensual culture in which we live, critical and engaged theoretical reflection is more important than ever before.